SHREWSBURY COLLEGE
060226

By the same author
LORCA: The Theatre Beneath the Sand

ACKNOWLEDGEMENTS

Un Chien andalou 1963; *L'Age d'or* 1963; *Tristana* 1971; *Le Charme discret de la bourgeoisie* 1973; L'Avant Scene du Cinema, Paris.

Los olvidados 1972; *Nazarín* 1971; *The Exterminating Angel* 1969; *Belle de Jour* 1971; L'Avant Scene du Cinema, Paris, and (in English translation) Lorrimer Publishing, London.

Permission to give my own English translation is gratefully acknowledged.

Stills for:
Los olvidados, Audio Brandons Films, New York.
Tristana, Audio Brandon Films, New York.
The Discreet Charm of the Bourgeoisie, Films Incorporated, Wilmette, Illinois.
and by kind permission:
L'Age d'or, Essential Cinema, London; Corinth Films Inc., New York.
Los olvidados, The Discreet Charm of the Bourgeoisie, Artificial Eye, London.
Tristana, Academy Cinema, London.
Un Chien andalou, Nazarín, Viridiana, Belle de Jour, Contemporary Films, London.

Quotations from Francisco Aranda, *Luis Buñuel: A Critical Biography,* trans. David Robinson, London: Secker and Warburg, 1975, by courtesy of the translator and the publishers.

THE DISCREET ART OF LUIS BUÑUEL

A reading of his films

THE DISCREET ART OF LUIS BUÑUEL

A reading of his films

GWYNNE EDWARDS

Marion Boyars
London . Boston

First Published in Great Britain and the United States in 1982 by
Marion Boyars Publishers Ltd.
18 Brewer Street, London W1R 4AS
and by
Marion Boyars Publishers Inc.
99 Main Street, Salem,
New Hampshire 03079.

Australian and New Zealand distribution by
Thomas C. Lothian Pty,
4-12 Tattersalls Lane, Melbourne, Victoria 3000.

Edwards, Gwynne
The discreet art of Luis Bunuel.
1. Bunuel, Luis
I. Title
791.43'0233'0924 PN1998.A3B757
ISBN 0-7145-2754-8 cloth

Library of Congress Catalog Card No. 82-71081

Printed and bound in Great Britain at
The Camelot Press Ltd, Southampton

CONTENTS

LIST OF ILLUSTRATIONS

PREFACE

Luis Buñuel is, with a handful of others, one of the truly great figures in the history of cinema. He is a film-maker who has always pursued his own fiercely independent vision, avoiding involvement with the truly commercial cinema, and he has never made a film in Hollywood. Although Buñuel is a Spaniard – and with Dalí, Lorca and Picasso one of a small number of creative Spanish artists who have helped to shape the art of our time – he has actually made few films in Spain. The lack of a Spanish film industry and the outbreak of the Civil War and its aftermath, have obliged Buñuel to work largely in Mexico and France. He has, indeed, often been thought to be a Frenchman, but the constant and essential feature of Buñuel is in fact his Spanishness, revealed unmistakably in his religious concerns, his humour and his literary heritage.

Buñuel's work is distinguished by a remarkable unity of theme and vision which has its roots in his own background acquiring a distinctive character during his association with the French Surrealists of the 1930s. Initially, Buñuel developed the surrealist fascination with the unconscious and his first film, the startlingly unique *Un Chien andalou* (1929), transferred to the screen the reality of dreams and unconscious desires. It is a vein which he has continued to explore to a greater or lesser degree in all his subsequent films. Secondly, Buñuel has always expressed a detestation of the bourgeoisie, born of his own bourgeois background and consolidated by his membership of the Paris surrealist group. His second film, *L'Age d'or* (1930), is a spirited assault on bourgeois values. Many of Buñuel's major films – *The Exterminating Angel* (1962), *Belle de Jour* (1966), *The Discreet Charm of the Bourgeoisie* (1972) combine his two major preoccupations. The main difference between his early and later work is that, with the passage of time, the tone and manner have become cooler, more objective and ironic.

Buñuel is not a director whose cinema technique immediately calls attention to itself. He is, on the contrary, an artist for whom technique is not an end in itself but merely a means to an end. To that extent his style is largely simple and direct. This is not to say, of course, that Buñuel eschews the lessons learned from his long experience (effects of slow motion, superimpositions, close-ups, angles, etc), but rather that he does not display them pointlessly. Inasmuch as technique serves argument and vision, Buñuel is clearly one of the masters of the cinema both in his visual presentation of the unconscious and in his visual social criticism, but in neither does he self-consciously parade his ingenuity. As he has escaped the influence of the commercial cinema in terms of his own intransigent moral viewpoint, so in an age of increasing technical advance he has avoided its often flashy effects.

The existing studies of Buñuel are largely of a general kind and, for all their many virtues, do not analyze his major films in any real detail. It is the purpose of this book to focus on those films that are generally regarded as Buñuel's best work, and to offer a close and detailed analysis of them that will be of interest both to the true Buñuel enthusiast and the more general student of the cinema. In the preparation of the book I have found it extremely useful to consult the scenarios of Buñuel's films which are generally available and to which the reader is recommended. Translations from the scenarios are in every case my own.

INTRODUCTION

Luis Buñuel was born in the small Aragonese town of Calanda, some 115 kilometres from Zaragoza, in 1900, the first of Leonardo and María Buñuel's seven children. Calanda itself, a backward and unsophisticated place, was poor soil for the cultivation of a genius, but, whatever its disadvantages, the young Luis had in his father the advantage of a man very different from the ordinary villagers. Leonardo Buñuel was a wealthy bourgeois who, having made his fortune in South America, had returned to his birthplace of Calanda at the age of forty-three, married María, then aged seventeen, and bought a large estate. The house in Calanda was, by all accounts, a very fine one, surrounded by a beautiful garden that ran down to the edge of the river, and it was here, in this comfortable bourgeois environment, that Luis, the future scourge of the bourgeoisie, was to spend much of his childhood. Even when, after Luis's birth, the family moved to a flat in Zaragoza, they would regularly visit their country house, and for many years Luis was to spend his summers there.[1]

Leonardo Buñuel, as well as being rich, was an intelligent and cultured man who mixed easily with the landowning intelligentsia of Zaragoza. He took a keen interest too in his children's education. In this respect Luis's upbringing, so crucial to his future attitudes, was both privileged and conventional. His mother, a very devout woman, ensured that her children were brought up strictly. At six years of age Luis was sent to the College of the Brothers of the Sacred Heart in Zaragoza and in the following year began attending the Jesuit College where he was to be a pupil for the next nine years. Luis proved to be a serious, well-behaved and hard-working boy who obtained good marks for piety. It was a background whose narrowness and essential Spanishness has been accurately described by Buñuel himself:

> My infancy slipped by in an almost mediaeval atmosphere (like that of nearly all the Spanish provinces) between my native town and Zaragoza. I feel it necessary to say here (since it explains in part the trend of the modest work which I later accomplished) that the two basic sentiments of my childhood, which stayed with me well into adolescence, are those of a profound eroticism, at first sublimated in a great religious faith, and a permanent consciousness of death. It would take too long here to analyze the reasons. It suffices that I was not an exception among my compatriots, since this is a very Spanish characteristic, and our art, exponent of the Spanish spirit, was impregnated with these two sentiments. The last civil war, peculiar and ferocious as no other, exposed them clearly.[2]

In the light of such comments it is easy to understand the sources of Buñuel's constant preoccupation both with the bourgeoisie and with religious belief and institutions.

Buñuel's childhood offers other revealing glimpses of the adult man; notably an interest in music and the theatre. Luis himself often pretended to be the priest saying mass, while all the children were fond of dressing up and taking part in dramatic entertainments of their own devising. Luis delighted, in particular, in a toy theatre, a gift from his parents, which had back-cloth and scenery, the cardboard figures of a King, a Queen, a jester and courtiers, and two sets representing a throne-room and a wood. As well as amusing himself, he organized theatrical shows for the boys and girls of the village, spending a week on preparations before the performance took place in one of the barns. At the age of thirteen he began to study the violin and revealed both an enthusiasm and an aptitude for it, while the piano had interested him from early childhood. After his three sisters had gone to bed, Luis would go to their bedroom and tell them – in the words of one of the sisters – 'A very Wagnerian tale', which he would accompany on the violin.[3] During the summers at Calanda, moreover, it seems that Luis even managed to form an orchestra which played during the various religious ceremonies held in the town. It is worth noting too that until the age of thirty Buñuel took part in one of Calanda's most theatrical religious occasions – the Easter Procession of the Drums, whose deafening noise is to be heard in some of his films.

In the countryside around Calanda the young Luis acquired a knowledge of nature and a love of animals and insects that are evident in many of his films. His sister, Conchita, has observed that the house at Calanda was always full of animals – monkeys, toads, frogs, snakes, lizards, mice, a ram, a horse – which belonged to Luis and which he cared for profoundly. All the children, through their constant and close contact with nature, developed both an affection and a respect for all living things, and in Luis's case it was to influence his subsequent choice of a university course.

At the age of seventeen Buñuel took a decisive step in his career when he left Zaragoza for Madrid and became a student in the famous Residencia de Estudiantes, a cultural centre of international reputation founded in 1910 and modelled on the English universities. He was persuaded by his father to pursue a course in Agricultural Engineering, but the compulsory study of mathematics during the three-year period more than off-set his interest in the natural sciences and, in his own words, led him to detest his studies. In 1920, therefore, he became a pupil of the celebrated Spanish entomologist, Dr Bolívar, director of the Museum of Natural

History in Madrid, and for two years devoted himself to the study of insects. The experience taught Buñuel, however, that he was less interested in the anatomy and physiology of insects than in their life and behaviour. This was also however a period in his life at the Residencia when, through the influence of his friends, he became more conscious of his literary and artistic inclinations. Consequently, he abandoned his scientific studies, entered the Faculty of Arts, and became a graduate of the University of Madrid in 1924. But if he officially turned his back on the natural sciences, their influence was to be a lasting one in many ways.

Buñuel's friendships at the Residencia de Estudiantes between 1917 and 1924 were to prove crucial in relation to his personal and artistic development. In 1919, for example, Federico García Lorca, later Spain's most famous poet and dramatist, began what was to become a ten-year stay there. Other talented young men who were either students at or connected with the Residencia included Salvador Dalí, Juan Ramón Jiménez, José Moreno Villa and Gregorio Martínez Sierra, whilst amongst the foreign residents were François Mauriac, H. G. Wells, G. K. Chesterton and Igor Stravinsky. From the Residencia, as well as from two similar institutions – the Institución Libre de Enseñanza and the Instituto de Escuela – were to emerge almost all the outstanding Spanish figures of the 1920s: Rafael Alberti, Dámaso Alonso, Ramón Gómez de la Serna, José Ortega y Gasset. Contact with other intellectuals, endless debate, the exchange of ideas, participation in literary discussions, attendance at poetry recitals and concerts, created an environment highly favourable to the encouragement of new creative energies.

Buñuel established a firm friendship with Lorca and between them they organized lectures at the Residencia and trips outside it. Through Lorca's influence, moreover, Buñuel's interest in the theatre developed a great deal. He was an enthusiastic amateur actor and took a leading part, as well as either directing or designing, in Zorrilla's famous

Romantic play, *Don Juan Tenorio*. From year to year Buñuel and Lorca alternated as designer and director, but it was Buñuel who always played Don Juan – by all accounts a bold, taut, exuberant performance. In addition, with Lorca and another friend, Juan Chabas, Buñuel developed an interest in the puppet theatre. The three of them had become acquainted with a man called Mayeau who presented shows for children in Madrid's Retiro Park. They subsequently helped him prepare more ambitious and sophisticated performances and even presented them at the Residencia. Buñuel's experience of acting and directing, even on this scale, would prove invaluable in years to come.

The Residencia, as well as Madrid intellectual life in general, was to prove decisive in relation to Buñuel's exposure to *avant-garde* movements, including those of a surrealist character, before his departure for Paris in 1925. From the end of the First World War both Madrid and Barcelona felt the impact of new and important foreign cultural influences. Between January and March 1917 Francis Picabia, whose role as an important figure in the early stages of Spanish Surrealism was recognized by André Breton in a visit to Barcelona in 1922, published the first four numbers of his Dada magazine, *391*[4]. In Madrid one of the most influential figures of the time was Ramón Gómez de la Serna who from 1915 conducted his literary circle at the Café Pombo. Familiar with Parisian *avant-garde* activities, he encouraged his associates to experiment in new art forms and, in relation to the cultivation of a life-style that struck a blow at tradition and convention, led by example: his delivery of a lecture from a trapeze and from the back of an elephant anticipate the extravagances of Dalí. These were the years that witnessed the Spanish *avant-garde* movements known as *creacionismo* and *ultraísmo*, the former associated with the Chilean poet, Vicente Huidobro, the latter with Gerardo Diego. *Creacionismo* sought to incorporate Cubism into Spanish poetry and to eliminate sentiment, while *ultraísmo* brought together aspects of

Cubism, Dadaism and Futurism and attempted to replace the traditional language of poetry with the terminology of geometry and physics; the language of the machine age. It is important to recognize too that from about 1909 Spanish writers were familiar with the same writers and literary traditions that inspired Breton, Eluard, Aragon and others: the Comte de Lautréamont, Rimbaud, the Marquis de Sade, the Gothic novel, a literary heritage which, in short, offered abundant examples of the eroticism, the cruelty, the horrific, irrational and the anti-traditionalist sentiment that in the years ahead would become the cult of the 'official' Surrealists. As for Buñuel himself, his first literary pieces reflect the *avant-garde* character of his generation and contain clear surrealist echoes. Such are 'Instrumentation', 'Downright Treachery' and 'Suburbs', published in 1922 and 1923. On the other hand, Spanish Surrealism, for all its debt to France, possesses its own essentially Spanish character and its own Spanish roots, for in the tradition of the picaresque novel, the prose writings of Francisco de Quevedo, and the later nightmarish paintings of Goya – acknowledged by Breton himself as a precursor of Surrealism – are to be found many of those elements of savage humour, cruelty, fantasy and anti-establishment attitudes that appealed so much to Buñuel's aggressive temperament. He was, in effect, already half surrealist before he left Spain.

The years spent at the Residencia also contributed greatly to Buñuel's knowledge of the works of Freud. Buñuel has himself stated, for example, that in 1921 he read Freud's *Psychoanalysis of Daily Life* in a Spanish translation by José Ortega y Gasset. Between 1922 and 1934 the works of Freud were translated into Spanish by the Biblioteca Nueva and during the 1920s proved to be a source of constant fascination for Spanish writers, including, of course, many of Buñuel's literary friends. In years to come Buñuel would bracket Freud with Lenin and Einstein as one of the three great men of the twentieth century, proof enough of his enduring admiration. There can be no doubt that even if direct contact with the Paris Surrealist group further contributed to Buñuel's familiarity with Freudian concepts, he would have had a sound enough knowledge of them long before. It is interesting to note in this respect that in discussing their plans for the making of *Un Chien andalou* Buñuel and Dalí adopted the practice of recounting their dreams to each other.

Having completed his studies at the University in 1924, Buñuel felt very undecided about his future. His father, who would certainly have pushed him into a respectable career, died in 1923, and, with his mother's permission, Buñuel took what was to prove for him the crucial decision of going to live and work in Paris. He arrived there in 1925 with a letter of introduction to the famous pianist, Ricardo Viñas, and was immediately persuaded by him to become involved in an ambitious production of Manuel de Falla's *El retablo de Maese Pedro*, to be presented in Amsterdam by the director of the Dutch orchestra, Mengelberg. Buñuel, having suggested to Viñas that the puppets in the work be played by actors, was made scenic director. He was surprised by his success, overawed at working with people as famous as Falla and Mengelberg, and fired with enthusiasm for the theatre. Shortly after this, moreover, Buñuel was to see Fritz Lang's *Les trois lumières (Destiny)*. The film made a great impression on him and he began to realize for the first time that the cinema possessed enormous powers of expression. It was not long before Buñuel was introduced to Jean Epstein, then the most famous director in France, and taken on by him as one of his assistant directors.

It was Epstein's practice to have around him a group of assistant directors who would help him in making his films. Buñuel worked with Epstein on two films: *Mauprat* and *The Fall of the House of Usher (La Chute de la Maison Usher)*, based on the story by Edgar Allen Poe: films which reveal in subject matter and treatment Epstein's love of romantic themes. *Mauprat* is distinguished by its violent personal relationships and its sombre settings of woods and castles,

The Fall of the House of Usher by its presentation of the crumbling house, its desolate landscapes, its evocative shots of flickering candles, gloomy vaults, and above all, of the death and burial of Lady Madeline. Buñuel was doubtless attracted by the subjects but Epstein's self-indulgent style was in many ways alien to his temperament and he has claimed that Epstein taught him nothing:

> The fact is that I learned very little from Epstein. When I began *Un Chien andalou* I knew very little about the cinema.[5]

Observation of Epstein's work, on the other hand, suggested to Buñuel how he might have proceeded and to that extent clarified his own ideas on the cinema:

> When I watched Epstein direct he frequently made me think – with the temerity of every newcomer – that this was not the way to do it, that the placing of the camera, lights or cast ought to be in such or such another way. Epstein was patient with me. Above all I learned by mentally elaborating the picture being made, seeing it in a different fashion.[6]

In addition, Buñuel must have learned from Epstein something about the techniques of making films. Both in his writings and in his pictures Epstein paid great attention to effects of slow motion and superimposition, while his use of the camera was, in general, highly subjective and poetic. They are effects which Buñuel was to use at given moments in most of his films.

During his apprenticeship with Epstein, Buñuel was anxious to make his own first film. Letters of 1927 and 1928 refer to plans to make a film with Ramón Gómez de la Serna, while other projects included a film to be called *La Sancta Misa Vaticanae* which, in its derisive and sacriligious tone, would have been an early *L'Age d'or*. None of these projects came to fruition, but in the early part of 1929 Buñuel worked with Salvador Dalí on ideas for *Un Chien andalou* and the film was made very quickly. Premièred in April, 1929, at the Studio Ursulines in Paris, *Un Chien andalou* had a notable triumph and became an immediate talking-point with intellectuals and cinema enthusiasts. Buñuel had succeeded in his very first film in transferring to the screen the language of Surrealism, in communicating through its disturbing succession of images the reality of the unconscious. It is worth noting, though, that at the time of its first showing André Breton, who had formally launched the Paris Surrealist group in 1924 with the publication of the *First Surrealist Manifesto*, had not heard of the film's directors and even planned a demonstration against it. Having seen *Un Chien andalou*, Berton declared roundly: 'Yes, this is a Surrealist film'. In the same year Buñuel joined the Paris Surrealist group. The two events pose two interesting questions. Why did Buñuel become an official member of the Surrealist group? And why did the Surrealists consider it important that there should be a surrealist film masterpiece?

Buñuel's surrealism, forged before his arrival in Paris and deeply ingrained in the nature of the man, extends beyond the limitations of any one particular movement and is as evident in his last film as in his first. His motive for joining Breton's official group in 1929 may well have been, therefore, a political one: the association of the group with the Communist Party. From 1925 Breton and his followers were in constant disagreement over the question of Surrealism's relationship with the Communists. The Surrealists' declared aim to achieve a 'revolution in consciousness' and 'to change life' had obvious connexions with the need to change the conditions in which people lived. This desire provoked Breton's intense interest in Communist theory and the events in post-revolutionary Russia. Breton's association with the Communist Party however proved to be a shaky one because he argued that it was possible to be a surrealist first and foremost and still support social and economic revolution. It was a stance that did not impress the

Communists themselves either in France or Moscow, and it would finally split Breton's group, but it may well have been the political and more practical aspect of the surrealist revolution which caused Buñuel to become an official member. He has himself referred to the fact that he was attracted to the Paris Surrealists both for artistic and political reasons.

In order to understand the reasons for Breton's acclamation of *Un Chien andalou* and the Surrealists' championing of Buñuel, it is necessary to consider both the importance they attached to film and the kind of films which they were making. For many, the cinema, with its unrivaled power of expression, was the perfect medium for communicating a surrealist view of life, a view put forward, for example, in René Clair's article of 1925, 'Cinema and Surrealism'. His own *Entr'acte*, made in 1924, attempted to present a flow of images without anecdotal argument. Objects are transformed one into another – a chessboard turns into the Place de la Concorde – and convey a surrealist defiance of logic. The same year saw the appearance of Fernand Léger's *Le Ballet mécanique*, another film without narrative. In 1926 Marcel Duchamp and Man Ray collaborated on *Anemic Cinema*, an abstract film composed of alternating shots of moving spirals and elaborate puns and anagrams, while Man Ray's own *Emak Bakia (Leave Me Alone)* is essentially a juxtaposition of unrelated images. Germaine Dulac's *La Coquille et le clergyman*, made in 1927 with a script by Antonin Artaud, had the promising subject of the temptation of a celibate priest but, through its reliance on cinematic tricks, appeared arty and pretentious. It was precisely the abstract and often 'arty' nature of such films and their failure to express ultimately the fantasies of human consciousness itself that in 1927 provoked Dalí's article 'Art Film – Anti-Art Film' with its specific criticism of Man Ray and Fernand Léger. For Dalí, the surrealist ideal, with its emphasis on the absurd, the illogical and irrational, was better expressed in the comic antics of Chaplin, Buster Keaton, Harry Langdon and

Harold Lloyd, and these, after all, were firmly rooted outside the world of art and abstraction. Buñuel shared Dalí's viewpoint, arguing that the comic films were the true surrealist cinema. In seeking his own inspiration here, as well as in commercial horror films and the serious films of Fritz Lang and Erich von Stroheim, Buñuel was expressing a clear preference for a cinema which contained and represented the themes so dear to the Surrealists in an imaginative yet concrete way, avoiding the kind of abstraction described above. When Breton acknowledged the Surrealism of *Un Chien andalou*, he was in effect acclaiming its triumphant fusion of form and content.

The success of *Un Chien andalou* led Buñuel to begin work immediately on another film. In its preparation he again collaborated with Salvador Dalí, but a disagreement between the two men created a permanent rift and considerable acrimony between them and Buñuel completed the filming of *L'Age d'or* alone. The circumstances surrounding its showing at the 'Studio 28' in Paris in December, 1930, are now cinema history. The right-wing press, in particular, reacted violently to a film which, in its eulogy to sexual passion and its contempt for the bourgeoisie, overthrew conventional social and moral values. Incited by the press, reactionary groups, including the League of Patriots and the Anti-Jewish League, attacked and damaged the cinema. With the threat of reprisals by the film's supporters, *L'Age d'or* was withdrawn on police instructions, and the surrealist group, as a protest against this infringement of human liberty, issued a detailed questionnaire. The outrage that surrounded the initial presentation of *L'Age d'or* would continue for a long time. It must have pleased Buñuel's anti-bourgeois sentiments as much as the making of the film contributed to his artistic evolution. *Un Chien andalou*, for all its merits, was a short, experimental film. *L'Age d'or* was, in contrast, the first full-length surrealist film. Moreover, inasmuch as its surrealist elements are contained within a recognizable narrative framework, it clearly anticipates Buñuel's mature work.

As a result of *L'Age d'or* Buñuel was offered a contract to make films in Hollywood but chose instead to go as an observer of American techniques of film-making. He stayed for only a month before returning to Paris in the spring of 1931, but during his stay in Hollywood encountered both Chaplin and Eisenstein. Buñuel's aggressive surrealist streak was revealed in an incident at Chaplin's Christmas party when a group of Spanish guests, armed with pruning shears and encouraged by Buñuel, attacked the Christmas tree, the symbol of bourgeois convention, and stripped it of its branches – much, it seems, to Chaplin's amusement. In 1932, however, Buñuel ended his association with the Paris surrealist group, for it seemed to him to have become too exclusive and to have abandoned its political aims:

> In 1932 I separated from the Surrealist group although I remained on good terms with my ex-companions. I was beginning not to agree with that kind of intellectual aristocracy, with its artistic and moral extremes, which isolated us from the world and limited us to our own company. Surrealists considered the majority of mankind contemptible or stupid, and thus withdrew from all social participation and responsibility and shunned the work of the others.[7]

Buñuel now had a variety of different jobs, ranging from that of a writer for Paramount Studios in Paris to that of 'dubbing' supervisor at Warner Brothers in Madrid. But the most significant event of these years was undoubtedly the making of *Land Without Bread (Las Hurdes)* in 1933 – a year which also saw Buñuel's marriage to Jeanne Rucar. With four companions Buñuel spent two months in one of Spain's most backward regions and, after very careful preparations, took a month to shoot his film. A documentary in character, it depicts in a ruthlessly objective manner the abject misery of a deprived and neglected people. To the pictures was added a cool, matter-of-fact commentary, while the heroic tones of Brahms's Fourth Symphony provided a suitably ironic accompaniment. Shocked by what they regarded as an insult to Spain, the Spanish Government banned the film, and it was not released until 1937. In relation to Buñuel's films in general *Land Without Bread* is a fine example of his liking for documentary, his direct, unfussy style, and that apparent objectivity which is simultaneously a burning commitment.

After the completion of *Land Without Bread*, Buñuel turned his attention to making films in Spain. Ricardo Urgoit, a wealthy Spaniard, had invited him to run Filmófono, a company which imported and distributed foreign films and which, under Buñuel's control, would make and show its own productions. In 1935 and 1936 Buñuel made four commercial films: *Don Quintín, the Embittered One (Don Quintín el amargao), The Daughter of Juan Simón (La hija de Juan Simón), Who Loves Me? (¿Quién me quiere a mí?),* and *Sentinel, On Guard! (¡Centinela alerta!).* Buñuel has subsequently dismissed the artistic quality of these films, but the value of his work with Filmófono lies far less in the merit of particular films than in the experience Buñuel acquired from doing the job of casting, writing, rehearsing, directing, and editing. Had Filmófono continued Buñuel might well have produced much better films, for his plans included his own adaptation of *Wuthering Heights*, of Valle-Inclán's novel, *Tirano Banderas*, and Galdós's *Fortunata y Jacinta.* But the outbreak of the Spanish Civil War in July 1936 brought Filmófono's activities to an end.

The years 1936-42 were significant in relation to Buñuel's already considerable interest in documentary. When the Civil War commenced, he was sent by the Republican government to Paris where he would gather and edit material for a full-length documentary on the war. *Loyal Spain, To Arms! (¡España leal, en armas!)*, reminiscent of *Land Without Bread* in its objective portrayal of horrific facts, is a fine example of Buñuel's skill as a film editor. In 1938 he was in Hollywood for the supervision of two American films about the Civil War, and from 1939 to 1942 he was involved in the production of documentaries of different kinds for the film department of the Museum of Modern Art in New York. Although Buñuel has described the nature of his job as purely administrative and uncreative, it is clear that through highly skillful editing he transformed a large amount of dull material into absorbing documentaries. Four years of dubbing, editing, and adding commentary and music deepened and broadened considerably Buñuel's practical experience. His work at the Museum came to an end in 1942 when his employers, informed of his part in the scandalous *L'Age d'or*, forced him to resign, though the real reason may well have been Salvador Dalí's claim that Buñuel was a member of the French Communist Party.

Returning to Hollywood, Buñuel worked for a while as a commentator for the Spanish versions of American Army documentaries, and then, from 1944 to 1946, was a dubbing director for Warner Brothers. It was a time in which the idea of making his own films was also very much in his mind. He was involved to some extent in the making of Warner Brothers' *The Beast With Five Fingers* and also prepared a number of his own projects, including *Goya and the Duchess of Alba*. Hollywood at this time was, however, in a state of depression, threatened by McCarthyist attacks as well as by the arrival of television, and in 1946 Buñuel left Warner Brothers. Inactive for a year, he finally made another crucial decision in his career – to make films in Mexico. After a gap of nearly ten years, Buñuel's renewed contact with a Spanish way of life – people, language, religion and institutions – proved to be a source of fresh and genuine inspiration.

Between 1946 and 1949 Buñuel made two films in Mexico – *Gran Casino* and *El gran calavera*. The former is a musical comedy set in Tampico in the oil era. Buñuel provided a poor subject with a good script, and parts of the film are typical of him, but otherwise it was a complete commercial flop which left him unemployed for two years. *El gran calavera*, on the other hand, though generally a poor film, was quite amusing, and was commercially successful in South America, Portugal and Spain. The importance of these films lies firstly in the fact that, in making them, Buñuel learned to work quickly and within limited budgets; and secondly, the success of *El gran calavera* led its producer, Oscar Dancigers, to give him a free hand in the making of another film. The result was his first great film for seventeen years, the masterly *Los olvidados*.

Los olvidados, made in 1950 and winner of the prize for the best direction at the Cannes Film Festival of 1951, marked Buñuel's return to the international scene, and in the next thirty years he was to make no less than twenty-six full-length films. *Los olvidados* was a landmark too inasmuch as it pushed Buñuel away from the overt surrealism of his first films into a more narrative tradition within which surrealism could still express itself. The tradition of the Mexican commercial cinema was, indeed, one of simple, strong, melodramatic stories laced with a good deal of action and violence. It was a recipe to which Buñuel, dependent upon his producers, had to submit, and one which he largely followed for ten years after the success of *Los olvidados*. *Susana* (1950), for example, presents us with a seductive heroine before whose charms the foreman on a Mexican ranch, the owner's son, and then the owner himself – all good Catholics – fall like ninepins, quarrelling over her amongst themselves. *The Brute (El Bruto)* (1952) has as its protagonist Pedro, the strong-arm man of a rich property owner, and, in its portrayal of his relationship with the latter, his victims, and the various women in his life, is full of passion and melodramatic incident. *He (El)* (1952) and *The River and Death (El río y la muerte)* (1954) have the same basic ingredients in varying proportions, as indeed does *The Young One (La Joven)* (1960), a joint Mexican-American production which, in a sense, marks the end of Buñuel's Mexican period.

The films of these years, for all their adherence to a

formula, rarely fail to reveal Buñuel's surrealist preoccupations. *Susana*, through the violent disorder created by its heroine, exposes individual and social tensions and the hypocrisy of conventional moral values. *El*, in the presentation of the central character's sexual inhibitions, lays bare the repressive influence of social and religious institutions. The themes are essentially those of *L'Age d'or*. Moreover, Buñuel's surrealist exposure of society's hollowness often goes hand in hand with the surrealists' other principal concern – the revelation of the inner life. *El* is the story of a man's obsession with a young woman and, after his marriage to her, of his insane jealousy, while *Susana* contains many incidents which suggest the sexual motivations of its characters. And in the two great films of this period – *Los olvidados* and *Nazarín* – the stark portrayal of external reality is consistently accompanied by Buñuel's concentration on his characters' private fixations.

The films made in Mexico bear witness in their themes and preoccupations to Buñuel's essential Spanishness, and it is not surprising, therefore, that he should have been anxious both to make films once more in Spain and to give a lead to a Spanish film industry in search of a genuine style and personality. Encouraged by a group of young Spanish filmmakers and enthusiasts, Buñuel returned to Spain in 1960 to make *Viridiana* and, after an absence of more than twenty years, was relieved to discover his old haunts and many of his old friends still extant.

If Buñuel's Mexican films had been governed by considerations of money, time and public taste, he had in the filming of *Viridiana* a relatively free hand. This did not mean, though, that Buñuel departed from the predominant style of his Mexican films, for *Viridiana* has the same narrative and melodramatic qualities, but it is a more polished and 'finished' film. The Spanish authorities, anxious no doubt to make the most of Buñuel's return to his native country, allowed *Viridiana* to be shown as the official Spanish entry at the Cannes Film Festival of 1961. In doing so the censorship had approved the film after a viewing without dialogue or sound, which were both added by Buñuel in Paris. In the event *Viridiana* won the 'Palme d'or' at Cannes but, as a consequence of its blasphemous implications, scandalized the Vatican. The film was subsequently banned in Spain, references to it in newspapers were forbidden, and many of those involved in its showing at Cannes lost their jobs. Buñuel had, it seemed, underestimated the repressive nature of the Franco regime. Elsewhere *Viridiana* was a great success and made a lot of money, but Buñuel returned to Mexico puzzled and, no doubt, saddened by the realization that it would be difficult to make another film in Spain.

Most of Buñuel's subsequent films were made in either Mexico or France. *Viridiana* was followed, for example, by *The Exterminating Angel (El ángel exterminador)*, which was made in Mexico in 1962, and which proved to be one of Buñuel's very best films of the sixties. Reminiscent in some respects of William Golding's *Lord of the Flies*, it depicts the bourgeois guests at a dinner party inexplicably trapped in the drawing-room and slowly but inevitably exposed to their own underlying savagery. Buñuel succeeds in this film, more, perhaps, than in any other, in combining a ferocious attack on bourgeois values with an exposure of unconscious motivation, for the progressive degradation of the refined company allows him to do both. Coolly received at the Cannes Film Festival of 1962, *The Exterminating Angel* has been seen by many critics as Buñuel's most surrealist film since *L'Age d'or*. Superficially it seems to be a less aggressive work and it is probably true to say that with the passing of the years Buñuel's manner is less overtly violent. But this is not to say that it is blunted by complacency. On the contrary, Buñuel's evolution since *Viridiana* is one in which aggression becomes a cool, detached, often documentary approach. For all that, its cutting edge is just as sharp.

In 1962 Buñuel returned to Spain with plans to film *Tristana*, a film based on the novel of the same name by the nineteenth-century Spanish novelist, Pérez Galdós. He evidently felt that two years after the scandal caused by *Viridiana* the Spanish censorship had become more tolerant. Buñuel was allowed to proceed with the practical arrangements for the making of the film, but at the last minute the censorship intervened, banning its filming on the grounds that, in its allusions to the practice of duelling, the script contravened the new code of censorship. Buñuel was not to make *Tristana* in Spain until 1970. Until that time he continued, as before, to work either in Mexico or France. *Le Journal d'une femme de chambre* was made in France in 1963 and *Simon of the Desert (Simón del desierto)* in Mexico in 1965. The former, based on Mirbeau's novel, depicts a bourgeois family in which its members, devoted to their own particular sexual fantasies, are isolated from the pressing political reality of the outside world. It is a withering exposé of bourgeois introversion. *Simón del desierto*, on the other hand, shows Buñuel grappling again with a religious theme. The idealism of the man who has spent the last fourteen years of his life perched on a tower preaching to those below him is seen, as in *Nazarín* to be wholly futile.

Buñuel's most famous film of the sixties – and also his most successful commercially – is undoubtedly *Belle de Jour*, made in France in 1966. It was the film for which he had most financial backing to date and it is thus in many ways his most lavish and 'glossy' film – though the word is not used here in any detrimental sense. Already in *Viridiana, The Exterminating Angel* and *La Journal d'une femme de chambre*, Buñuel had suggested through expensively and even oppressively furnished rooms the crippling weight of bourgeois conventionality. The settings of *Belle de Jour* – rich apartments, tennis clubs, holiday resorts – emphasize precisely the superficiality and reliance on appearance of its characters' lives. In contrast to this Buñuel reveals in the protagonist, Séverine, the turbulent, subversive emotions that boil beneath the surface. It is a film which is full of arresting dream-sequences, as surrealist in its exposure of the unconscious as *Un Chien andalou* or *The Exterminating*

Angel. Belle de Jour is also Buñuel's first colour film. He uses colour not merely as a decorative element but to create even more effectively the atmosphere of bourgeois comfort and elegance which is then consistently undermined.

The Milky Way (La voie lactée), made in France in 1969, is one of Buñuel's most original films. Religious themes characterize to a greater or lesser extent all Buñuel's work, but *The Milky Way* is unusual inasmuch as it deals with religious questions – in this case the heresies involved in Catholic dogma – in a much more central and abstract way. It is the kind of film which Buñuel had long wanted to make. In 1970, moreover, he fulfilled another of his aims by finally making *Tristana* in Spain. Although eight years had passed since the abortive attempt to make the film, there were still problems with the Spanish censorship and Buñuel waited six months for work to begin. In some ways *Tristana* is one of his most muted and restrained films, for it has hardly any of the surrealist elements of *Belle de Jour*. Nevertheless, its restrained manner does not prevent us from appreciating Buñuel's cool and ruthless exposure of the backwardness and narrowmindedness of Spanish provincial life, both social and religious. He had remarked of Toledo that 'it is old and stinks of piss'[8] and in *Tristana*, filmed in Toledo, Buñuel captures precisely that sense of an old, decaying way of life that is also symbolic of much of Spanish society as a whole.

In the seventies Buñuel's creative energies have shown little sign of faltering. In three major films he has pursued his favourite themes with the same enthusiasm and ingenuity as in the past. *The Discreet Charm of the Bourgeoisie (Le Charme discrèt de la bourgeoisie)*, a French production of 1972, combines a satiric onslaught on the bourgeoisie with a surrealist exposure of the characters' inner lives. It is a film that is reminiscent of *The Exterminating Angel*, but its tone is generally lighter and more amusing. *The Phantom of Liberty (Le Fantôme de la liberté)*, made in 1974, also has many surrealist qualities. Buñuel's last film to date, a French production of 1978, is *That Obscure Object of Desire (Cet Obscur objet du désir).* If Buñuel makes no more films, *That Obscure Object* will surely be a fitting epitaph. Its central character, Mathieu, is Buñuel's smug bourgeois whose cosy life is disrupted by a persistent sexual passion. Played superbly by Fernando Rey, who had served Buñuel so well as Don Jaime in *Viridiana* and Don Lope in *Tristana*, Mathieu is very reminiscent of these earlier bourgeois gentlemen. Buñuel's films have, from beginning to end, a remarkable unity of theme and vision. It is highly appropriate that, as *Un Chien andalou* opens with its famous assault upon the eye (spectator's as much as character's), *That Obscure Object* should end with a mighty explosion.[9]

Buñuel's views on the cinema have been expressed over many years in essays, interviews and conversations. He has, of course, invariably expressed his disapproval of the commercial cinema; for the commercial artist is always in the hands of others, of the need to compromise, and, in particular, of the need to conform to conventional moral standards. Before making *Nazarín* Buñuel made the following comments on the commercial film in general:

> The cinematic 'churro' [i.e. a fritter] can often be made with wonderful technique, fine actors and sparkling dialogue. The 'churro' can easily win an Oscar or be acclaimed at film festivals. There is no fixed price. In Mexico we have made a lot of them for 600,000 pesos, while Hollywood will spend as much as 10 million dollars for just one. The 'churro' is distinguished by a mentality that is as sterile as it is out-of-date. It is the usual range of emotions – love, hate, sorrow, etc. – measured according to the basest standard: the murderer must be executed, the prostitute must be saved, Good must defeat Evil – it is all absolute mental laziness![10]

Luis Buñuel

A similar view of the stultifying effect on artist and audience of the commercial cinema was expressed in answer to a question put to Buñuel by a film critic:

> How is it possible to hope for an improvement in the audience – and consequently in the producers – when every day we are told in these films, even in our most insipid comedies, that our social institutions, our concepts of Country, Religion, Love, etc., etc., are, while perhaps imperfect, unique and necessary? The true 'opium of the audience' is conformity; and the entire, gigantic film world is dedicated to the propagation of this comfortable feeling, wrapped though it is at times in the insidious disguise of art.[11]

In conjunction with his distaste for the commercial film-industry Buñuel has often expressed his dislike of the so-called 'stars' of the cinema.

While the commercial cinema propagates the conventional values of a conformist and moneyed middle class, Buñuel has always opposed such values. From his first film, *Un Chien andalou*, he has launched a fierce onslaught on accepted and established attitudes, moral, social and artistic. In *Un Chien andalou* his purpose was not to please but to provoke. Asked to define his moral standpoint, Buñuel has stated:

> Morality – middle-class morality, that is – is for me immoral. One must fight it. It is a morality founded on our most unjust social institutions – religion, fatherland, family culture – everything that people call the pillars of society.[12]

Elsewhere he has emphasized the unwavering consistency of his philosophy:

> The thought that continues guiding me today is the same that guided me at the age of twenty-five. It is an idea of Engels. The artist describes authentic social relations with the object of destroying the conventional

> ideals of the bourgeois world and compelling the public to doubt the perennial existence of the established order. That is the ultimate meaning of all my films: to say time and again, in case someone forgets or believes otherwise, that we do not live in the best of all possible worlds. I don't know what more I can do.[13]

If Buñuel's purpose is to confront us with the harsh reality of the world in which we live, he does not, on the other hand, have any better world to offer. His earlier films, notably *L'Age d'or*, are a fierce assault on existing values and institutions. In later films – and it is already evident in *Los olvidados* – Buñuel's attention is preoccupied, not with remedies, but with the notion of man as he is in all his flawed and often grotesque humanity. His view of the world is, as he has himself said, basically simple:

> It's no good telling people that all's for the best in this best of all possible worlds . . . I believe that you must look for God in man. It's a very simple attitude.[14]

Man's eyes should not, in other words, be turned away from the world towards some comforting and soporific idealization of things, be it social or religious ideology, but towards it, in order to apprehend, understand and cherish man in all his imperfections. Nothing illustrates the point better than the hideous beggars of *Viridiana*. When their banquet is suddenly frozen by Buñuel into an image of *The Last Supper*, he divests saints of a traditional sentimentality and endows the most monstrous of men with a spark of saintliness. For Buñuel religious, social and political ideals give men false concepts of themselves. Nazarín, for instance, is a man filled with religious idealism whose principal concern it is to change the world. He has his counterpart in Viridiana, whose head is filled with notions instilled in her by her convent training. Séverine, in *Belle de Jour*, is a woman initially ruled by conventional and puritanical bourgeois morality, a woman cast in its joyless image. In each case these characters are, through their experience of the world, born again – born, that is, to an understanding of their fellow men and of themselves, and in the process slowly stripped of their false illusions. It is the process which we see at work in a particularly sharp and heightened form in *The Exterminating Angel* as the bourgeois guests, locked in the drawing-room and deprived of food and water, are confronted with the reality of their own physical and moral degradation.

In the light of this, Buñuel's preoccupation with the unconscious – for the surrealists the true reality – is entirely logical. For him the cinema is the perfect medium through which to express it:

> In the hands of a free spirit the cinema is a magnificent and dangerous weapon. It is the superlative medium through which to express the world of thought, feeling, and instinct. The creative handling of film images is such that, among all means of human expression, its way of functioning is most reminiscent of the work of the mind during sleep. A film is like an involuntary imitation of a dream. Brunius points out how the darkness that slowly settles over a movie theatre is equivalent to the act of closing the eyes. Then, on the screen, as with the human being, the nocturnal voyage into the unconscious begins. . . . The cinema seems to have been invented to express the life of the subconscious. . . .[15]

In this lecture, delivered at the University of Mexico in 1953, Buñuel restated what in practice he had done in *Un Chien andalou* twenty-four years earlier and what he has done in all his films. He has spoken elsewhere of his absorbing interest in a 'life with ambiguities and contradictions'.[16] In *Belle de Jour* Séverine's real self is expressed not in her daily life, hemmed in and circumscribed by meaningless and empty social habits, but in her uninhibited dreams, to which in the course of the film her actions slowly adapt themselves. Similarly, Viridiana's touching of the cow's teat and her contact with the phallic handles of the skipping-rope awaken in her, and reveal to us, her awareness of forces within her that are deeper, more powerful and more 'real' than the values superficially imposed upon her by her convent education. Inasmuch as so many of Buñuel's characters are born again to a greater understanding of themselves, it is an understanding which responds progressively to the significance of their own inner lives which, for the most part, have been buried beneath the suffocating layers of mindlessly accepted attitudes. Gaston Modot, Séverine, Tristana are people who, casting aside their bonds, live out their own inner vision.

As far as the technical side of the cinema is concerned, Buñuel has consistently aimed at simplicity and directness, be it to portray external reality or the unconscious. In a description of one day in the shooting of *Viridiana*, Francisco Aranda has drawn attention to these qualities in Buñuel's direction:

> Given its [the shot's] complexity, a script and direction less skilled would have made endless shots and takes. Buñuel controlled the filming precisely, despite his apparent inaction.... Later Quintana came in. 'This man is great. Every day of shooting makes me more aware of it. He simplifies everything to mathematical precision. Where other directors would get into a great muddle, shouting and making all sorts of scenes, he resolves the problem with no fuss; and, moreover, films exactly what has to be filmed. Out of a thousand possibilities, he infallibly chooses the best'.[17]

Jean-Claude Carrière, who has worked closely with Buñuel on many films since 1963, refers to the economy of his technique:

> He steers clear of unusual angles or sophisticated camera work.... The solution is usually the simplest, or sometimes just the easiest.... Once he's satisfied with a take, he goes on to the next.... He has the reputation

> of being well-organized and very economical, never behind schedule. . . .[18]

Music, too, is employed only when it serves a specific purpose. In 1954 Buñuel observed:

> Personally I don't like film music. It seems to me that it is a false element, a sort of trick, except of course in certain cases.[19]

He has used music sometimes for ironic effect, as in *Viridiana*, sometimes to underline a given moment, as in the love sequence of *L'Age d'or*, but never as mere ornament or background. Like all great artists, Buñuel has reduced the complex art of the cinema to a simplicity which is the source, at least in part, of his enduring appeal.

Finally, in relation to his cinema in general, it is important to emphasize that Buñuel is both a very literate and a highly literary man and that literature has exercised a deep and lasting influence upon his work. Reference has been made in the preceding pages to Buñuel's friends at the Residencia de Estudiantes, most of whom were writers, to the *avant-garde* movements with which he became familiar, most of which were literary, and to his own early creative writing. Themes and images which in later years are expressed in the language of cinema can often be found in Buñuel's prose and poems of the 1920s. 'Instrumentation', published in 1922 in the Spanish journal, *Horizonte*, is a surrealist description of orchestral instruments which anticipates an episode in *The Exterminating Angel*. 'Suburbs', which also belongs to 1922, looks forward to the seedy buildings, the hovels and the wasteground of *Los olvidados*. 'Palace of Ice' and other surrealist pieces were written for the unpublished *The Andalusian Dog (El perro andaluz)*, which preceded *Un Chien andalou*. In addition, during the 1920s Buñuel wrote poems and short stories of a more traditional kind which were influenced by such literary genres as the Spanish picaresque novel and which also found expression in many of his films.

Between 1928 and 1932 Buñuel worked as a cinema critic for the influential *avant-garde* Spanish magazine, *La Gaceta literaria*, and also became editor of its cinema section. In the pages of *La Gaceta* he published his critical assessments of such films as Carl Dreyer's *Jeanne d'Arc* and Abel Gance's *Napoleon*, as well as highly perceptive essays on cinema technique, such as 'Cinema, Instrument of Poetry'. At the same time he contributed to the Catalan literary journal, *L'Amic de les arts*, and in 1927 he was cinema critic for *Cahiers d'art*. Subsequently, as a maker of films, Buñuel was to abandon film criticism, but he has expressed himself in a very articulate manner in the many interviews which he has provided for journals.

Buñuel's most important literary activity is to be found in his scripts, for either singly or with a collaborator, he has written the scripts for all his important films. The range of subjects reflects Buñuel's varied literary interests: the Spanish picaresque novel and Cervantes in *Los olvidados* and *Nazarín*; in the latter and in *Tristana* the influence of the nineteenth-century Spanish novelist, Galdós; and the English novel in *Wuthering Heights* and *Robinson Crusoe*. The surrealist character of many films points, too, to an intimate knowledge of the works of both the precursors of Surrealism – Rimbaud, Lautréamont, Sade – and to the works of Freud. But the true significance of Buñuel's scripts is to be found in their own literary merit, for to see a film like *Viridiana* is to become aware not merely of the suggestive power of the visual images but of the expressive power of the spoken word.

NOTES

[1] I am particularly indebted for biographical information to Francisco Aranda's very detailed book, *Luis Buñuel: biografía crítica*, Barcelona: Editorial Lumen, 1969. My references are to the English translation by David Robinson, published by Secker and Warburg, 1975.

[2] Aranda, p. 12. The extract is taken from Buñuel's unpublished autobiography, written in English in 1938 for the New York Museum of Modern Art.

[3] See Aranda, p. 18.

[4] For a very informative study of this subject see C. B. Morris, *Surrealism and Spain, 1920–1936*, Cambridge: At the University Press, 1972.

[5] Quoted by Aranda, p. 34.

[6] Aranda, pp. 34-35.

[7] Aranda, p. 88.

[8] In an interview on French television.

[9] Useful general studies of Buñuel's films include: Freddy Buache, *The Cinema of Luis Buñuel*, trs. Peter Graham, London and New York: Tantivy/Barnes, 1973; Raymond Durgnat, *Luis Buñuel*, London: Studio Vista, 1967; Ado Kyrou, *Luis Buñuel: an Introduction*, New York: Simon and Schuster, 1963; and *The World of Luis Buñuel, Essays in Criticism*, ed. Joan Mellen, New York: Oxford University Press, 1978.

[10] In an interview published in *Mexico en la cultura*, no. 478, May 1958. The translation is my own.

[11] Quoted by Aranda, p. 185.

[12] See Donald Richie, 'The Moral Code of Luis Buñuel', *The World of Luis Buñuel*, p. 111.

[13] Quoted by Victor Casaus, *'Las Hurdes: Land Without Bread'*, *The World of Luis Buñuel*, p. 184

[14] See David Robinson, ' "Thank God – I Am Still an Atheist": Luis Buñuel and *Viridiana*', *The World of Luis Buñuel*, p. 239.

[15] Quoted from Buñuel's essay 'Poetry and Cinema', reprinted in *The World of Luis Buñuel*, pp. 105-110.

[16] See Aranda, *Luis Buñuel*, p. 212.

[17] Aranda, p. 197.

[18] See 'The Buñuel Mystery', *The World of Luis Buñuel*, pp. 93-94.

[19] Aranda, p. 91.

1
UN CHIEN ANDALOU

CAST

The Young Man	—	Pierre Batcheff
The Young Woman	—	Simone Mareuil
Priest	—	Salvador Dalí
Man with razor	—	Luis Buñuel

Script	—	Luis Buñuel Salvador Dalí
Design	—	Pierre Schilzneck
Photography	—	Albert Duverger
Editor	—	Luis Buñuel
Producer	—	Luis Buñuel
Director	—	Luis Buñuel

Buñuel's first film, *Un Chien andalou*, received its première in June, 1929, at the Studio Ursulines in Paris.[1] It was an immediate success, acclaimed by cinema critics, writers, painters and intellectuals alike, and proclaimed by André Breton as a true surrealist film. To Buñuel's astonishment it subsequently ran for the general public for nine consecutive months at the Studio 28 and became the subject of controversy and of innumerable articles. Although so-called surrealist films were made both before and after *Un Chien andalou*, none of them attracted such attention or became the focal point of so much argument.

As far as the film's origins are concerned, Buñuel stated in a letter to José Bello in January, 1929, that he was about to spend a fortnight working with Salvador Dalí 'on some mutual and very cinematographic ideas' and expressed the intention of commencing shooting at the beginning of April.[2] In another letter of February 10 he observed that he and Dalí had produced a wonderful scenario, unique in the modern cinema, and that filming would begin in March. At this stage the film was to be called *It is Dangerous to Lean In (Dangéreux de se pencher en dedans)*, a play on words on the inscription in French railway carriages. *Un Chien andalou*, the eventual title of the film, was the title of a book of poems which Buñuel and Dalí were planning to write together. It was a title which Buñuel said had made him and Dalí 'piss with laughter', for there was no dog anywhere in the book, but it was a good title and, as well as being funny, was totally idiotic. At all events the film was eventually made quite quickly and in the same year the scenario was published in the official surrealist journal, *La Révolution Surréaliste*.

Dalí's role in the final making of the film seems to have been less than his contribution to the preparations for it, though it is probably true that his initial association with it was, perhaps more than Buñuel's, a guarantee of its success. In subsequent years, following the break with Buñuel, Dalí has claimed the film for himself. For his part, Buñuel has observed that the plot was a joint effort, that Dalí suggested the title, and that the agreement to exclude from the film all sense of narrative and logic was a mutual one. Prior to shooting they both recounted their dreams and selected from those images they thought most suited to the film. But as far as its making was concerned, Buñuel has observed that Dalí was present only on the last day of filming and played the part of one of the two priests who are dragged on the end of the rope in one of its central sequences. The final product, in terms of its cinematographic quality and style, was, with the exception of a few small details, pure Buñuel.

Buñuel has described his intentions in *Un Chien andalou* in the following way:

> In the film are amalgamated the aesthetics of Surrealism with Freudian discoveries. It answered the general principle of that school, which defines Surrealism as 'an unconscious, psychic automatism, able to return to the mind its real function, outside of all control exercised by reason, morality or aesthetics'.
>
> Although I availed myself of oniric elements, the film is not the description of a dream. On the contrary, the environment and characters are of a realistic type. Its fundamental difference from other films consists in the fact that the characters function animated by impulses, the primal sources of which are confused with those of irrationalism, which, in turn, are those of poetry. At times these characters react enigmatically, in as far as a pathological psychic complex can be enigmatic.
>
> This film is directed at the unconscious feelings of man, and therefore is of universal value, although it may seem disagreeable to certain groups of society which are sustained by puritanical moral principles. . . .[3]

The concern with the revelation of 'the unconscious feelings of man' is, of course, in true surrealist manner, an important feature of the film, the source, indeed, of much of its lasting value. But other factors too were important in its making.

The element of joke, of outrageous surrealist humour, can never have been far away and, in addition, there was, of course, that other surrealistic requisite – the need to shock.

Buñuel's aggression had been a marked feature of his character during his stay at the Residencia de Estudiantes in Madrid, much commented upon by those who knew him. When in 1929 he joined the surrealist group in Paris, he identified completely with what he saw as their 'moral and artistic intransigence' and fully shared their hatred of conventional, stultifying moral and artistic values. His letters of the period reveal a violent hostility that would last until *L'Age d'or.* Of *Un Chien andalou* he wrote in *La Révolution Surréaliste* that his aim was to provoke, not to please, that the film was not an 'aesthetic' exercise but 'a desperate appeal to murder'.[4] He repeated the idea when the film was shown later in the Cineclub of Madrid:

> I do not want the film to please you but to offend you. I would be sorry if you were to enjoy it.

In more recent years Buñuel has written:

> . . . the film represents a violent reaction against what in those days was called 'avant-garde', which was aimed exclusively at artistic sensibility and the audience's reason. . . . In *Un Chien andalou* the film-maker for the first time takes up a position on a poetic-moral plane. . . . His object is to provoke instinctive reactions of revulsion and attraction in the spectator. . . .[5]

The extent of Buñuel's attempt to reveal the unconscious and, by so doing, to shock his public into both a new awareness of themselves and of the hypocrisy of many of their values, may be gauged by Henry Miller's account of the Madrid performance of the film:

> Afterwards they showed *Un Chien andalou.* The public shuddered, making their seats creak, when an enormous eye appeared on the screen and was cut

> coldly by a razor, the drops of liquid from the iris leaping onto the metal. Hysterical shouts were heard.[6]

Un Chien andalou begins with one of the most disturbing sequences in the history of the cinema. A title on the screen suggests the commencement of a fairy tale: *Once Upon a Time*. The mood is enhanced by a shot of a man looking out through the window at the moon in an almost cloudless sky and by the face in close-up of a young, wide-eyed girl. Then, in a series of alternating shots the fairy-tale mood, and any complacency the spectator might have had, are ruthlessly destroyed. A thin cloud moves towards the moon. A razor moves towards an eye. The cloud slices the moon. The razor slits the eye. Buñuel, taking the part of the man who wields the razor in the film, compels us to pay attention to it, shatters our comfortable illusions, and destroys our accustomed way of looking at things, making us look anew.[7] In its illogicality, its dissolves and its shifting focus, the sequence has too the character of dream and of the unconscious that is to distinguish the film as a whole. The images also have particular Freudian connotations and point to the consistency of the film's symbolism in this respect. Razor and eye are the male and female sexual organs and, inasmuch as the man uses the razor on the woman, the incident anticipates the film's sexual violence. But it has too, beneath the surface, a very conscious artistry that is equally characteristic of Buñuel.

The prologue becomes another subtitle: *Eight Years Later*. The film's protagonist, a young man, is seen cycling along a Paris street. He wears a dark grey suit and on his head and around his shoulders and waist there are white, frilly trimmings. He carries around his neck a box with diagonal stripes and he rides the bicycle in a listless, mechanical manner. Both dress and movement indicate sexual immaturity and emotional paralysis, even castration, while the box symbolizes female sexuality.[8] The suit points too to his bourgeois respectability. He is the first of the many bourgeois cripples that people Buñuel's films.

The young man has his bourgeois counterpart in a young woman who is seen seated at a table in a room, reading a book. She becomes suddenly agitated, goes to the window in time to see the young man fall from his bicycle into the mud, rushes downstairs to his assistance and begins kissing him passionately (in Freudian terms falling indicates sexual anxiety while ascending or descending stairs is synonymous with sexual desire). The young woman, clearly, feels the sexual drive that the young man lacks. She trembles inexplicably before she sees him, as though in response to some deep and powerful impulse. Her rejection of the book in response to her instinctive feelings represents an overthrowing of the inhibiting influences – tradition and culture – that have shaped her upbringing, and of which the young man, lying inert in the gutter as she kisses him, is already the crippled victim. In their first encounter Buñuel has given expression to one of the film's most important themes: the power and the frustration of love.

A new sequence begins with a close-up of hands removing a striped tie from the box that the young man carried around his neck.[9] The diagonal stripes link the tie, the paper in which it is wrapped, the box in which it is carried, the rain falling in the street, and the shirt of the man with the razor. The diagonal stripes are a recurring motif which strongly underlines sexual aggression (especially in connection with phallic metaphors like the tie) and also make a connection between apparently disjointed episodes in a way which endows them too with the obsessive character of dream. The hands become the young woman who is looking at the frills, the plain tie and the stiff collar. Worn earlier by the young man, they are laid out now on the bed as though worn by an invisible man, this impression heightened by the rumpled bedclothes. The clothes that lack a body point again to the young man's castration and indicate that the woman's search for passion is still

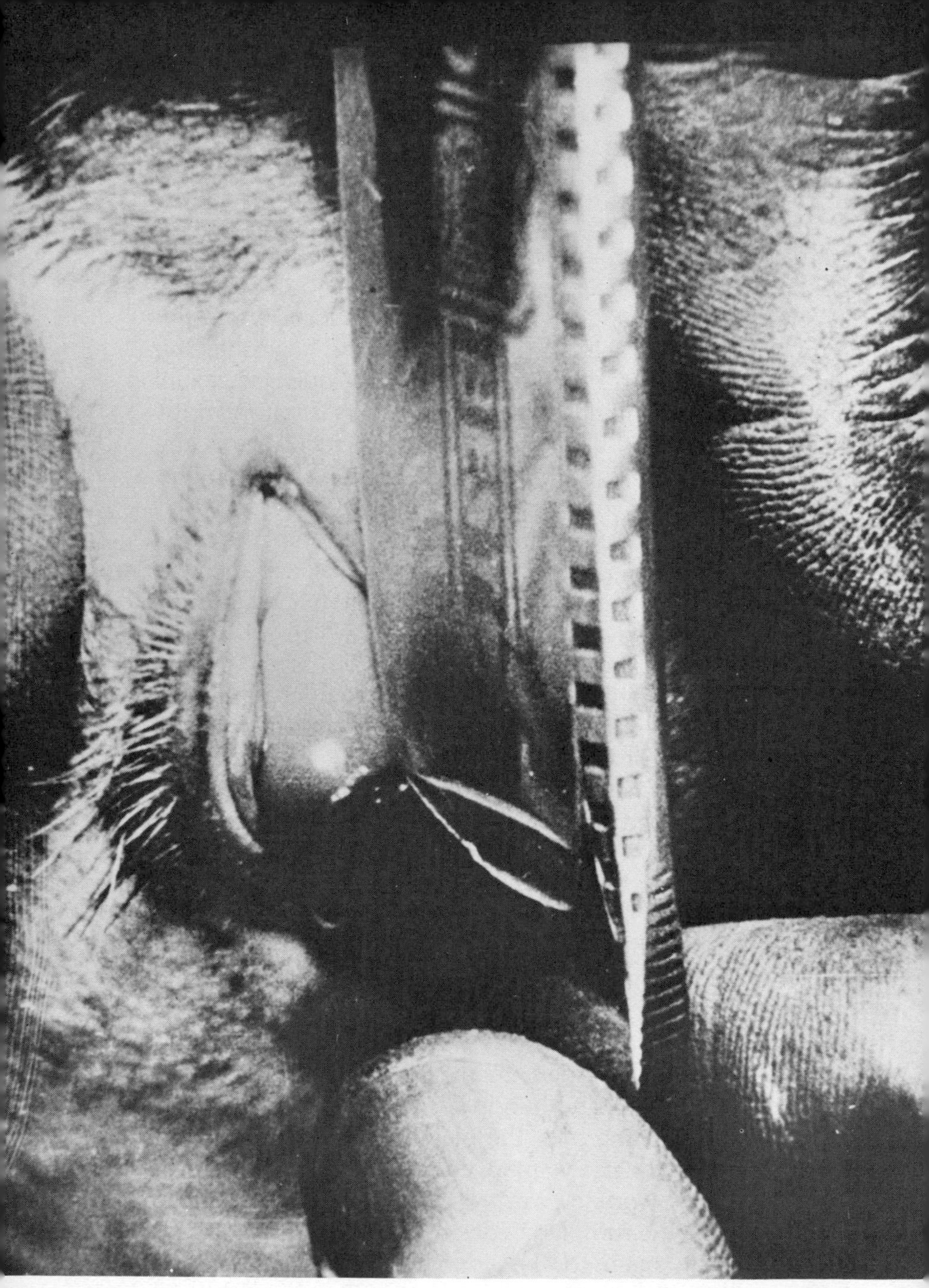

The slicing of the eyeball

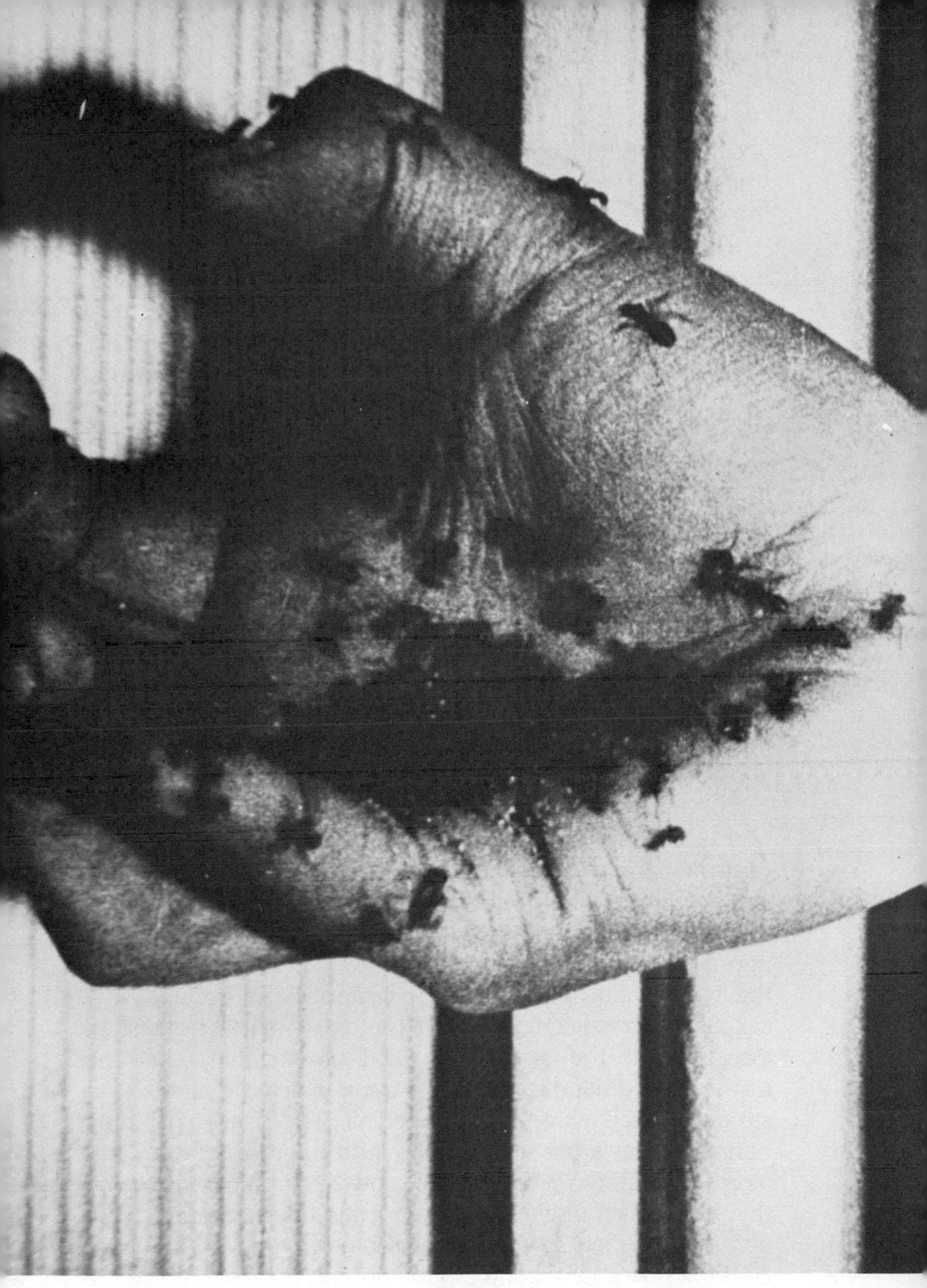

Awakening sexuality

unsatisfied. When she removes the plain tie in favour of the striped tię, it indicates a search for passion that, even if it is more aggressive, retains a respectable facade.

The young man, devoid of his frills, is no longer sexually infantile. He is seen, however, gazing motionless at his hand, and a close-up of the hand reveals a hole in the palm from which ants are beginning to crawl.[10] The mutilated hand, symbolic of sexual mutilation, is an important recurring motif, while the young man's frozen stance, echoing the inertia of his earlier fall, underlines the extent of his emotional frigidity. The crawling ants, suggesting putrefaction in one sense, indicate in another the beginnings of new activity and, together with the discarded frills, point to the young man's imminent sexual awakening. It is suggested to us in a typically evocative Buñuelian series of dissolves whereby the inner life of the character is projected in purely cinematic terms. The image of the hand becomes the close-up of hair under a woman's armpit as she sunbathes in a field; then the spines of a sea-urchin undulating gently; and this in turn the head of a woman who is prodding a dismembered hand with a stick. The transition from the female armpit – a vaginal image signifying the young man's castration – to the woman's efforts to arouse the lifeless hand represent progressive sexual arousal.

The woman who in the final dissolve has been seen from above is revealed now as having a somewhat masculine appearance and is standing in the street near the spot where the young man fell from the bicycle. She is evidently the sexually aggressive side of the young woman who rushed downstairs to the assistance of the young man, while the dismembered hand is his lifeless penis which she attempts to stir to renewed activity. The stick which she uses to prod the hand also has a phallic meaning, and the roles of man and woman are here reversed. The crowd that gathers to watch the scene, both fascinated and horrified by it, expresses the attitude of society towards a display of uninhibited sexuality. And the policeman, coercing the young woman to place the hand in the box, is, of course, as he is in other Buñuel films, the agent of repressive forces, portrayed as impassive and lacking in any depth of feeling. For her, the possession of the hand (the male sexual organ) in the box (vagina) signifies her physical possession of her lover, while for society it is sufficient that overt sexual activity be kept nicely hidden away. Suddenly, in a moment which parallels the young man's fall from the bicycle, the young woman is killed by a passing car. The crowd, which reacted to her sexual activities, is indifferent towards her death, and only three individuals approach the horribly mutilated body.

The scene has been observed from the bedroom window by the young man and the young woman. It is clear that they have been observing their own drama. They are unmistakenly linked to the woman with the box by the fact that the intense rapture on her face as she caresses the box is reflected in theirs too. In terms of their own relationship, the woman's death can be interpreted in several ways. On the one hand, it points to the fact that her aggressive role is about to end as the young man's sexual appetites begin to dominate. In Freudian terms to be run over symbolizes sexual intercourse and the incident points to the young woman's violation. On the other hand, inasmuch as the car which runs down the woman is a symbol of bourgeois society, the episode anticipates the final frustration of passion for both the young man and the young woman. The policeman's impassive application of moral standards has its counterpart in the machine that crushes the ecstatic lover beneath its wheels.[11]

At all events, the young man assumes now a sexually aggressive role and advances on the girl who withdraws before him. The earlier close-up of the maimed, useless, inactive hand is now a close-up of the hands of the young man reaching out, finding, squeezing the young woman's breasts through the material of her dress. In a highly expressive series of dissolves that reveal, once more in Buñuel's very distinctive style, the workings of the young man's mind, the breasts are seen naked and then, still fondled and squeezed by the searching hands, are transformed into the young woman's naked buttocks. They are images which convey thoughts, emotions and the raw, primitive force of passion. And it is expressed visually too in the trickle of blood that runs from the corner of the young man's mouth, an image of pure animal appetite.[12]

The reversal of roles is underlined by the young woman's defence of herself with a tennis racket, the counterpart in reverse of the stick with which in the earlier sequence the woman prodded the hand. And the tennis racket is also perhaps, and most certainly would have been in the late 20s, an image of the bourgeois whose sexual inhibitions have driven the young woman onto the defensive. It is, indeed, this theme which gains momentum now in a bizarre but highly witty sequence. The young man, seeking something that will help him in his efforts to possess the girl, grasps the ends of two ropes. He advances towards her but is suddenly held back by a great weight attached to the ropes. As the weight is hauled into view, it is seen to be composed of priests, pianos and dead mules – the dead weight of tradition that hinders the progress of passion. The priests, slightly bemused but otherwise unconcerned, continue praying as they are dragged across the floor, their hands together in an image of all the inflexible ritual of the Catholic Church. The grand pianos, like the book read previously by the young woman, are the weighty symbols of culture and education whose oppressive influence is expressed in the lifeless bodies of the sightless mules that are draped over them. We are reminded both of the bloody, mutilated hand that lay in the street and of the girl's eye sliced by the razor. And they are images, too, like the woman's body mutilated by the car, of what the young man and the young woman will become. The young man, struggling to assert himself, continues his slow advance and, in a gesture of rebellion that will be repeated in subsequent films, kicks aside the furniture, another symbol of the neat and comfortable bourgeois world.[13] But even now his defeat is signalled by the reappearance of the motif of the mutilated hand. The young woman, terrified by the violence she has provoked, runs into another room and, as the young man tries to follow her, slams the door on his hand. A close-up of the hand reminds us of the dismembered hand lying in the road. As the hand opens to reveal the ants that swarm over it, it suggests the continuing presence of life and energy, but in its evocation of maiming also points to the fact that passion is about to be extinguished. The subsequent shot is, indeed, one of the young man lying on the bed dressed in his frills and with the box placed upon his chest. He is motionless, his eyes fixed and staring. He has, in every sense, reverted to his former state. His expression recalls the mechanical way in which he rode the bicycle, his inertia, his fall from it, and his frills confirm his return to a state of infantile sexuality. The feminine association of the box underlines the abandonment of his aggressive male role. The young woman, throwing aside her bourgeois inhibitions, had succeeded in overcoming his, in awakening the deep, human feelings buried beneath the suffocating weight of fear, anxiety, doubt and guilt instilled by conventional morality. But in yielding to these things once more, she condemns him and is herself condemned to that stultified condition exemplified in the powerful image of the inert figure on the bed.

A title introduces the third and final section of the film: *Towards Three in the Morning*. A new character arrives outside the young man's room. He has run up the stairs – suggestive of sexual desire – and he rings the doorbell vigorously. Two hands appear through holes in the door shaking a cocktail shaker. The door is opened by the young woman and the newcomer bounds into the room. His face is concealed from us throughout the sequence but it is already clear from his manner that he is in every respect the opposite both of what the young man was and of what he has become again. The hands shaking the cocktail shaker suggest masturbation, the newcomer's vibrant energy and, in evoking the maimed hand of the young man, especially the most recent image of it trapped in the door, sharpens the contrast between the two men. And they remind us too of the young man's hands clasping the girl's breasts, of the sexually active phase from which he is now removed.

The newcomer, seeing the young man inert on the bed, boldly confronts him, orders him to rise, strips him of his frills and hurls them, together with the box, through the window. As a punishment he commands the young man to stand facing the wall and, as he turns to the camera, we see the newcomer's face for the first time. His features are those of the young man and are distinguishable only by the fact that the newcomer's face looks finer and younger. He is clearly a version of what the young man was several years ago. The sequence as a whole is, in effect, the enactment of the young man's thoughts and feelings, a projection of his inner drama as he lies on the bed and dreams of the active man he once was. The frills and the box, hurled through the window by the newcomer, are the symbols of repressed sexuality and femininity which another, aggressive form of the young man will not accept, while the punishment is an expression of the young man's guilt.

The room in which the young man and the newcomer find themselves is seen to contain a school desk with inkwell and pen, and on top of the desk are a number of books and other scholastic objects. It is as though the thoughts of the young man are regressing in time beyond the stage represented by the newcomer. We are in the presence of the young man's early educational influences, and the theme suggested earlier by the book and the pianos is the subject of another variation. The newcomer takes the books from the desk and a close-up of the hands holding the books echoes the earlier shots of hands. It is sustained by another shot of the young man's hands as he takes the books from the newcomer and, with one in each hand, points them at him. In a moment that is both dramatic and meaningful in terms of the film's themes, the books are transformed into revolvers. In dreams both guns and shooting represent the sexual act. Here the meaning is the opposite, for the revolvers are really books, synonymous with education and therefore destructive of uninhibited sexuality. When the newcomer is shot by the young man he is the embodiment of all that is alive and purposeful destroyed by the deadly and deadening forces of tradition. The hand that holds the book, the hand that points the gun, the maimed and lifeless hand, the bleeding, dismembered hand – the images are repeated tellingly, the shifting and apparently illogical surface of the film underpinned by a tightly-knit logic. And as the newcomer falls dying, we recall once more the young man's fall from the bicycle. The point that they are both the same, destroyed by a common enemy, is forcibly made.

The newcomer falling in the room becomes a shot of the newcomer falling in a park and recalls too the young man's fall from the bicycle with its implication of sexual anxiety and failure. A naked woman is seated with her back to him, and, as he falls, the newcomer's fingers brush the bare skin of the woman's back. The figure remains motionless and fades away. The setting of the park with its bushes and trees and the statuesque nude provides a romantic backcloth to the newcomer's death. Her pose brings to mind the Venus de Milo and suggests that the nude figure is the newcomer's dream of feminine perfection. He has always sought her but in the very moment when his search seems over, she eludes him and his fingers clutch at empty air while she is oblivious to his anguish. And, like a dream, she vanishes, leaving him bereft of all illusion. His failure is also an echo of the young man's, for the hands reaching out for the nude woman recall the young man's hands on the naked breasts and buttocks of the young woman. To the extent that the newcomer is a facet of the young man, an imagined form of him, the sequence is again the visual representation of the young man's turbulent thoughts as, defeated by the young woman's rejection of him, he lies on his bed and broods on his own futile search for love.

The sequence in the park has a social dimension. As the newcomer lies in the grass, a few individuals approach the body, one attempts to listen to his heart-beat and another raises his left arm. Near them two passers-by are totally engaged in their own conversation. The latter, in particular, reflect the indifference of society that is expressed in many of Buñuel's films, while the actions of the former, though well-intentioned, give to the newcomer's death a touch of absurdity.[14] It is heightened as he is carried off in a kind of funeral procession, for the Wagnerian music that accompanies the moment has an incongruity that is totally ironic.

A new sequence reveals the room in which the young man shot the newcomer. The young woman is looking for him but cannot find him. Instead, her eyes are drawn to a dark spot on the blank wall. It grows larger as the camera draws nearer until, in a close-up that fills the screen, the spot becomes a moth which has on its back the pattern of a skull. The death image, evoked very powerfully in the sequence in the park in relation to another, more active facet of the young man, is relevant now to his present, repressed self. The death's head becomes the young man himself dressed in his frills. Moreover, we see now, as he takes his hand from his face, that his mouth has disappeared. If previously he has been repressed sexually, he has now lost all sexual drive, for the mouth is its symbol, and the face with no mouth recalls the earlier scenes of sexual aggression in which the blood dripped from the corner of the young man's mouth or when, lasciviously, his mouth sought the young woman's naked breasts. She, as though to emphasize her sexuality, paints her mouth with lipstick, asserting, as it were, the existence of her labia. Another shot of the young man reveals hair growing where the mouth was, a suggestion, perhaps, of female pubic hair and of his total loss of masculinity. But the young woman, for all her display of sexual aggression, is affected too, for the hair has disappeared from beneath her arm, an ominous pointer to her fate. We are reminded of an earlier shot of hair beneath the arm of a young woman, an image of erotic significance which clarifies the meaning of this later incident. The young woman sticks out her tongue at the young man in a gesture as defiant and as assertive of her sexuality as the painting of her lips. It is a gesture which should be seen, though, in the light of the young man's ultimate failure to assert himelf.

The shot of the young woman walking out of the room into the next room is transformed, for the final sequence of the film, into a shot of the young woman on a beach. A man is standing facing the sea, dressed in a striped sweater and plus-fours. The young woman calls to him, he turns and they meet happily. The scene is, in every sense, an image of bourgeois love. The setting is the sentimentalized setting of young lovers in a Hollywood film. The man's golfing-trousers, like the earlier shot of the girl's tennis racket, evokes his class and origins. And the happiness of the young couple as they meet on the beach which they alone inhabit is the dream, the fairy-tale come true, of every conventional young couple. The man is not the young man we have seen before but a mixture of the different aspects of him, perhaps a respectable compromise that, in her search for love, the young woman has settled for. There are echoes of earlier episodes. A close-up of the man's clenched hand close to the girl's face, a transformation of the mutilated hand, suggests passion. As they walk along the beach and kiss each other from time to time, we are reminded of the young woman rushing downstairs to kiss the fallen cyclist. The wind which blows through the scene is the strong wind of passion that will blow through the girl's bedroom in *L'Age d'or*. But if there are positive echoes of earlier scenes to suggest that the couple's dream will come true, there are negative reminders too. The young man's frills and the striped box wash against the young couple's feet. Is their presence a pointer to an imminent stage of sexual inhibition, or an indication that all that is in the past, these objects the forgotten flotsam of earlier experience? The man's rejection of them, reminiscent of the newcomer's throwing of the frills and the box through the window, suggests a new and positive sexual maturity. And the couple, walking arm in arm into the distance, walk into a future that is everyone's dream of cosy, sentimentalized love.

As the couple continue walking, words appear in the sky: *In the Spring*. Like the opening title of the film – *Once Upon a Time* – they evoke a kind of fairy-tale, the blossoming of true love. But, in contrast to the optimism of the words, everything has changed. The idyllic beach has become an endless desert. The couple who walked happily on the sand are buried in it. The sun beats down on them mercilessly, they are blind, and the insects slowly devour them. The dream of love has become a nightmare. The man and the young woman, for all their hopes of love, are the paralyzed, mutilated, dying prisoners of their and society's bourgeois values, the final reality of the images that have dotted the film like sign-posts on a fatal journey. The film ends as it began, with mutilated eyes, and the shock sequence of the prologue – moon and cloud into eye and razor – returns – beach into burning desert, romantic illusion into nightmare – and stamps it with a final, inescapable sense of logic.

Buñuel's cinematic style and technique is often described as simple and straightforward. Jean-Claude Carrière has observed:

> His technique is commonplace. He is completely free of artiness.[15]

Raymond Durgnat makes a similar assessment:

> His style is self-effacing.[16]

Un Chien andalou is, however, by its very nature more complex than many of Buñuel's films, for to reveal the unconscious requires more than a simple technique. In his first film Buñuel employs the style and the cinematic language that he has since made his own. They are used here, however, with a greater density and consistency than in the later films.

Buñuel's intention to shock is often achieved by a startling juxtaposition of opposites. The prologue is a good example, for when the moon and the silvery cloud become, without warning, the blade slitting the eye, it is like an ambush on our unsuspecting sensibilities. In another episode the young woman, totally immersed in ecstatic thoughts, is suddenly killed and horribly mutilated by a car. In the final section of the film the young couple walk hand in hand along an idyllic beach and then, in a sudden transformation, are buried in the sand of a burning desert. The sense of shock in these and in other sequences is sharp and immediate, for Buñuel's manner is direct, matter-of-fact, objective, in the style of documentary devoid of all comment. It makes the scenes all the more shocking.

The revelation of unconscious thoughts and feelings, the film's constant preoccupation, is achieved in a great variety of ways. Because he was making a silent film, Buñuel was obliged to express the inner life of his characters in purely visual terms, and facial expressions and body movements became an unusually important part of the film's language. In one shot the camera focuses on the young man's empty, blank expression, in another on his hand as he stares at it, motionless. The faces of the young man and the young woman express their rapture and ecstasy as they watch the woman in the street. The blood dripping from the corner of the young man's mouth represents his violent but contained passion, while the fingers feverishly seeking the girl's breasts convey its awakening. Every shot is a bold, telling image, revealing unequivocally those emotions which we seek to conceal beneath the surface.

Buñuel communicates the thoughts and the feelings of his characters in another way too: exteriorizing them in a manner that has become a feature of his style. The young man's sexual castration and gradual arousal are, for example, projected in the very expressive images of the hair beneath a woman's armpit and the undulating spines of a sea-urchin. Later, as he squeezes the young woman's breasts, we suddenly see them naked in the way that his inflamed imagination dwells on them. And when the young woman looks down on the street, the woman prodding the hand with the stick is the physical representation of her own desire.

The process of exteriorization of the inner life of the characters is one which is true not merely of single shots or short sequences but of whole sections of the film. Its entire third section, from the moment of the newcomer's appearance, may be seen at the expression of the young man's thoughts and imaginings, the passing before his inner eye of his experiences and of another form of himself. It is even possible – a measure of the film's innovative and thoroughly experimental character – to regard the whole of its action as the representation of the young man's confused and shifting thoughts from the moment of his first appearance on the bicycle.

The projection of the subconscious demands sudden transitions, unexpected dislocations, and inexplicable leaps in time and space in the images conveyed to us on the screen. When, for example, the young woman walks out of the door of the young man's room, she walks onto a beach. Similarly, when the newcomer is shot in the young man's room, he falls to the ground in a park. In terms of cinematic technique, dissolves, fade-outs and fade-ins, transitions and changes of focus continually suggest the fluid, shifting, uncertain and irrational character of dream and fantasy.

If these techniques reflect the fluidity of mental processes, the close-up, a very important feature of this film, expresses their obsessive character. The examples are numerous, as the preceding analysis suggests. As the mind fixes on its obsessions, seeing them both large and clear, so the camera copies that process. The many disturbing and insidious images of the film linger with us long afterwards just as our own phobias are imprinted on our minds. *Un Chien andalou* contradicts in this respect the frequent assertion that Buñuel rarely uses close-ups. On the other hand his use of them in this film is for a specific purpose rather than merely a virtuoso show of effects.

Although *Un Chien andalou* is in many ways Buñuel's most poetic film, it is never sentimental. It is characterized, as are his other films, by what Raymond Durgnat has described as a 'fast, hard style', almost the style of documentary, albeit a documentary of the mind. In terms of its subject matter and its style, Buñuel's first film was not only extraordinary in its day but remains still a milestone, a remarkable innovatory achievement in the history of the cinema.

NOTES

[1] In his autobiography Buñuel gives June, 1929, as the date of the première. Francisco Aranda, *Luis Buñuel* . . . , p. 59, refers to the première as taking place in April of that year.

[2] For the text of the letters, see Aranda, p. 58.

[3] Quoted by Aranda, pp. 56-57.

[4] *La Révolution Surréaliste*, no. 12 (December 1929).

[5] *Art in Cinema*, San Francisco Museum of Modern Art, 1947.

[6] *The Cosmological Eye*, London, 1945, p. 57.

[7] Buñuel has observed that to produce in the spectator 'a state which could permit the free association of ideas, it was necessary to produce a near traumatic shock at the very beginning of the film; hence we began it with a shot of an eye being very efficiently cut open. The spectator entered into the cathartic state necessary to accept the subsequent events of the film'. See Aranda, p. 67.

[8] For Buñuel's knowledge of Freud, see the Introduction. The sexual symbolism of boxes, eyes, razors, ties, and many of the other objects prominent in the film are fully documented in Freud's *The Interpretation of Dreams*.

[9] The tie, according to Freud, has a phallic significance.

[10] Raymond Durgnat, *Luis Buñuel*, p. 27, makes the interesting point that the French expression 'avoir les fourmis' *('to have ants')* means 'to have pins and needles' and that the appearance of ants here signifies the awakening of a limb that was dead.

[11] Raymond Durgnat, p. 28, suggests that the car represents the public and is therefore a symbol of society. He also links it to the young man's desire to kill the girl.

[12] In *L'Age d'or* Modot's passion for Lya Lys is similarly expressed by a gush of blood from his mouth.

[13] In *L'Age d'or* Modot vents his frustration against society by wrecking the drawing-room of his lover's wealthy parents.

[14] *Un Chien andalou* is usually described as a 'poetic' film or as revealing the inner self, and little is made of its social dimension. Although the latter is not Buñuel's principal concern here, there are, nevertheless, many pointers to his later attacks on bourgeois values.

[15] 'The Buñuel Mystery' in *The World of Luis Buñuel,* p. 92. The article first appeared in *Show* (April 1970).

[16] *Luis Buñuel,* p. 15. On Buñuel's technique in *Un Chien andalou* see Aranda, pp. 65-67.

2
L'AGE D'OR

CAST

The Man	—	Gaston Modot
The Woman	—	Lya Lys
The Bandit Leader	—	Max Ernst
Pemán	—	Pierre Prévert

SUPPORTING ACTORS

Caridad de Labaerdesque; Lionel Salem; Madame Noizet; Liorens Artigas; Duchange; Ibáñez; Pancho Cossío; Valentin Hugo; Marie Berthe Ernst; Jacques Brunius; Simone Cottance; Paul Eluard; Manuel Angeles Ortiz; Juan Esplandío; Pedro Flores; Juan Castañe; Joaquín Roa; Pruna; Xaume de Maravilles.

Script	—	Luis Buñuel Salvador Dalí
Design	—	Pierre Schilzneck
Photography	—	Albert Duverger
Editor	—	Luis Buñuel
Producer	—	Le Vicomte de Noailles
Director	—	Luis Buñuel

In a letter of March 25, 1929, Buñuel indicated to José Bello his intention of making a second film and suggested that it would be completed by the beginning of May.[1] The film was not, in fact, finished until the following year and it received its première on November 28, 1930, at the Studio 28 in Paris. Buñuel, once again, planned the film in collaboration with Salvador Dalí but, before shooting commenced, ended his association with him. Buñuel has since observed that Dalí had nothing to do with the filming and that he retained Dalí's name in the titles out of respect for their former friendship.[2] For his part, Dalí has accused Buñuel of betraying his ideas. At all events the film was made at the Billancourt Studios in Paris, without Dalí's presence, and the shooting took a month. Financed to the tune of a million francs by the Vicomte de Noailles, Buñuel had complete control over his choice of subject. *L'Age d'or* was one of the first talkies made in France. It was also the most scandalous film of its generation.

The showing of the film at the Studio 28 in the autumn of 1930 precipitated violent controversy. At first there was relatively little trouble, but on December 3 members of the *Jeunesses Catholiques*, the *Ligue des Patriotes*, and the antisemitic *Ligue Antijuive*, attacked the cinema, slashed the seats, threw ink and acid on the screen, and destroyed many of the surrealist paintings exhibited in the foyer. In the days that followed, the right-wing press expressed their opposition. Richard Pierre Bodin, writing in *Le Figaro* on December 7, observed:

> A film called *L'Age d'or*, whose negligible artistic quality is an insult to any kind of technical standard, combines, as a public spectacle, the most obscene, disgusting and tasteless episodes. Country, family and religion are dragged through the mud . . .[3]

Another critic, in the *Eco de Paris* on December 10, added:

> . . . With the intention of relieving the dreadful tedium

> of every centimetre of this film, the director has introduced scenes of the lowest and most despicable pornography.

It was a reaction whose violence finally caused the Paris Chief of Police to intervene in order to avoid further reprisals. The manager of the cinema, M. Mauclaire, was fined, the film was officially banned on December 11, and on the following day all copies of it were seized.

The wave of condemnation had, of course, its counterpart. Henri Tracol, writing in *Vu* on December 3, 1930, was full of enthusiasm:

> The role of sound and speech in this film is evidence of Buñuel's amazing sense of the new possibilities of the cinema.

Léon Moussinac, in *L'Humanité* on December 7, 1930, expressed his admiration for the film's power and originality:

> Never before in the cinema, or with such force, such disdain for 'conventions' and for bourgeois society and its trappings – the police, religion, the army, morality, the family, the State itself – has there been such a violent assault, such a kick up the backside . . .

For their own part, the Surrealist group, in response to right-wing reaction, issued a questionnaire in which they queried the actions of the police, their support of fascist and anti-semitic groups, and the suppression of their own freedom to attack established values.[4] The document was signed by Maxime Alexandre, Louis Aragon, André Breton, Luis Buñuel, René Char, René Crevel, Salvador Dalí, Paul Eluard, Max Ernst, Georges Malkine, Benjamin Péret, Man Ray, Georges Sadoul, Yves Tanguy, André Thirion, Tristan Tzara, Pierre Unik, and Albert Valentin. As to the positive value of *L'Age d'or*, they had no doubt:

> . . . the social usefulness of *L'Age d'or* must be determined by the extent to which it meets the destructive

> needs of the oppressed, and perhaps too by the way in which it panders to the masochistic inclinations of the oppressors. Despite the danger that it may be banned, this film will, in our opinion, serve the very useful purpose of blazing through skies that are never as lovely as those seen in the mirror [of Lya Lys's dressing table].

Buñuel has described the purpose of *L'Age d'or* in his autobiography:

> The story is also a sequence of moral and surrealist aesthetic. Around the principal characters, a man and woman, is disclosed the existing conflict in all human society between the sentiment of love, and any other sentiment of a religious, patriotic, humanitarian order; . . . the hero is animated by egoism, which imagines all attitudes to be amorous, to the exclusion of control or of other sentiments . . . It is a romantic film performed in full surrealist frenzy . . .

In relation to *Un Chien andalou, L'Age d'or* marks a significant advance. Like the earlier film, it lays bare men's primitive, subconscious urges, especially sexual instinct. Its aims are, however, more clearly political than those of *Un Chien andalou*, and its attack on established social and moral values is more central and sustained. In the presentation of the clash between man's instinct and the repressive nature of the institutions which surround, challenge and threaten to defeat him, *L'Age d'or* looks forward to Buñuel's major films in a way that *Un Chien andalou* does not. Some critics, great admirers of Buñuel, have seen *L'Age d'or* as a magnificent celebration of love. Ado Kyrou, for example, though fully aware of the film's social and religious implications, praises in particular its exaltation of love:

> Buñuel is the most honest and sincere man that I know. Untouched by the filth of the cinema business, he has expressed himself, expresses himself and will

> continue to express himself with simplicity, freedom and boldness. He has spoken and will always speak of love and the enemies which love must fight.[5]

Henry Miller, on the other hand, one of Buñuel's greatest advocates, pinpoints with precision and perception the film's broader central conflict:

> Being normal, instinctive, healthy, gay, unpretentious, he [Buñuel] finds himself alone in the crazy drift of social forces. Being thoroughly normal and honest, he finds himself regarded as bizarre. Like Lawrence again his work divides the world into two opposite camps – those who are for him and those who are against him. There is no straddling the issue. Either you are crazy, like the rest of civilized humanity, or you are sane and healthy like Buñuel. And if you are sane and healthy you are an anarchist and you throw bombs . . .[6]

In an interview in 1965 Buñuel suggested to Manuel Michel that with the passing of the years and our growing immunity to shock, the original impact of *L'Age d'Or* has been diminished.[7] He suggested too, though, that the moral oppression which then existed has remained unchanged, for it has simply assumed another disguise. Whatever his own reservations about the film's relevance to our own rapidly changing world, it is equally true that in terms of its message as well as its art, *L'Age d'or* remains an immensely impressive work.

L'Age d'or begins in the manner of a documentary. The camera shows in close-up three scorpions pursuing each other, and a struggle in which a scorpion kills a rat. The sequence of pictures is accompanied by titles which provide factual information:

> *The tail is composed of five prismatic joints . . . The claws, which bring to mind the great claws of the*

crayfish, are instruments of attack and information . . .

In relation to the film as a whole, the opening suggests that we must see what follows not as a work of the imagination but as a documentation of the real world. Society is about to be examined and, like the scorpions, revealed to us in close-up.[8] In a thematic sense, the scorpion may be seen as Buñuel's symbol for the fierce and aggressive sexual passion which threatens conventional moral and social values and of the aggression of a destructive and venomous society towards such passion. In another sense, the film is itself a scorpion, for its sting, like the razor at the beginning of *Un Chien andalou*, threatens our complacent acceptance of the world we live in.

A second sequence, longer than the first, commences with a title: *A Few Hours Later*. A bandit who is acting as a look-out on a rocky shore witnesses the arrival of four arch-bishops in full regalia and singing the *Dies Irae*. He stumbles away to warn his companions of the danger and, with the exception of Pemán, who is already dying, they attempt to make their escape. They fall exhausted one by one until only the leader is left, despairing and in a state of collapse. The archbishops are seen as skeletons in the rocks, but they are succeeded by ten to fifteen boats which bring ashore a governor, a nun and various dignitaries. They disembark and proceed to the laying of a foundation stone.

The scorpions of the first sequence have become the bandits and the archbishops and the dignitaries of the second, and the struggle between the scorpions is now the clash between the rebels and the religious and social institutions that, even though they may appear to decline and die – skeletons in the rocks – constantly renew themselves in their efforts to retain their deadly hold.[9] The bandits, the part of their leader played in the film by the surrealist painter, Max Ernst, personify rebellion against the moral and the social order, the spirit exalted throughout the film. But their defeat is already ominous, an echo of the vanquished scorpion or of the rat killed by the scorpion. It is the fight to the death of these opposing forces that is the film's central concern.

The broad statement of the theme assumes now a more precise and specific form. The governor clears his throat in preparation for a solemn speech but is distracted by ecstatic cries from the background. The camera focuses on the wild embraces of a man, Gaston Modot, and a woman, Lya Lys, both of them oblivious to the ceremony and immersed totally in their sensual enjoyment of each other:

> *A close-up near the ground, of a man and a woman embracing, with great lasciviousness, both rolling about in the mud.*[10]

Love makes its spirited assault on society's pomposity. Buñuel expresses, with a mixture of lyricism and aggressive irreverence, the rapture and ecstasy of passion and the lovers' total commitment to it. As the woman is dragged from her lover, the camera pinpoints her face:

> *The woman turns her head and, with a look of anguish and tenderness, stares fixedly towards her lover.*

As for Gaston Modot, he is a visionary whose passion for the girl illuminates his whole existence:

> *A close-up of the man. His eyes are half-closed and he seems to be contemplating an ineffable vision. His face expresses intense happiness and his head sways gently as though moved by the rhythm of his voluptuous vision.*

The excitement of his feelings and the erotic nature of his thoughts are conveyed to us, as in the case of the hero of *Un Chien andalou*, by a series of highly expressive images, the film's representation of external reality transformed into the evocation of an inner landscape. In quick succession the woman is seen seated on a lavatory seat of great whiteness; the seat is empty and the toilet-paper blazes fiercely; and boiling lava runs from a volcano, interspersed with a shot of Gaston Modot's rapturous expression. The images have the character of dream, of the illogical and arbitrary workings of the mind, and they have too Buñuel's typically irreverent wit.

Society reacts to the lovers' shameless sexuality with shock and horror. Gaston Modot is marched away by two brutal and impassive policemen, agents of repression. Buñuel's hero, on the other hand, acts spontaneously and in accordance with his instincts, breaking away from his captors and venting his feelings on a dog which he kicks in the air and an insect which he crushes beneath his foot. The point is clearly made that sexual repression leads to destructive and violent acts, responding to violence with violence.

The picture of society is now expanded. A fade-out leads into a sequence in which the governor completes the ceremony of laying the foundation stone. The cement he places on it is seen to consist of excrement. The stone bears an inscription:

> 'In the year of our Lord 1930, on the spot occupied by the bones of the four Majorcans, there was placed this first stone for the foundation of . . .'

The shot becomes, in turn, an aerial view of Rome in the style of documentary and accompanied by two titles. Firstly: *Imperial Rome.* Secondly: *The Ancient Lover of the Pagan World Has Become with the Passing of the Centuries the Secular Seat of the Church. Some Views of the Vatican, the Strongest Pillar of the Church.* The picture has opened out from its initial focus on the island to present us with a powerful symbol of society, pagan and Christian, ancient and modern, but a society founded on excrement. The documentary nature of the sequence with its explanatory titles and its aerial views indicates, as in the case of the shots of scorpions, that the detailed picture of society about to be presented is in every respect authentic. Rome, with its traffic problems, its milling crowds, its fine buildings, its parks, its decaying and collapsing houses, and its mixture of normal and bizarre incidents, has, moreover, the rich and complex fabric of any other modern city and is thus the symbol of our civilization. Inasmuch as its exterior is impressive but does not conceal the cracks beneath the surface, it is also an image of a society whose outward sophistication hides a deep, underlying viciousness.

A fade-out leads into a shot of Gaston Modot. Still in the clutches of the police, he is no longer on the island but a member of modern society. A new and particularly brilliant sequence, a variation on the earlier revelation of his erotic thoughts, suggests the magical power and the triumph of love over all constraints and barriers. A close-up reveals the hand and forearm of a woman in an advertisement for hand-cream. It becomes a close-up of a real hand, similar to that in the advertisement and balanced elegantly on a fingertip. The board of a passing sandwich-man displays a pair of glamorous, silk-stockinged legs, slightly apart. And a photograph in a window in which a girl's head is thrown back seductively bears a close similarity to Modot's lover. He may be separated and apart from her, impeded by society from enjoying her, but love triumphs in other ways, transcends the limitations of time and space, and even uses the commercialism of the modern world to its own advantage. Moreover, the succession of shots suggests not only Modot's imagining of Lya Lys but her feelings and emotions at the moment of his imagining of her.

Lya Lys, like Modot, is placed now in the context of society. She is seen in a room whose elegance proclaims its bourgeois character. Her mother is sitting and she holds a book in her hand. The girl takes a book from a table and we see that her ring-finger is bandaged.[11] She discusses with her mother the arrangements for a party, and mention of her father introduces a shot of him in his chemist-shop in which his ring-finger is seen inside the neck of a bottle. The drawing-room setting, anticipating that of *The Exterminating Angel*, and the books, reminiscent of *Un Chien andalou*, are the symbols of wealth and education, and the latter, as in the earlier film, of sexual inhibition too. The girl's bandaged finger, evoking injury and thus sexual frustration, is equally a phallic image and therefore a pointer to her sexual longing. The father's finger inserted in the bottle – in Freudian language all hollow objects represent the uterus – indicates a sexual gratification otherwise denied by a cold and repressive marriage. The link between the daughter and the father, established by the finger, suggests too a sexual bond between them the importance of which emerges later.

The theme of society's domination is sustained when the girl enters her bedroom and sees a cow lying on her bed. It is an image of her mother's large and oppressive presence on the one hand and of the police, perhaps, on the other, for '*vache*' is French slang for police. In another sense the cow might be regarded as a super cat or poodle, a suitable measure of bourgeois extravagance. Its expulsion from the bedroom is either a sign of its obedience to its mistress or a pointer to her imminent freedom from those forces to which she has until now been subjected. In any case, Modot's earlier imagining of her now becomes, in a very striking and original sequence, her imagining of him, the representation of her fantasies announced by the tinkling of a bell:

> *Her face reflects a great serenity. Her expression, lost in some vague dream, conveys the inner contemplation of some beloved image.*

The mirror into which the girl looks reflects not her face but her erotic vision. The form in which Gaston Modot is presented is that shaped by her imagination as she visualizes him at this particular point in time, sharing her emotions and even her physical posture. As for him, wherever he is, he will also be dreaming of her. It is a rapturous and ecstatic union which, defeating time and distance, is communicated to us in linked shots of the lovers biting their lips. Lya hears too the barking of a dog and is moved by it, while in another shot Modot looks tenderly at a dog which is barking at a passer-by. In the mirror, we see a beautiful sky with white, oval clouds, a sunset, a tree in the foreground. A wind begins to blow from the mirror, moving the girl's hair and clothes. The sequence is one in which images and sounds combine perfectly to express the magical and transcendental force of love.[12]

With Modot's release from custody, Buñuel's manner becomes ironic. His hero has been chosen by the Ministry of Good Works to embark on a special mission. The camera focuses in close-up on the overblown, pretentious wording of a document:

> 'The International Assembly of Good Works names from this day Mr X . . . as its worthy delegate and royal commissioner responsible for its new mission'.

There follows a shot of important officials, of the president, and of the dignified presentation to Modot of the document in the name of the homeland, a piece of pomposity mocked and undermined firstly by Modot's words and then by his behaviour. Modot's reading of the document is like a child's mechanical recitation of a multiplication table. No sooner has he finished than he makes his escape, bent not on the execution of the Ministry's good works but on the completion of his own greater mission of seeing his lover again. As a blind man is about to enter a taxi, Modot unceremoniously knocks him aside in order to appropriate it for himself. It is an incident which, in its violent treatment of a figure to whom conventional society normally extends its sympathy and sentiment, is designed to shock. But it is also designed to illustrate the aggression to which frustated sexual feeling may be driven.

A fade-out leads into another title and another close-up of society:

> *Near Rome in his Magnificent House the Marquis of X and his Wife Prepare to Receive their Guests.*

The arrival of the guests at the country house, a favourite Buñuel situation which will open *The Exterminating Angel,* has all the hallmarks of formalized bourgeois ritual. The cars draw up one after the other, the servant opens the door, the guests descend, enter the house, another car arrives, and the process is repeated. The guests are accompanied too by ritual objects, for the open door of a car reveals a reliquary reminding us of the Christian values of the society portrayed to us. Actions and gestures, formal greetings, polite conversation, the grouping of figures in the drawing-room, contribute to the carefully documented picture of the aristocracy at home.

A new sequence, bizarre, witty and indignant, exposes the indifference of this introverted circle to the world outside it. A cart pulled by mules and containing the driver and two drunken peasants lumbers across the drawing-room while the Marquis and the guests, totally oblivious to it, continue their conversation and, when necessary, allow the cart to pass between them. As a comment on their lack of sensibility, it is a wonderfully comic moment, an elaboration on the episode in *Un Chien andalou* when, despite the newcomer's death, two men cannot be drawn from their conversation. A much more biting incident involves a fire in the kitchen. Flames and smoke belch through the kitchen door and a servant-girl runs in terror into the drawing-room and falls unconscious at the feet of the guests. Insensitive to the girl's plight and suffering, for it is outside their ritual and range of feeling, the guests are unperturbed. A third incident, bizarre and shocking, moves them a little more. It involves the gamekeeper and his mongol son who, eager to play a trick on his father, snatches his cigarette and runs away, playfully making gestures at his father. The latter, enraged by his son's mischievous behaviour, takes his gun, wounds the boy with his first shot and kills him like a rabbit with the second. A close-up of the child twitching on the ground communicates the horror of the incident. Linking shots portray the guests in the drawing-room. Some of them, drawn to the balcony by the sound of gunfire, observe what has happened, express their mild disapproval and return inside:

The spectators leave the balcony and move to different parts of the room (and we should not forget that many of the guests did not move at all when they heard the shots).

A society which has been shocked by unbridled sexuality and quickly stamped on it, remains unmoved by the spectacle of human suffering and violent death.

Gaston Modot's arrival at the party points to the imminent unleashing on this aristocratic gathering of the explosive passion that earlier disrupted the solemn laying of the foundation stone. The girl, even before she sees her ardent lover, is filled with longing and sexual desire. Oblivious to the idle chatter of a friend, she is seen in close-up playing with a ring on her finger. The shot links with an earlier one of the girl's bandaged finger and its clear phallic significance is repeated in another close-up of a servant rubbing a carafe of wine. Gaston Modot's immaculate appearance, which identifies him superficially with the other guests, barely conceals his passion, symbolized here in his dragging behind him a woman's dress. Beneath his dinner-jacket he is a primitive cave-man. That Lya is to be his conquest is evident from a close-up of the dress draped over a chair, for its angle is the same as that of her own seated posture.

The ensuing sequence brings Modot into violent conflict with the bourgeois company. The faces and expressions of the guests have a polite and dignified formality. Modot, in contrast, bites his lips in a frenzy of unconcealed excitement, an open display of primitive sexuality. Lya responds, if somewhat less openly, to this animal display of male, scorpion-like aggression. The episode is in every sense an extended and witty variation of our introduction to the erotic couple. The sparks of passion fly between them, joining them in a common cause and spirit that denies both the values and the existence of the materialistic things around it. Modot's mental ravishing of Lya, whom he eyes with unashamed lechery, is interrupted by the marchioness when she sits beside him and commences her inane, interminable prattling. Enraged by her interference and infuriated further when she spills some wine on him, Modot ignores all social niceties, throws the wine at her and viciously slaps her face. Society, of course, is scandalized by this flaunting of its rules and Modot, as before, is set upon, held by a guest and threatened by a servant, the equivalent of the police in the previous incident. But for the victim of love only love has meaning. Modot is absorbed by the vision of his lover:

> *. . . the aggressor pays no attention to what is happening around him and he gazes at his lover with a great desire, almost devouring her . . .*

Lya is equally enraptured by him:

> *. . . a great tenderness in her eyes. Everything that he does seems to her heroic . . .*

Their passion is on the point of consummation. When Modot leaves the drawing-room dragging the dress behind him, a derisive gesture in the direction of society's polite sophistication, his cave-man conquest of Lya's body is about to begin.

The lovers' rendezvous in the garden of the Marquis' house constitutes the film's climax. The setting of the garden, bushes, trees and elegant wicker chairs is both conventionally romantic and unmistakably bourgeois; a fitting backcloth for formal assignations and the exchange of suitably refined sweet-nothings. Within it Modot's outrageous unconventionality strikes an incongruous and beautifully comic note:

> *The entrance to a dark avenue in the garden. The girl is there waiting for her lover. He enters the frame rapidly and, without preliminaries, launches himself at the girl. Seizing her forcibly by the waist, he disappears down the avenue with lascivious haste.*

It is an incongruity wittily sustained throughout the scene. A series of shots reveal the guests emerging in orderly fashion from the drawing-room into the garden, and rows of nicely and neatly ordered seats where they will sit to listen to a concert. The rows of musicians in dinner jackets, obedient to the conductor's every instruction, complete the image of bourgeois formality and good taste. Alternating close-ups of Modot and Lya reveal their passionate gropings and the wicker chairs overturned by love's ferocity. In a sequence which conveys without words the lovers' mounting ecstasy, Modot bites Lya's finger and she his. Close-ups of their faces reveal their rapture and a shot of Lya gnawing at her lover's fingers shows them to have disappeared. The picture of passion, both lyrical and witty, has its sombre side. Modot and Lya, seated in typically bourgeois garden chairs, find their shape an obstruction to their passionate enjoyment of each other. As he seeks to draw her closer to him, she slips to the floor, bringing him with her, and he, kneeling, attempts to kiss her in a posture that is as absurd as it is uncomfortable. Society's constraints upon the lovers are constant and insidious, the setting for the rapturous expression of their feelings as impracticable as it is ultimately daunting. Love is a noble aspiration transformed into farce and tragedy.

Further inconveniences present themselves. As the lovers indulge in a further frenzy of passion, a servant summons Modot to the telephone. The Minister of the Interior wishes to speak to him on a matter of national importance, for, in pursuing Lya, Modot has neglected his duty to mankind. Love is hampered by another sacred cow, but love for the moment triumphs, turning society's weapons and instruments against it. Lya in one of the film's most erotic sequences, is seen ecstatically sucking the toe of a statue, using a symbol of bourgeois culture and good taste to maintain her level of sexual excitement. For his part, Modot bellows down the telephone, stilling the voice that threatens love.[13] For love nations must fall, thousands must die, and even Ministers must shoot themselves. The shot of the

Frustration thwarted

Minister with a bullet in his head adds to the list of love's trophies. Dogs, blind men, marchionesses, Ministers of State – the list is increasingly impressive.

Modot and Lya are reunited and the theme of love, for all the various distractions, approaches a triumphant climax. Modot's vision of his lover is now reality, Lya the flesh and blood form of the advertisements which earlier excited his imagination:

> . . . *her head is thrown back, and her lover, touching her knees, opens her legs.*

It is the triumph of love over an unfeeling and callous world. It is a passion, moreover, which, projected into the future, conquers time. In a very lyrical sequence its initial frenzy and excitement is seen to acquire a new tranquillity and tenderness:

> *From this moment their attitudes change. They are no longer moved by powerful desire but both are overcome by a great tenderness.*

Modot, in a sequence which exteriorizes his thoughts, sees Lya twenty years from now. Her face reflects a state of peace, a true happiness. He caresses her cheek and she rests her head on his shoulder. Close-ups reflect a rapturous, idyllic union. The slow movement of the scene underlines and enhances its spiritual quality. Blood on Modot's face, echoing an incident in *Un Chien andalou*, symbolizes the ecstasy of love. And it accompanies a climactic, orgasmic cry:

> My love, my love, my love!

The words have as their ascending, pulsating accompaniment the music of Wagner's *Tristan and Isolde* which is played passionately by the orchestra in the garden.[14] It is a true celebration of love's transcendental and blinding majesty. At the same time, though, Tristan and Isolde, for all their passion for each other, die. The ecstasy of Lya and Modot is thus a prelude to their defeat, to the fact that, even if age cannot wither them, there are other insidious forces which can.

At the moment of love's fulfilment, the influence of Lya's father asserts itself, obstructing the lovers. Modot's ecstatic cries – 'My love, my love, my love! – have their counterpart in the father's unrestrained weeping. Lya, moreover, her eyes half-closed, blind to all but Modot's charms, suddenly has them opened to the reality of the bond – social, moral and emotional – that ties her to her father:

> *She, her eyes half-closed, dreaming, her lips parted, is about to kiss her lover, but suddenly her eyes open wide and a cry comes from her throat.*

When she abandons Modot, rushes to her father, and they kiss passionately, the point is made that his hold upon her is complete, her desertion of him for Modot an act of total betrayal. Her embracing of her father is, in effect, her embracing of everything he stands for.

Modot's rapture becomes in the ensuing sequence his frustration. Hurling himself upon a bed in a bedroom of the Marquis' house, he begins to tear the pillows, venting his anger on this symbol of conventional marriage. He seizes a plough, which happens to be present in the room, and wields it like a giant phallus, scattering the furniture. The sexual aggression of the young man in *Un Chien andalou* acquires a more intense form. And as the newcomer in the earlier film hurls the frills and the box, the symbols of sexual repression, through the window, so Modot disposes of society's sacred objects, including a bishop complete with staff. But Modot's rebellion, for all its energy and violent aggression, is also his defeat, a heroic but futile gesture, for the repressive forces of society will, like the phoenix, rise again. The bishop, hurled from the window, lands on his feet, seizes his staff and scuttles away to continue his work elsewhere.

A dissolve leads into the final sequence which, in its violence and savagery, is thematically linked to the scorpions

Frustration rampant

that introduce the film. To that extent the ending of *L'Age d'or*, which has often been seen by critics as puzzling and disappointing, is truly the final sting in the tail. The episode is, in the first place, based on the Marquis de Sade's *One Hundred and Twenty Days of Sodom* and its central character is the murderous debauché of Sade's novel, the Duke of Blangis. Buñuel accompanies the dissolve from the portrayal of Modot's violent sexual frustration with a documentary-type title:

> *At the Precise Moment When These Feathers, Torn Out By his Furious Hands, Were Covering the Ground Below the Window, At This Very Moment, We Were Saying, But Very Far From There, the Survivors of the Chateau de Selliny Were Emerging In Order to Return to Paris.*

A medieval castle is seen on a steep mountain. Another explanatory title passes across the screen:

> *In Order to Celebrate the Most Bestial of Orgies, Four Known and Savage Criminals Had Locked Themselves in the Impregnable Castle For One Hundred and Twenty Days. They Had No Law But Their Own Depravity. They Had No God, No Principles, No Religion, and the Least Wicked Amongst Them Was Tainted With Greater Evil Than Can Be Imagined. In Their Eyes the Life of A Woman, No, of All the Women on the Surface of the Earth, Had No More Value than a Fly. They Had Taken With Them to the Chateau, For Their Own Despicable Ends, Eight Lovely Young Girls, Eight Magnificent Adolescents, and to Provide Stimulus for Their Already Jaded Imaginations, Four Depraved Women Who Would Constantly Fire With Their Tales the Criminal Lust of the Four Monsters.*

A close-up of the castle gates reveals the four men and another title:

And Here Leaving the Chateau of Selliny Are the Survivors of the Criminal Orgies. The First and the Leader of the Four is The Duke of Blangis.

Buñuel's ending works on two levels. Inasmuch as the film culminates in a savage orgy which has a clear derivation from Sade, one of the Surrealists' favourite writers, it can be seen as a final celebration of the wild, irrational passion, a law unto itself, which has driven Modot throughout the film to overthrow social rules and conventions. The aggression of unrestrained sexuality – Modot, the Duke of Blangis – is the scorpion that attacks and is feared by polite society. On the other hand, in its attempts to repress instinctive feeling, bourgeois society itself displays a scorpion-like ferocity. The Duke of Blangis, robed and bearded, bears a remarkable similarity to Christ. When a young girl, one of the orgiasts' victims, follows them from the castle, the Duke displays a Christ-like tenderness towards her, takes her back inside and, after a hideous shriek is heard, emerges once more with an expression of great piety. The final shot is of a cross bedecked with female scalps. Looked at in terms of its religious implications, the sequence can be seen to be a withering attack on a Christian society which, in the name of morality, represses spontaneous feeling, displays towards its women respect and tenderness and in so doing violates them, for in such circumstances true sexual freedom is transformed into sadism. In its final indictment of a cruel and repressive society, the ending of *L'Age d'or* is firmly linked to those scenes in the rest of the film where Modot's attempts to express freely his passion for Lya have been ruthlessly crushed by a scandalized society. It is entirely logical that in a single sequence the themes of sexual freedom and repression should be fused in such a memorable image.

From a technical point of view, *L'Age d'or* marks an

advance on *Un Chien andalou*, though in some respects its aims and methods are very similar. It shares with the previous film a primary concern with the revelation of the feelings of the two main characters. To this end, therefore, close-ups of Gaston Modot and Lya Lys are an important part of the film's cinematic language. Secondly, as in the case of *Un Chien andalou*, the thoughts and emotions of the characters are sometimes revealed in a sequence of visual images; the inner workings of their mind exteriorized. Such is Modot's erotic imagining of Lya seated on the lavatory of immaculate white porcelain, followed by shots of blazing toilet-paper and boiling lava; the white heat and jumble of the lover's inflamed imagination. Similarly, in a number of evocative and brilliant sequences, the lovers' vision transforms reality in its own image. Modot sees Lya everywhere – on advertisements, on sandwich-boards, in photographs. She sees him reflected in the mirror of her dressing-table, time and place conquered by their unity of spirit. And because, unlike *Un Chien andalou*, this is a talking-picture, sounds as well as images are used to link the lovers. Both Modot and Lya hear the barking of the dog. And the sound of the wind which blows out of her mirror is, in addition to its movement of her hair, an evocation of the elemental power of her passion. There is, too, throughout the film, a significant use of body-language and of the physical manifestation of passion. In the mirror-sequence Lya and Modot are seen biting their lips simultaneously. In the drawing-room, amongst the guests, Modot's biting of his lips communicates his desire to Lya. Her rubbing of her finger, her father's finger inserted in the bottle-neck, the servant's hands on a decanter, are all physical symbols of erotic desire. And in the garden-scene, the blood on Modot's face, like the blood on the girl's breast in the final sequence (both reminiscent of *Un Chien andalou*) is the outward sign of inner anguish.

L'Age d'or also shares with *Un Chien andalou* the desire to shock and, like the earlier film, often achieves that aim through simple, incongruous juxtapositions and quickly alternating shots. Early in the film, for instance, shots of the dignified laying of the foundation stone alternate with those of the shameless lovers rolling in the mud. Later, images of dignified guests and neat rows of chairs are interspersed with shots of chairs overturned and the lovers groping at each other on the ground. And in the extended sequence in the drawing-room, the ritual conversation and the formal poses of the refined company have as their incongruous counterpoint the appearance of the rustic cart, the explosion in the kitchen, and the shooting of the child. The episodes clash and collide violently and often unexpectedly and produce within us not merely a sense of shock and disturbance but of unease as well, of a tension based on a feeling of uncertainty. It is a frame of mind, an overthrowing of our sense of comfort and security which, once achieved, Buñuel can exploit further. In this particular sense music plays its part too. Sequences of romantic music – Wagner's 'Forest Murmurs' from *Siegfried* and 'Death of Tristan' from *Tristan and Isolde*; Beethoven's *Fifth Symphony*; Mendelssohn's *Fourth Symphony* and *Fingal's Cave*; Mozart's *Ave Verum*; and Debussy's *La Mer est plus belle* – are used sometimes to accompany and underline visual sequences but on other occasions to clash with them, creating a violent discord between what is seen and heard. The image-sound counterpoint idea had been discussed in 1928 by Eisenstein, Pudovkin and Alexandrov in their *Manifesto on Cinema sound*. Buñuel may not have read it, but he had sufficient cinematic instinct and intuition to put the theory into practice in his own first talking-picture, and would continue to do so in the years ahead.

If the above suggests a degree of artiness and over-sophistication, this is by no means the film's main impact. On the contrary, it is its simplicity which impresses. As Francisco Aranda has pointed out, it was a central principle of surrealism not to want 'to make art'; a theory which Buñuel himself embraced wholeheartedly. The camerawork is therefore unpretentious, simple and direct, devoid of any mere striving for effect. The cameraman, Albert Duverger, avoiding unusual angles, produced an effect distinguished by its lack of polish and sometimes by its crudity. It is an effect that is, of course, deliberate and part of the film's documentary intention. From the outset, through his use of documentary-like sequences and detailed explanatory titles, Buñuel insists that his aim is to show us how things are in the society in which we live, to frame his lovers with the reality that surrounds them. This is not to deny the uplifting and transcendental power of love which is communicated to us in many of the film's more lyrical sequences, but inasmuch as reality intrudes in its myriad forms and guises, touching upon and ultimately thwarting the lovers' dream, the technique is something which serves to remind us at every step of that inevitable and desolate truth.

NOTES

[1] See Francisco Aranda, *Luis Buñuel . . .*, p. 68.

[2] See Aranda, p. 69.

[3] All translations into English, unless otherwise stated, are my own.

[4] Aranda, pp. 70-71, gives a detailed account of the questionnaire which was later reprinted in *Le Surréalisme au Service de la Révolution* (1931).

[5] See 'Amour, érotisme et cinéma', *Le Terrain Vague* (1957).

[6] See *The Cosmological Eye*, London, 1945. The section on *L'Age d'or* is reprinted in *The World of Luis Buñuel*, pp. 166-179.

[7] See Freddy Buache, *The Cinema of Luis Buñuel*, London, 1973, pp. 28-29.

[8] See Ado Kyrou, *'L'Age d'or'*, in *The World of Luis Buñuel*, p. 155: 'A documentary-like opening announces that the film is an account of fact . . .' Tony Richardson, in 'The Films of Luis Buñuel' in the same collection of essays, p. 126, makes the same point: 'By its first sequence, a brusque documentary account of scorpions, the film asks to be accepted as fact rather than fiction'. The respective essays appeared originally in *Buñuel: An Introduction*, New York, 1953, and in *Sight and Sound* (January – March, 1954).

[9] Raymond Durgnat, *Luis Buñuel*, p. 39: 'The Bishops, though dead, triumph'.

[10] All quotations are taken from the script of the film published in *L'Avant-Scène du cinéma*, No. 27/28, Paris, 1963. The English translations are my own.

[11] The finger, with its Freudian implications, is a recurring symbol. In *Un Chien andalou* the hand in its different forms and meanings played a significant part. In *Viridiana* feet are prominent. In each case the overtones of such images endow the scenes in which they occur with a haunting and memorable quality.

[12] Of the mirror sequence, Ado Kyrou, *'L'Age d'or'*, p. 157, observes: 'The most perfect example of the meeting of cinema and surrealism is the mirror sequence, which I think is the most magnificent poetic sequence in the history of the film'.

[13] Raymond Durgnat, *Luis Buñuel*, p. 41, interprets the voice on the telephone as 'the still small voice' of Modot's conscience.

[14] The music can, perhaps, be seen here both as accompaniment and as ironic counterpoint – ironic in the sense that it anticipates the frustration of Modot's passion. For Raymond Durgnat, *Luis Buñuel*, p. 51, 'the "Liebestod" in *L'Age d'or* is lyrical', while in most Buñuel films the 'use of classical music is conspicuously ironical'.

[15] Of the somewhat enigmatic ending, Joan Mellen makes this observation: 'In this episode, borrowed from the Marquis de Sade, Buñuel's Christ appears ready to participate in the very perversities of those he is presumed to have "saved". Whether religious or political, repression breeds the acts it presumes to prevent – an ongoing Buñuelian theme'. See 'An Overview of Buñuel's Career' in *The World of Luis Buñuel*, p. 6.

[16] *Luis Buñuel*, p. 83. Aranda has some interesting observations on aspects of Buñuel's technique in *L'Age d'or*. For a more general study, See Raymond Durgnat's 'Style and anti-Style' in *Luis Buñuel*.

3
LOS OLVIDADOS

(The Young and The Damned)

CAST

Pedro	—	Alfonso Mejía
Marta	—	Estella India
Meche	—	Alma Delia Fuentes
Julián	—	Javier Amézcua
Judge	—	Héctor López Portillo
Jaibo	—	Roberto Cobo
Blind Man	—	Miguel Inclán
Poxy	—	Efraín Arauz
Little-Eyes	—	Mario Ramírez
Reform School Director	—	Francisco Jambrina

Photography	—	Gabriel Figueroa
Editor	—	Carlos Savage
Art Directors	—	Edward Fitzgerald W. W. Claridge
Music	—	Rodolfo Halffter: themes by Gustavo Pittaluga
Sound	—	José B. Carles (RCA)
Production	—	Ultramar Films Oscar Dancigers
Script	—	Luis Buñuel Luis Alcoriza
Assistant Director	—	Ignacio Villareal
Director	—	Luis Buñuel

After his classic documentary, *Land without Bread*, of 1932, Buñuel disappeared from the international film scene and embarked on a variety of projects which involved him in work in Spain, Paris, Hollywood, New York and finally, Mexico. It was here in 1950, twenty years after *L'Age d'or*, that he made *Los olvidados* and emerged once more from what have sometimes been described as the forgotten years.[1]

Francisco Aranda has observed that the budget for the film was very small. With the exception of Estella India (Marta), a well-known Mexican actress, Buñuel's cast was relatively unknown, although some had acting experience. Roberto Cobo (Jaibo) had played in the music-hall, Miguel Inclán (the Blind Man) was a professional actor, and even the young girl who took the part of Meche had done some acting. The sets, of course, were readily available in the hovels and derelict sites of Mexico city itself. Realizing, no doubt, that *Los olvidados* represented an opportunity to make a film of true quality, Buñuel worked hard yet, as was his custom, quickly. In the event he emerged from the wilderness into the full glare of international publicity. Despite his fears and reservations, *Los olvidados* was shown at the Cannes Festival of 1951 and won the prize for the best direction. The jury of the International Press gave him a special award for his work in general. And as for *Los olvidados*, it received considerable critical acclaim. Buñuel had arrived again, and this time would never return to the wilderness. His arrival marked instead the beginning of thirty years in the course of which he would make at regular intervals his most outstanding films.

Buñuel has drawn attention to the social purpose of *Los olvidados:*

> During the three years I was without work (1947-49) I was able to explore Mexico City from one end to the other; and I was impressed by the misery in which many of its people lived. I decided to base *Los*

> *olvidados* on the lives of abandoned children; and in my researches I patiently examined the records of a reformatory. My story is completely based on real cases. I tried to state the wretched conditions of the poor as they really are, because I detest films that make the poor romantic and sweet.[2]

At the same time he has emphasized that the film, for all its social implications, is not to be seen as presenting a thesis:

> For me *Los olvidados* is, quite honestly, a film with a social argument. To be true to myself I had to make a film of a social type. But, apart from this, I did not in any way want to make a thesis film.[3]

On the particular point of its lack of thesis and its moral objectivity, Freddy Buache has made a useful comparison between *Los olvidados* and other films with similar subjects:

> . . . he is not concerned with putting across a thesis about rehabilitation methods; his whole film is on a different level from Delannoy's self-indulgent *Chiens perdus sans collier*, Truffaut's autobiographical *Les 400 Coups*, the facile optimism of Nikolai Ekk's *The Way to Life* and Donskoi and Legoshin's *Song of Happiness*, or the repulsive sentimentality of all those films that bring tears to the eyes of the charitable by depicting the plight of waifs and strays.[4]

Buñuel was less concerned with making facile moral judgements about the society which breeds delinquents than in portraying it as it is, as a grim and inevitable fact of life.

The film reveals too Buñuel's continuing fascination with Surrealism. In speaking of its social implications he had also observed:

> I had seen things which had distressed me very much, and I wished to portray them on the screen, but always with that love of the instinctive and the irrational that I have and which is to be found everywhere.[5]

The characters of *Los olvidados* are convincing precisely because Buñuel consistently probes beneath the surface of their otherwise drab and ordinary lives, revealing to us the psychic world of *Un Chien andalou* grounded now in a tangible reality. Superficially *Los olvidados* is, like *Bitter Rice* and other films of the 1950s, neo-realist, but it also has, of course, a dimension that they totally neglected. Of Pedro's dream of his mother, Francisco Aranda has said:

> Only Buñuel could conceive such a scene. The unbridled eroticism, the underlying Freudian and Surrealist references which give it intellectual weight and exclude any pornographic interpretation; the way in which such a scene is interwoven with banal incidents, show that after twenty years of comparative inactivity, Buñuel remained completely himself.[6]

This particularly vivid sequence has a parallel in the scene portraying Jaibo's death where the voice on the soundtrack is his own inner voice and the mangy dog the outward representation of his fear of death. And there are, too, many other incidents where, even if the inner life of the characters is not externalized in the way described above, it is revealed to us through their contact with and reaction to the physical world around them. Rarely, indeed, is Buñuel's film a superficial image of the real world. Given the character of his early films, it would be surprising had it been so.

For many critics *Los olvidados* remains one of Buñuel's masterpieces. Francisco Aranda, on the other hand, considers that its merit has, perhaps, been overrated, that its violence is both excessive and monotonous, and that for Buñuel the fusion of social and surrealist concerns proved an uncomfortable marriage.[7] What cannot be denied, however, as Aranda himself concedes, is the film's immensely powerful portrayal of human beings who are the victims both of their own natures and to an even greater degree of their harsh environment. Buñuel, using as his material the raw and often melodramatic elements of popular Mexican cinema, succeeded in giving it something of the awesome inevitability and moving grandeur of Greek tragedy.[8]

The credits are followed by a series of dissolving shots of real cities: the port of New York, the island of Manhattan, the Eiffel Tower, Big Ben, and Mexico City. Buñuel's manner is, as in the opening sequence of *L'Age d'or*, documentary, his purpose to suggest that, no less than in the ruthlessly objective *Land Without Bread*, he is once more presenting us not with a fiction but with a closely observed picture of the real world. A superimposed voice enhances the effect of newsreel. It has, however, a glib complacency which Buñuel's irony will quickly undermine:

> 'Concealed behind the impressive structures of our great modern cities are pits of misery which contain unwanted, hungry, dirty and uneducated children. . . . Mexico, a great modern city, is no exception to this universal truth . . . and this film, based on real life, is not optimistic . . . but leaves the solution to this problem in the hands of the progressive forces of our time.'

The opening shots of impressive cities become a shot of waste ground inhabited by rough and ugly urchins, the intractable material confronting the 'progressive forces of our time' and the real focus of Buñuel's uncompromising vision.

The city is quickly shown to be a concrete jungle in which, both in appearance and deed, the youngsters' proximity to the animal world is firmly underlined. As the boys play their games a close-up makes the point:

> *Close-up of the boy who is playing the enraged bull. He bares his broken teeth, charges with lowered head, his forefingers pointing forward like horns.*

Shots of Sour-Face, clinging to and climbing a pillar, suggest his approximation to a monkey. Jeering, mocking faces, aggressive gestures, and a sense of bristling hostility add to the impression of a world in which the difference between the animal and human world is only (and sometimes less than) skin deep.

A dissolve introduces Jaibo, one of the film's main characters. He has escaped from a reformatory and is being ruthlessly hunted by the police. A shot of a black police car, stalking Jaibo like some black panther, sustains the idea of the jungle, the hunter and the hunted. In the context of his initial picture of the ferocity of human nature and of simple and savage laws, Buñuel reveals in all its absurdity the idea of the triumph of human progress. Jaibo's experience in the reformatory has merely sharpened his wits, providing him with the ammunition to defeat the progressive forces which seek to help him. As in his other major films, notably *Nazarín* and *Viridiana*, Buñuel is intent on exposing the futile and self-defeating nature of any kind of false idealism.

Another dissolve reveals a busy market-place where Carmelo, a blind man, entertains the crowd with his one-man band. In his patter and his cunning he is a figure straight out of the Spanish picaresque novel of the sixteenth and seventeenth centuries whose influence on Buñuel is particularly strong: a good example of the frequently literary sources of his films. In particular, Carmelo is reminiscent of the blind man in the first chapter of *Lazarillo de Tormes*.[9] The picaresque world, in which only the fittest survive, is precisely the world of *Los olvidados*, and in the episode which follows, when Jaibo and his gang attempt to steal the blind man's money from the satchel on his back, he is like some unsuspecting animal cornered by his enemies. It is a world whose primitive savagery is embodied in close-ups of Skinhead's razor blade as he tries to cut the satchel, the sharp nail in the blind man's flailing stick, and the stick slashing the boy's legs. Buñuel portrays the scene with objectivity and avoids moral and sentimental clichés. The blind man, a traditionally sympathetic figure, is seen to be just as vicious as Jaibo. But neither does Buñuel condemn:

these people are what they are, their morality that of the world which shapes them in its image. The boy's dialogue evokes a world where no one has compassion for them and they have little for each other:

> SKINHEAD: The bastard! He had a big nail in the end of the stick.
> THIRD BOY: Your guts will fall out!
> SHOESHINE: Does it hurt? Get your mother to see to it.
> SKINHEAD: My mother? You must be daft. She doesn't want me. That's why I left home.

For them to steal, to injure or be injured, is something to be measured not according to some nicely adjusted moral scales but in relation to the simple, black and white necessities of their own desperate existence.

The scene switches to the outskirts of the city, to another patch of wasteland where the boys, bent on vengeance, hunt the blind man. He seeks refuge in his habitual, assumed role of the helpless unfortunate:

> Have pity! Have pity on a poor, helpless, blind old man!

His plea is abruptly answered by a clod of earth hurled at his face. Pity is denied him in a world which has no pity and the boys proceed to smash the old man's instruments. They have no scruples in depriving him of his living, as he has none in attempting to deprive them of life and limb. He is left lying amid the wreckage of his instruments, an indifferent cockerel the only witness of his fate:

> *The camera tracks and pans sideways as he lifts his head, his face plastered in mud, and finds himself eye to eye with a black cock. Ironical musical effect, as the camera holds on the cock.*

In the blind man's downfall there is, after all, a rough justice.

Another sequence presents the chicken run of a house where Pedro, another of the film's main characters, lives with his mother and her three other children. The opening shot of Pedro stroking a hen and examining the hen's eggs has evident sexual overtones (Pedro's need of his mother). It also underlines the close proximity of the world of animals and human beings and the essentially primitive nature of human motives. Within the house Marta's children follow their mother, clamouring for food with all the eagerness of open-mouthed chicks pursuing the mother hen. Pedro is left to go hungry, for Marta will not feed him when he can work but does not. In the end, unseen by her, he steals some food and makes his escape. The rules which operate are as stark, simple and clear-cut as those of the natural world.

The point is also made by another scene set in a different but otherwise similar hovel. Poxy, another of the boys, sharpens his knife while his mother lies on the bed, moaning with pain, in her own view less important than the animals:

> I count for less than the animals round here. Look at Meche and you two. You'll leave me to die on my own!

In the stable, where Jaibo, Pedro and Little-Eyes have appeared, the closeness of the human and animal world is reflected constantly. Jaibo holds a black kid in his arms. Later he and Pedro attempt to milk an ass. At the same time Little-Eyes lies beneath a nanny goat, drinking from her udder.[10] And all around them are the sounds of nature, epitomised in the cackling of the hens. The fact that the house and the stable are adjacent has, clearly, a metaphorical as well as a physical significance. And in Jaibo's sexual advances to Meche, Poxy's young sister, there is a pure animal spontaneity and a kind of bantam-cock bravado.

A dissolve reveals some waste ground near a building site where Jaibo, accompanied by Pedro, is bent on vengeance against another youth; Julián. In the ensuing scene, one of the most violent in all Buñuel's films, Jaibo hurls a large and heavy stone at Julián's head and, when he falls to the ground, clubs him savagely with a thick branch. It is an episode of frightening brutality but none of it gratuitous, for in Jaibo's actions is contained the instinctive behaviour of a character for whom violence is the normal currency of daily life. Buñuel portrays the incident with the stark objectivity with which in *Land Without Bread* he shows a donkey stung to death by a swarm of bees.

The violent instincts of these people have their counterpart in their primitive superstitions. A fade-in reveals the market place from which the blind man, led by Little-Eyes, makes his way to Pedro's house. He has come to treat the boy's mother with his folk remedies, and, as she calls on the Virgin Mary to ease her suffering, so he rubs her naked back with a white dove, which is also a pointer to his own lust:

> This will help you. Look at the dove. All the pain you had, you have passed to him. When he dies, you will be well again.

Similarly, Little-Eyes wears around his neck a dead man's tooth to ward off illness. For Buñuel the mother's invocation of the Virgin is as much an empty superstition as the blind man's cure or the boy's charm. The blind man's final, purely realistic comment, as he drinks from a bottle of milk, undermines, in true Buñuelian fashion, all the mumbo jumbo:

> Ah! There's nothing like ass's milk for health.

A brief scene centres on a legless cripple seated on a small cart or trolley. Jaibo and the boys surround him, demand cigarettes, and, when he defies them, lift him off the cart, empty his pockets, dump him on the pavement, and send the cart careering down the road, while the cripple vainly calls for the police. The scene is short but extremely vivid, and it is portrayed, like the other violent episodes of the film, with an impressive objectivity, as though Buñuel had merely filmed things as they happened. There is no excessive pity for the cripple. He expects no pity for himself, nor does he ask of the world what he knows it cannot provide. If anything, the scene has an element of grim humour that is markedly picaresque.

The largely external action of the film becomes now a remarkable sequence that takes us into the psychic world of *Un Chien andalou*, as Buñuel exposes Pedro's fears and obsessions. A dream-sequence in slow motion is full of disturbing images and associations. The dream-form of Pedro rises from the bed which contains his sleeping figure, looks beneath it and sees Julián's battered and bloodstained body grinning at him. His obsession with the crime is accompanied too by thoughts of his relationship with his mother, who is seen sitting on her bed in her nightdress. Pedro is haunted by the fear of her rejection of him:

PEDRO'S VOICE: Why don't you ever kiss me? ... Mama! I promise I'll be better ... I'll look for work. You will be able to rest.

In the illogical yet meaningful world of dream the mother's refusal to give her son food assumes a form both clear and ambiguous. Marta, her hair flying in the wind, her face illuminated by lightning, advances towards Pedro and holds towards him a piece of raw, bleeding meat. As Pedro extends his hand to take it, another hand appears from beneath the bed to snatch the meat from his grasp. Pedro and Jaibo struggle over it until the victorious Jaibo withdraws once more beneath the bed. In one sense the meat is, of course, another form of Julián's bleeding and mutilated face, another ghastly projection of Pedro's obsessive thoughts. In another sense, like the mutilated hand of *Un Chien andalou*, it has clear sexual implications, and Pedro's conflict with Jaibo is a conflict for possession of Pedro's mother, born out of Pedro's fear of his rejection by her. And it is a projection too of Pedro's fear of Jaibo, who looms ever larger in the boy's tormented mind, a demon figure of dangerous and threatening proportions. Buñuel, as in his first film, captures in highly suggestive images the fearful and confused world of dream, endowing the film's narrative with a characteristic poetic depth.[11]

A new sequence depicts the stable of Pedro's house.

Meche squats on the floor milking an ass and the milk is heard running into the pail. Above in the loft Jaibo watches her. Meche's fingers grasping the animal's teat pinpoints Jaibo's sexual desire while the spurting milk is a clear equivalent of ejaculation. The scene also looks forward to *Viridiana*. Similarly, the spectacle of Meche's naked thighs as she bathes them with the ass's milk awakens in Jaibo the growing desire aroused in the ageing Don Jaime by the sight of Viridiana's white and naked flesh. Meche is, for her part, innocent, and yet, for all her tender years, already shaped by the reality of the world in which she lives to profit from her charms. Surprised and frightened by Jaibo, she is also quick to negotiate the price of a kiss. The shot of her naked thighs, together with her bargaining, is a finely judged pointer to her unconscious but inevitable drift into eventual prostitution. Towards Little-Eyes, on the other hand, she is capable of tenderness, for he tries to protect her from Jaibo. Meche is already, in a sense, the conventional tart with a heart of gold, transformed by Buñuel's deft and sure touch into a figure of extraordinary conviction.

Meche's awakening to the world about her has its parallel in Little-Eyes. A dissolve to a building-site reveals his encounter with Jaibo who threatens to kill him if he admits to having seen him. The violent incident is followed by another in which the blind man, sensing Jaibo's presence, questions Little-Eyes and twists his ear to extract the truth. It is an episode in which the young boy is seen to respond inevitably to the violent world in which he finds himself and of which he is a victim. He reacts to the blind man's cruelty by picking up a piece of concrete, and for a moment we are presented, in a highly suggestive shot, with a virtual reconstruction of Jaibo's murder of Julián:

> *The BLIND MAN sits in back view as he peels the potatoes. Beyond him, LITTLE-EYES picks up a large chunk of concrete and approaches, poised to throw it at him.*

The boy resists the temptation, but just as Meche is a prostitute in the making, so Little-Eyes is close to becoming another Jaibo. The end of the sequence reveals the blind man brandishing his knife:

> *He brandishes his knife threateningly, and then begins slicing the potato savagely . . .*

Both he and Jaibo personify the savagery from which Little-Eyes can never escape and to which, if he is to survive, he must adapt.

Buñuel's subtle treatment of the material of the film is seen again in an incident involving Pedro. The black cock, an earlier witness to the blind man's downfall, appears on the fence above the chicken run, bent on mating with the hens. His appearance is accompanied by the same ironic music as before, but now, in contrast, it is a prelude to his own fate. The cock, like the black kid, is also an evocation of Jaibo, both of his lustful, strutting nature and his ultimate downfall. And there is, too, a third dimension to the scene. When Pedro's mother seizes a broom, rushes from the house to the chicken-run and begins to belabour the cock with all her might, the episode becomes for Pedro a reconstruction of Jaibo's savage murder of Julián, its horror further sharpened in his mind by the anguished cries of the dead boy's drunken father:

> They've killed my son. They've killed him. If I find out who did it . . .

When Pedro calls to his mother, 'Mama! Stop it! Don't hit him again!', Buñuel exposes clearly the mental images that flash before the boy's eyes. If, as in the dream-sequence, he is a master at revealing the world of fear and fantasy, Buñuel is also someone who employs the incidents and objects of everyday, prosaic reality to display the inner life of his characters.

Jaibo's hungry eyeing of Meche's thighs has its counterpart now in another episode involving Marta. Visual links establish both parallels and differences:

> *. . . We first see MARTA'S legs as she washes them in a basin of water. Then the camera moves back and reveals her standing with her dress tucked up to her thighs. She wears a low-cut blouse . . .*

Meche, desirable as she is, becomes in Marta a mature and sexually experienced woman, Jaibo's sexual hunger correspondingly sharpened: *He gazes lustfully at MARTA'S thighs . . . JAIBO gazing at her breasts . . . he smiles, staring at her legs.* The camera is, in effect, the mirror of Jaibo's desires at a more advanced and developed stage. Buñuel, indeed, conveys in the structure of his film, in the relationship of scene to scene, episode to episode, not merely the development of an action but the growth and development of the characters, particularly the boys who are part of it. The personalities of Jaibo, Pedro and Little-Eyes unfold before us with an authenticity as great as that which distinguishes the camera's portrayal of physical reality. It is one of the film's outstanding qualities.

When the scene changes to a street in a rich quarter of the city, shots of shops, cinemas and cars evoke the 'impressive structures of our great modern cities' of the film's initial sequence. Pedro is being hunted by the police for a theft committed by Jaibo. Inasmuch as he is now a fugitive he is already another Jaibo, as was Little-Eyes in his murderous intentions towards the blind man. But the real focus of this scene is the well-dressed, middle-aged man with moustache and goatee beard, the bourgeois child molester who accosts Pedro in the street. The landscape of the film has been transformed; slums into rich thoroughfares, wasteground into elegant buildings, rough and dirty urchins into well-groomed individuals. On the other hand, the bourgeois gentleman is no different from Jaibo. He attempts to buy the boy just as Jaibo purchased the kiss from Meche. And he is, of course, part of the 'progressive forces of our time'. Buñuel comments on the incident through the actions of a policeman. He has observed the bourgeois but merely shakes his head in disapproval. Elsewhere the police are vigorously continuing the search for the two delinquent boys.

Two brief episodes reaffirm the violent world of the film. The camera reveals a piece of waste ground where Pedro has been sleeping in a rough shelter of stones, bricks and corrugated iron. In the background is a pile of old tyres, paper and scrap metal from which two tramps emerge to threaten him. Buñuel's equation of material and human dereliction is one which is seen in several of his films, notably in the beggars' orgy of *Viridiana* and the drawing-room sequence of *The Exterminating Angel.* As Pedro is, in a sense, a version of Jaibo, so he is also a form of the two tramps. Indeed, it is a constant feature and merit of Buñuel's film that between its various characters the points of contact are always clear, its hardened rogues the mirrors of a younger generation. When, in another brief episode, the owner of a merry-go-round at a fair hits Sour-Face savagely, the boy's look of hatred parallels directly the older man's hostility towards him and points to his own future. The shot of the fairground with its jolly music creates an ironic counterpoint to the human motives that dominate the episode.

In another scene set in Pedro's house, Jaibo's longing for Marta, and her own sexual frustration, reach a climactic point. Close-ups of Jaibo looking greedily at Marta, devouring her with his eyes, emphasize his animal longing for her. As for Marta, a shot of her half-open thighs as she squats to pick up some chicks is suggestive not only of Jaibo's inflamed desires but of her own subconscious yearnings:

> . . . *Unconsciously, she half opens her thighs.*

Marta is an ordinary woman, poor, uneducated, widowed, but for Buñuel as worthy of attention as any human being. His portrayal of her, like his portrayal of many of the film's characters, avoids the superficial and exposes the real and pressing needs that lie beneath the surface. None the less, for all his sympathetic although unsentimental treatment of human beings, the Buñuelian irony is rarely far away. The human passions enacted in the house have as their accompaniment a shot of performing dogs in the street, and the analogy with human beings is very clear:

> *. . . The dogs are made to dance on their hind legs. . . .*
> *We see the dogs dancing, dressed in skirts and hats. . . .*

The same fascination with the complexity of human motives distinguishes the ensuing confrontation between Marta and Pedro. The boy has returned after running away from home. He needs his mother's love but encounters only her hostility. Her anger is, of course, natural, but her attitude towards her son is partly coloured too by a sense of guilt linked to her own affair with Jaibo. Because of it, she misinterprets Pedro's observation, seeing it (quite wrongly) as a comment on the association:

> PEDRO: You are annoyed because of Jaibo. It's his fault.
> *Incensed by this remark, MARTA turns and hits her son violently across the face.*

For his part, Pedro cannot understand her violence towards him:

> Why did you hit me?

Mother and son become increasingly moving and touching figures. When Pedro threatens her with a chair, an instinctive action that goes against the grain, it is an action that points to the nature of his tragedy, a tragedy that lies in the violence done to a basically good and tender human being.

A new sequence introduces the juvenile court of a government department; an example, clearly, of one of the 'progressive forces of our time'. Shots of filing cabinets, desks and formally dressed officials evoke a tidily ordered world at the opposite extreme from the piles of rubble, the wretched hovels and the human derelicts that populate the film. It is the world which seeks to order Pedro's life, to rehabilitate him on a school farm from whence he will emerge a new and enlightened citizen. In the figure of the judge however, Buñuel embodies moral clichés whose irrelevance to the lives of Pedro and Marta speak for themselves, and which are given their true perspective by Marta's observation:

> JUDGE: Sometimes I believe that it is you who should be punished for the things you do to your children. You offer them neither love nor affection, so they look for it elsewhere.
>
> MARTA: Perhaps it is true, but I have to spend my days washing floors for other people so that I can eat.

Marta's tragedy lies partly in the fact that, although she knows Pedro's needs much better than the system ever can, the system itself denies her the opportunity of fulfilling them, offering only moral platitudes instead.

The cold formality of the scene has its opposite in Marta and Pedro's farewell. Embittered by his mother's apparent coldness, Pedro accuses her of a lack of genuine affection for him. Moved by his sincerity, Marta accepts that he is innocent of theft, and, deeply touched by his despair, kisses him. It is a moving scene, simple and devoid of undue sentiment. There is pity in it too, for although the characters do not know it, their reconciliation has come too late and they will never meet again. The focus of the film has moved, in the course of its development, away from Jaibo's violent exploits to a subtle and penetrating exploration of the slow destruction of Pedro's innocence. Jaibo is at the end of a road that Pedro travels still, but the journey is the same.

Buñuel's portrayal of the Director of the farm school is sympathetic. His benign and kind appearance is paralleled by his good intentions, and he displays towards Pedro both tolerance and understanding. Pedro, on the other hand, reacts with violence towards a world which, in his view, violates his liberty. When, in a powerful scene, he seizes a stick and sets about the chickens in the chicken run, the incident evokes the blind man's flailing stick, Marta's vicious attack on the cockerel, and Jaibo's murder of Julián. Pedro is already cast in the image of his elders, and the Director recognizes sadly the futility of his own idealism:

> DIRECTOR *(smiling sadly)*: . . . I was only thinking. If we could lock away poverty and not the children.

The familiar sound of the crowing cock, as the sequence ends, is Buñuel's comment on the incident.

Subsequent events confirm the Director's recognition of his own impotence. He continues to treat Pedro with kindness and, because he is anxious to allow the boy to prove himself, sends him on an errand to the tobacconist's shop. Pedro gratefully accepts the opportunity and responds eagerly to the Director's faith in him:

> *He looks towards the gate with joy.*

It is, however, a moment whose optimism quickly fades, for in the street Pedro is accosted by Jaibo who proceeds to steal the Director's money from him. The Director's good intentions, as well as Pedro's response to them, founder in a world where Jaibo and others like him will always thwart them. Jaibo, however, is presented not as a deliberately evil individual worthy of condemnation but as an inescapable fact of life; an immovable obstacle in the face of which all human aspirations seem inevitably doomed. When Pedro pursues Jaibo in an attempt to recover both the Director's money and his own good name, he succeeds only in getting himself into a fight in which, accusing Jaibo of killing Julián, he puts himself within the ambit of Jaibo's violent revenge. But if Pedro cannot escape the unmitigated harshness of the world, neither can Jaibo. The blind man has not forgotten him. Grasping eagerly at Pedro's revelation of Jaibo's part in Julián's murder, the blind man plans to denounce him to the police. In this world of 'dog eat dog' Jaibo can no more

top, The violence of the world
bottom, The blind man's lust

escape the blind man's malice and vengeance than can Pedro evade Jaibo's unremitting violence.[12]

The blind man's viciousness, exposed throughout the film, is seen to be accompanied by his lust. When Meche brings him some milk, he sits her on his knee, puts his arm around her, and draws her close to him:

> BLIND MAN: Ah, little Meche! Sit here. You're a very nice little girl. *(He puts her on his knee.)* Your hair smells nice.

Beneath his fawning compliments his desire for even a fleeting physical contact is very clear. Moreover, his attempt to bribe her with sweets links him to the bourgeois gentleman's efforts to buy Pedro. For Buñuel both are utterly unpleasant characters but both are human too. In presenting us with another facet of the blind man's character, Buñuel deepens and rounds it further, allowing us to see, as in the case of the other individuals, beneath the surface.

A scene in the stable of Meche's house presents Pedro's final confrontation with Jaibo. Jaibo is asleep in the hayloft when, ignorant of his presence there, Pedro arrives and accidentally disturbs him. In the ensuing fight Jaibo kills the younger boy by hitting him over the head with an iron bar. This reconstruction of Jaibo's murder of Julián underlines the point that in a world like this the pattern of violence is self-repeating. Throughout the film, the recurring motifs of stones, bricks, flailing sticks, brooms and iron bars construct a network of savagery in which the characters are both enmeshed and inextricably linked. The shot of Pedro lying on his back, with blood trickling from his mouth, is remarkably like the shot of the bleeding Julián in Pedro's dream. It is a shot, moreover, which underlines the expendable nature, the virtual insignificance of human lives. As Pedro's body lies in the straw, a white hen stands on his chest, indifferent to his fate, as was the black cock to the blind man's downfall.

This impression is reinforced by the film's final sequences.

Jaibo is shot by the police as he attempts to escape. Superimposed over a shot of his face as he lies dying is a shot of a mangy dog, and a voice is heard calling:

Look out, Jaibo. The mangy dog is coming.

The dog, a wretched and miserable creature, underlines the insignificance of Jaibo's death, the total absence of any kind of heroism or dignity. And there is about it too a terrible sense of isolation. The voice, Jaibo's inner voice, is heard again:

No . . . no . . . I'm falling into a black pit. I'm alone.

Furthermore, while Jaibo's body lies amidst dereliction, Pedro's corpse is thrown by Meche and her grandfather onto a vast rubbish dump. It is a logical if terrifying ending for those who, like empty cans and bottles, society merely casts aside. In a sense, the ending contains a glimmer of hope, for Marta loves her son enough to search for him, and fear is accompanied by pity on the old man's face, as he disposes of Pedro's body. But the fact that Marta's search is pointless and the old man's pity ineffective is the final unavoidable truth that obliterates all hope.[13]

Los olvidados, unlike *Un Chien andalou* and *L'Age d'or* but like Buñuel's other Mexican films, has a clear-cut story line. It moves from beginning to end in a simple, direct and incisive manner, with all the speed and clarity of the better Spanish picaresque novels. In some ways the documentary nature of the film's beginning sets the tone for what comes afterwards, for a matter-of-fact, unsentimental presentation of events is the very essence of *Los olvidados*. Certainly, nothing in Buñuel's work fits better Raymond Durgnat's definition of his 'fast, hard style'. In this respect, as Durgnat has himself observed, Buñuel may be compared with certain American directors, notably those of the twenties and thirties, for whom speed was money.[14] And it is important to bear in mind, of course, Buñuel's own experience of Hollywood, for it clearly left its imprint.

The rapid movement of the film has its roots in Buñuel's largely objective standpoint, for it enables him to present things as they are, without comment, sentimentality, or moral overtones. The camera does not dwell unduly, for instance, on either character or incident. When the clod of earth hits the blind man in the face, Buñuel does not linger on it. He could easily, in his presentation of destitutes and cripples, have sentimentalized them by over-emphasis, or made horrific incidents, like Jaibo's murder of Julián, more horrific still by portraying them at greater length and in greater detail. The effect of Buñuel's approach is that neither character nor incident are exaggerated within the general context of the film. They maintain the importance that they have in the lives of the people presented to us on the screen, and to this extent the film is, in a sense, truly 'documentary'; a truthful evocation of the reality of the delinquents of Mexico City. Francisco Aranda is therefore surely wrong when he speaks of the film's excessive violence.[15] It is precisely the predictability of violence, its normality in the lives of these people, as well as its desensitizing effect, which gives to the film its essential truthfulness.

While Buñuel's technique is unquestionably simple and straightforward, close-ups play an important part in evoking the reality of a harsh and ugly world. The close-up of Poxy's face in the opening sequence pinpoints a physical ugliness that personifies the brutal existence of such children. It is echoed in other marvellously suggestive faces through the course of the film, from the arrogant superciliousness of Jaibo to the rough, leathery, indestructible features of the blind man: a truly Goya-like gallery of portraits. Close-ups of objects also convey the predominant violence in which the characters live. We are shown the razor blade in Skinhead's hand, the blind man's stick slashing the boy's legs, the stone in Jaibo's hand, the piece of concrete held by Little Eyes, the knife brandished by the blind man, the broom wielded by

Marta, the chair used by Pedro against his mother, the stick with which Pedro kills the chickens, the iron bar with which Jaibo kills Pedro. These objects, emphasized in close-up and echoing each other in a hauntingly obsessive pattern, create the impression of a reality both violent and claustrophobic which constantly surrounds the characters and from which they cannot escape. And thirdly there are the landscapes of the film, which, like the objects described above, seem to repeat themselves endlessly, defining with their harshness the enclosed world in which the characters move – the pieces of waste ground, the derelict construction sites, the decaying houses, the mounds of rubbish. They are as much a part of the film's essence as the characters – the physical, external image that frames with its own violence and ugliness the lives of the people contained within it.

While the film's technique conveys all this, it suggests very powerfully too, in a way which separates it entirely from Italian neo-realist films, the inner lives of its characters. The most vivid and eloquent sequence in this respect is Pedro's dream. The dream atmosphere is recreated in part by slow motion. The figures drift and glide. The voices that accompany the dream are the voices of the characters but superimposed. The climactic section, depicting Pedro's struggle with Jaibo, is accompanied by lightning and a howling wind. These are all in themselves highly accomplished and effective cinematic effects, but, for all this, the haunting, memorable quality of the episode lies esentially in its power to touch on (and to embody in meaningful images) feelings deeply embedded in the human psyche. The most memorable image is thus the image of the raw, bleeding piece of meat invitingly extended by the smiling mother to her son. In its sexual implications alone it is very strong. Buñuel has gone beyond the merely technical devices of the cinema to capture, in a moment of insight and poetic intuition, an emotion, a relationship of universal relevance. Similarly, as Jaibo dies and the mangy dog is seen approaching along a wet road that shines in the sun, Buñuel conveys the fear, the wretchedness, and the loneliness of death that affects us all. His great achievement is to penetrate not only the minds of his characters but ours too and to pinpoint the common ground of our humanity.[16] In doing so he uses the camera as a poet uses language.

Elsewhere in the film the inner life of the characters is revealed through the portrayal of external reality. When Meche pours the milk over her thighs, the camera focuses on her white flesh as though the camera itself were Jaibo's eyes as he watches her from the loft. Later Marta's legs are seen in close-up as she washes them. In both cases Buñuel exteriorizes Jaibo's lust. Other emotions are displayed with equal force. When Marta attacks the black cock with the broom, a medium close-up of Pedro reveals his mouth hanging open, and his eyes staring. In short, Buñuel exposes in relation to a particular incident the terrible emotion that Pedro felt, and continues to feel, in relation to another – Julián's murder. Indeed, for all its apparent emphasis on the portrayal of external reality, the film's true quality lies very much in the inner reality of its characters. And in this particular sense, Buñuel, twenty years on from *Un Chien andalou* and *L'Age d'or*, is still a true Surrealist.

NOTES

[1] For the biographical and historical background see Francisco Aranda, *Luis Buñuel . . .*, pp. 100-136.

[2] In an interview given to *Nuevo Cine*. The translation is my own. See too Aranda, p. 137.

[3] In an interview given to *Cahiers du Cinéma*. The translation is my own. See too Aranda, pp. 137-138.

[4] *The Cinema of Luis Buñuel*, p. 49.

[5] Quoted in the interview given to *Cahiers du Cinéma*. See note 3 above.

[6] Aranda, p. 141.

[7] Aranda, p. 143, suggests that the 'violence always present in Buñuel, here seems at times to be pitched to a forced note. The astonishing brutalities shock us with a regularity that becomes predictable . . .'

[8] For some perceptive observations on the tragic nature of the film see Raymond Durgnat, *Luis Buñuel*, pp. 60-68, and André Bazin, *'Los olvidados'*, in *The World of Luis Buñuel*, pp. 194-200. Bazin's article appeared originally in *'Qu'est-ce que le Cinéma? III: Cinéma et Sociologie*, Paris: Editions du Cerf, 1961.

[9] The literary influences upon Buñuel, particularly the Spanish literary influences, have often been mentioned by critics and quite rightly so. Aranda, for example, observes that 'he has followed literary trends much more closely than might appear at first sight ... His letters reveal his passion for literature' (p. 46). Carlos Rebolledo discusses the influence of the picaresque novel, notably *Lazarillo de Tormes*, in 'Buñuel and the Picaresque Novel', *The World of Luis Buñuel*, pp. 139-148. The article is, unfortunately, ruined by factual errors, the most serious being the attribution of the anonymous sixteenth-century tale to Francisco de Quevedo, a seventeenth-century author. Other errors include a wrong date – 1557 – for the appearance of *Lazarillo* (1554) and a discussion of a Part II of the book, also, presumably, by Quevedo.

[10] We can compare the incident with a similar episode in *Viridiana*. In both films the world of natural instincts forms a background to the behaviour of human beings.

[11] André Bazin has expressed very well both the effectiveness and the true universality of this particular sequence: 'We can never forget this piece of meat, palpitating like some ghastly sea creature, offered by a mother who smiles like a madonna ... Buñuel has furnished us with the only contemporary aesthetic expression of Freudian symbolism that works. The surrealists used it too selfconsciously; we cannot respond to symbols too obviously and abritrarily chosen. By contrast, in *Un Chien andalou*, *L'Age d'or*, and *Los olvidados* these psychological situations are presented in all their profound and irrefutable truth. Whatever the plastic form Buñuel gives to the dream (and in this case, it is highly ambiguous) his images pulse with the life and feeling of dreams. The dark, thick blood of the unconscious circulates in these scenes, and drenches us, as if an artery has been opened into the soul' (See *'Los olvidados'* in *The World of Luis Buñuel*, pp. 196-197).

[12] Joan Mellen observes that 'all are victims in Buñuel, the despoiling and the despoiled ... for even the vicious are victims of forces of which they are as much the shaped as the shapers'. See 'An Overview of Buñuel's Career', *The World of Luis Buñuel*, pp. 18-20.

[13] Francisco Aranda, in particular, underlines the film's pessimism: 'The world is a kind of inferno, with no way out. The human being, like a homunculus, bears his destiny ...' See p. 145.

[14] *Luis Buñuel*, 'Style and Anti-Style', p. 15.

[15] See n. 7 above.

[16] See n. 11 above.

4
NAZARÍN

CAST

Nazarín	—	Francisco Rabal
Andara	—	Rita Macedo
The Sacrilegist	—	Ignacio López Tarso
Chanfa	—	Ofelia Guilmaín
La Prieta	—	Rosenda Monteros
Beatriz	—	Marga López
Ujo	—	Jesús Fernández
The Parricide	—	Luis Aceves Castañeda
Pinto	—	Noé Murayama

and:
Ada Callasio, Antonio Bravo, Aurora Melina,
David Reinoso

Photography	—	Gabriel Figueroa
Editor	—	Carlos Savage
Art Editor	—	Edward Fitzgerald
Sound	—	José Pérez
Production	—	Manuel Barbachano Ponce Productions Barbachano Ponce
Script	—	Luis Buñuel Julio Alejandro (from the novel by Benito Pérez Galdós)
Assistant Directors	—	Ignacio Villareal Juan Luis Buñuel
Director	—	Luis Buñuel

In the eight years that separate *Los olvidados* and *Nazarín* Buñuel made the extraordinary total of thirteen films, of which the first eleven were all Mexican and the last two French-Italian and French-Mexican productions respectively. Despite the great success of *Los olvidados*, Buñuel was obliged to continue making his commercial Mexican melodramas, in the production of which, limited budgets, a lack of time and the nature of popular taste and demand were all important factors. Nevertheless, within the evident limitations of these films, Buñuel's achievement was often considerable. *El*, for example, made in 1952, portrays Francisco, a rich bourgeois forty-year-old virgin who, inhibited by his puritanical upbringing in which religion figures prominently, becomes obsessed with a young woman and, having married her, develops an insane jealousy. The mixture of sexual motivation and religious inhibition, together with a fascination with the protagonist's inner life, exemplifies the way in which Buñuel endowed the typical Mexican melodrama with his own particular brand of genius. Especially interesting too in this respect are his two interpretations of the classics: *Las aventuras de Robinson Crusoe* (1952) and *Cumbres borrascosas (Wuthering Heights)* (1953). In the first of these (as in the case of *El* and so many of his other films) Buñuel lays bare his protagonist's inner conflict, notably his sense of solitude and of social and sexual deprivation, while Crusoe's encounter with Friday, which reveals his social and racial prejudices, strikes another familiar Buñuelian chord.[1] *Wuthering Heights* was, for obvious reasons, a favourite work of the Surrealists, and it is no coincidence that Buñuel had originally wanted to make *Cumbres borrascosas* at the time of *L'Age d'Or*. With its concentration on powerful and uninhibited passion, the Bronte novel remained very close to Buñuel's heart and the film is, in Francisco Aranda's view, one of Buñuel's masterpieces.[2]

Buñuel had wanted to make *Nazarín* for ten years or so and the script, with several others, lay idle, waiting for a producer courageous enough to take it on. Oscar Dancigers, who since 1946 had produced or co-produced ten of Buñuel's films, would not touch the subject, and in the end Buñuel turned to Manuel Barbachano Ponce, who had produced *Raíces, Torero* and *Méjico mío* for Carlos Velo. Because the film was made in Mexico, Buñuel, as in the case of most of his Mexican films, was compelled to work within a limited budget and time-scale, although he was given six weeks to shoot it instead of the normal four. In talking about *Nazarín* before shooting began, Buñuel had referred to the vast amounts of money spent by Hollywood on films with lavish sets, fine actors and a wholly stereotyped, conventional, bourgeois morality in which evil must always be conquered, good must always triumph.[3] His own films, of course, had always been, from the moment when *Un Chien andalou* exploded on the screen, precisely the opposite, and *Nazarín*, in its scrutiny of conventional religious beliefs and attitudes, is no exception.

Nazarín, reflecting again Buñuel's literary interests, is based on the novel of the same name by the great nineteenth-century Spanish novelist, Benito Pérez Galdós. The novel describes a priest, Don Nazario Zaharín, whose aim in life it is to live as closely as possible in accordance with the teachings of Christ. Accompanied by the prostitute, Andara, and later by the beautiful Beatriz, Nazarín travels from village to village, teaching the Christian virtues of love, compassion, forgiveness and resignation, and turning the other cheek to the malice and scorn that are invariably aimed in his direction. When Nazarín is struck down by typhus and lapses into delirium, he sees himself walking towards Golgotha, hoping to be crucified. Christ appears and speaks to him, expressing the belief that Nazarín's suffering is in His name and that, after his recovery, he will continue his work. The end of the book establishes, in effect, a close parallel between Nazarín and Christ.

In many respects Buñuel remained faithful to the novel. On the other hand, Freddy Buache asserts quite correctly that Buñuel has stamped with his own personality everything that he took from Galdós and that in his hands the film acquired quite a different emphasis.[4] While the novel stresses, for example, Nazarín's exemplary Christian behaviour and the redeeming nature of his suffering, Buñuel reveals only his futility and the pointlessness of a Christian life in a world that is both incapable and unworthy of it. The ending of the film omits Nazarín's dream of his meeting with Christ (which in the novel gives him strength) and focuses instead on his growing despair and disillusionment, on his alienation both from the Church itself and from his own Christian idealism. Nazarín's journey through the world is one that progressively leads him to an acceptance of it and of man's imperfection, and to that extent looks forward to one of the principal themes of *Viridiana*.

While Buñuel was directly influenced by Galdós's novel, it is also important to note certain points of contact between the film, the Spanish picaresque novel, already referred to in relation to *Los olvidados*, and Cervantes's *Don Quixote*.[5] *Nazarín* contains precisely those social types together with their environment of poverty and suffering that are the particular province of the Spanish picaresque. If the blind man of *Los olvidados* seems to have stepped directly out of the pages of the anonymous *Lazarillo de Tormes*, then the dwarf Ujo, the prostitute Andara, and especially the criminals, the Parricide and the Sacrilegist, seem to belong to the harsh, grotesque and violent world of Quevedo's *La vida del buscón (The Life of the Swindler)*. With regard to Nazarín himself, Buñuel observed of him and his two female companions as they began their pilgrimage, 'There goes Don Quixote with his two Sanchos'.[6] The comparison is not a superficial one, and Buñuel was well aware of it, for Nazarín, setting out to travel the world armed with his Christian idealism, is the equivalent of the champion of chivalry. Buñuel, moreover, like Cervantes before him, unfolds a story of disenchantment, of a burning, unquenchable idealism often made ridiculous and finally defeated by the nature of the world it seeks to change.

The credits appear against a series of prints depicting Mexican scenes around the year 1900.[7] They are accompanied by the cries of pedlars, the clatter of horses' hooves, barking dogs, and snatches of song sung to the tune of a barrel organ. The last print is followed by a shot in which its figures, arranged in identical positions, come to life. The introduction is designed to create both a sense of historical perspective and of real life, to point to the fact that the material of the film, although set in the past, is more documentary than fiction. Buñuel's fondness for documentary is still very much in evidence.

The opening scene establishes too a characteristic Buñuelian irony. The camera picks out the name of an inn which will figure prominently in the film – *The Inn of the Heroes*. The sign is cracked and faded. Its somewhat tatty character is reflected too in the people who pass by:

> *... shot of a square in the day time and poorly dressed people are passing to and fro. The men are wearing sombreros and the women large, drab shawls. In a wall in the background, a doorway leads into a wretched building ...*

In this shabby context, implications of heroism take on a richly ironic incongruity. Buñuel quickly and effectively presents a world of anti-heroes and anti-heroic sentiments, very characteristic of the Spanish picaresque, in which the moral idealism of Nazarín will inevitably seem, like the name of the inn, incongruous and comic. The introduction of the prostitutes underlines the point. Andara accuses Camella of stealing her buttons when, in fact, she has herself stolen them from someone else. The world of *Nazarín*, like that of *Los olvidados* and *Viridiana*, is one whose morality obeys essentially pragmatic laws, and one in which the Christian principles of Nazarín himself, like those both of the director of the reformatory and of Viridiana, are doomed to founder.

An engineer is seen engaged in the process of installing electricity in the village. He represents the forces of social progress, but, as in the case of *Los olvidados*, Buñuel presents the 'progressive forces of our time' against the background of ignorance and poverty that constantly deny it. The engineer's scientific calculations are set against the spectacle of shabbily dressed people and a donkey having its coat clipped, while the affirmation of social advance has its opposite in the down-to-earth assertions of Chanfa, proprietress of *The Inn of the Heroes*:

MAN: Electricity is an indication of social progress, madam.

CHANFA: There's no social progress in this place, I can tell you that, only a lot of poor people.

But what is true of social and material progress is true of moral enlightenment too, and it is no accident that the engineer, whose confidence Chanfa so rudely shatters, should now give way to Nazarín. The appearance of this symbol of Christian virtue is accompanied, significantly, by Chanfa's lack of charity towards a lodger:

> You'd better get the rent by this evening, you lazy good-for-nothing, or you'll be sleeping in the street.

Buñuel establishes with almost every detail the context in which Nazarín's beliefs and principles must operate.

In relation to the villagers, Nazarín displays the traditional Christian virtues of compassion, charity, humility and patience. They, in return, show none towards him. The girl who cleans his room has stolen his food and his clothes. His landlady treats him with disrespect. The prostitutes abuse him, and a neighbour, taking advantage of his charity, strips him of the little he has left:

> The children have broken my cooking pot and I came to get yours.

Just afterwards she adds:

I'm taking this little bit of wood, Father . . . since you won't be needing a fire.

The flock which Nazarín attempts to lead along the path of righteousness clearly has the appetite of wolves. Confronted by the aggressive prostitutes, Nazarín can merely accept their insults. He is saved, in fact, by the engineer who hustles them away, displaying towards them a vigour which the priest cannot muster. The engineer, for all Buñuel's irony regarding the 'progressive forces of our time', is seen to be, like Jorge in *Viridiana*, a man whose practical approach to life is at least more effective than Nazarín's futile turning of the other cheek.

A new sequence develops the point. In the stable of the inn a young woman, Beatriz, is seen in the act of trying to hang herself. Chanfa's comments on her vain attempt at suicide, as well as on the cause of it, are ruthlessly devoid of sentiment:

When you really want to kill yourself, choose a stronger beam. . . . And even if you did really want to do it, you shouldn't give him the pleasure – he's not worth it.

In addition, her actions, like the engineer's, are practical and to the point, for she takes the girl to the kitchen, gives her some work, and provides her with food. For all her harshness, Chanfa is, in the true sense, a compassionate and understanding woman. In contrast, Nazarín, face to face with a truly desperate soul, can only offer useless advice to a girl who, on account of her dishonour, would find herself despised by family and friends:

You've been seduced, have you not? You should go back to your village and your family.

Almost immediately Beatriz is deserted by Pinto, her cruel and heartless lover:

He does not seem in the least concerned by the bad effect which his departure is having on BEATRIZ. As he leaves, he laughs cruelly, opens the door and goes out.

Framed on one side by Chanfa's pragmatism and on the other by Pinto's cynicism, the irrelevance of Nazarín in a world like this is further emphasized.

A scene set in a tavern suggests that the poor people of the village seek their consolation less in Nazarín's platitudes than in the wine and the women to be found there. It is a scene that also places Nazarín's piety against the raw and naked passions of people who, as in the case of *Los olvidados,* are little better than animals. The two prostitutes, Andara and Camella, confront each other with bristling hostility. In the fight which follows Buñuel portrays them like two squabbling hens, scratching and clawing, petticoats flying, while the spectators, their own emotions as primitive as those of the fighting women, show their approval:

> ... *The screen is a flurry of limbs and undergarments ... the cries of the women, just like the squawking of hens, continue off.*

The powerful reality of passion of another kind is reflected in Beatriz. As she observes the close physical contact of the two struggling women, she is moved to erotic thoughts of her own sexual encounters with her lover. A flashback to her bedroom reveals a scene of passionate lovemaking. Pinto caresses her feverishly, buries his face in her neck, and she, responding to him, bites his lip until the blood runs – echoes of *Un Chien andalou* and *L'Age d'or.* It is a sequence which, portraying both the animal aggression of the two prostitutes and the raw power of erotic passion, depicts a reality with which Nazarín can never contend.

The image of the world in all its harsh and lurid colours becomes in a new sequence a series of religious images: a painting of Christ on the wall of Nazarín's room, a rosary, Nazarín crossing himself and kissing the rosary. Subsequently, in a very suggestive episode, the two are juxtaposed as Andara, the prostitute, comes to the priest's room, and

Buñuel develops a scene that is full of incongruous and ironic possibilities. Andara, wounded in the fight with Camella, seeks Nazarín's help. He is, of course, concerned with her spiritual being and his words to her are appropriately pious:

> Think of your sins . . . you must have many on your conscience. . . . And commend your soul to God and the Holy Virgin. . . .

Andara's earthy language provides a richly comic counterpoint. Moreover, when Nazarín is obliged to bathe her shoulder, her naked flesh teasingly confronts his spirituality. A shot of the open wound in her shoulder has unmistakable vaginal associations:

> *Close-up of ANDARA'S shoulder as NAZARÍN'S hands remove the clothing and reveal an open wound still wet with blood.*

When the girl faints, Nazarín is compelled, to his great discomfort, to put his arms around her. The distant barking of a dog, a favourite motif of Buñuel's, points once more to the existence of a world of instinct and natural passion that Nazarín consistently seeks to avoid but with which in the end he must inevitably, like Viridiana, come to terms. As the sequence ends, Andara looks at the picture of Christ who is seen to be laughing heartily, amused no doubt by Nazarín's uneasiness. The image of the laughing Christ provides a characteristic Buñuelian perspective on Nazarín's Christianity.[8]

Subsequent events underline both the futility and the disastrous consequences of his charity. When the priest, Don Angel, pays Nazarín for taking Mass, he spends the money on Andara, revealing himself to be in every sense the true Christian. For her part, Andara is concerned only with her own skin and, in particular, with evading the police. On the other hand, Prieta, having discovered Andara's whereabouts, seeks only to be paid for keeping quiet. In the end Andara, to avoid detection and cover her tracks, sets fire to Nazarín's room. Consistently deprived of clothes and food by grasping neighbours, he is finally deprived of shelter. Such is the world's response to Nazarín's compassion. It seems appropriate that the statue of Saint Anthony should be consumed by the flames lit by a prostitute.

A new sequence is set in Don Angel's house. Nazarín, it is revealed, has informed the local judge both of his knowledge of the women's fight and of his subsequent concealment of Andara. In a world of malice and suspicion the truth of a good and honest man is, however, regarded as a confession of his guilt both of a sexual association with a prostitute and of an involvement in the fire. As a consequence of these events Nazarín loses his ministry, and, as a further consequence of the shame attached to this, his room in Don Angel's house. Buñuel portrays the chain of events with irony but reserves for Don Angel, the epitome of the orthodox clergy in all its self-justifying bigotry, a particularly pointed barb. Shocked by Nazarín's resolve to travel the roads and beg for alms, Don Angel defends the dignity of the cloth, of a clergy which has, in effect, abandoned one of its own for telling the truth:

DON ANGEL: What? A priest begging for alms! Have you forgotten the dignity of the clergy?

And secondly, Don Angel's concern with the dignity and sanctity of the Church has as its accompaniment his own preoccupation with his stomach as he dunks his bread in his chocolate drink. The final shot of the sequence – of the table with the chocolate drinks and the bread rolls – places his moral and spiritual cliches in a suitably ironic perspective.[9]

Dismissed from his ministry and Don Angel's house, Nazarín begins his journey through the world. He is seen working on a railway track in exchange for food. A short distance away three men observe him, incensed by the fact that others are prevented from working for a wage, and, when one of them approaches and threatens Nazarín, he is obliged to leave. The behaviour of the workman, which undermines the foreman's authority, brings about his intervention, he strikes one of the men, and another hits the foreman with a shovel. The camera focuses on the two groaning men lying on the ground. Meanwhile, Nazarín is seen well away from the incident, oblivious to the violence and the sound of gunshots:

> *NAZARÍN is seen walking through some trees; the camera pans and tracks in front of him. He hears shots from the direction of the construction site. He pauses and picks a small branch from an olive tree at the side of the path. He seems concerned but simultaneously divorced from what is happening.*

The effect of Nazarín's Christian way of life is, ironically, to set his fellow men against each other and leave in his wake a trail of devastation.[10]

Continuing his journey Nazarín encounters Beatriz in a village street and is persuaded by her, as an act of charity, to visit her sister's sick child. The women who await the priest's arrival are highly emotional and superstitious:

> JOSEFA *(in an exhausted tone)*: A terrible fever is burning her up. It is sapping her strength. I knew it would be bad because the day she fell ill an owl hooted all through the night and when I went out three dogs barked one after the other.

For them religion is itself, of course, part and parcel of a generally superstitious attitude, and Nazarín, arriving barefooted in their midst, is endowed by them (and totally against his will) with a Christ-like significance. In another of the film's beautifully comic scenes the good man, asserting his own humility and condemning the women's blasphemy, is undone by his own goodness and transformed by hysterical women into the opposite of what his sense of his own unimportance wants him to be. Moreover, to Nazarín's growing consternation and our own amusement, the

The priest worshipped

women's feelings acquire increasingly obvious sexual overtones. One of them, screaming hysterically, is reminiscent of Beatriz in an earlier erotic scene:

> *. . . he is surrounded by the hysterical women, all kneeling, shouting out supplication. One of them rises and falls backwards on the ground, screaming with hysteria.*

Beatriz's own expression is ecstatic, while the women surround Nazarín and their hands reach out to touch him:

> *The camera tracks in on NAZARÍN. The women's hands touch and caress him. He bows his head, troubled but apparently resigned, and the women continue shouting and chanting . . .*

Nazarín's charity continues to be a source of trouble to him. Furthermore, the child recovers, and for the women Nazarín's saintliness is seen to be a proven fact. Like Christ he acquires his disciples – in this case Beatriz and the prostitute, Andara, who resolve to accompany him wherever he goes. The irony of the priest, beset, as it were, by his own Christianity, is a comic vein which Buñuel exploits quite delightfully. As the two women express their firm intention to follow Nazarín in the path of virtue, the mooing of cows off-screen provides an appropriate commentary.

The scene changes to a road where a horse has broken its leg. At the side of the horse is the sweaty, portly figure of a colonel, whose carriage the horse has been pulling, and a priest, while the colonel's wife stands at a distance from them with a sunshade in her hand. The colonel, devoid of all compassion for the wretched animal, can only rant and rave over the inconvenience of its injury. But if the horse incurs his wrath, so does a poor peasant who now appears along the road and who, failing to see the colonel and the priest, fails to accord them due respect:

COLONEL *(in a threatening manner)*: What's wrong

with you, you numbskull? Don't you know you should salute a colonel, and even more so a priest?

The colonel is a typical bourgeois, a man for whom respect means only that deference of others towards him that is all to do with social and class distinctions. Buñuel presents the colonel's brutish insensitivity much as he does that of the aristocratic gathering of *L'Age d'or*. He makes his comment too in a particularly telling shot:

> *The COLONEL appears on the left and the two men* [i.e. the colonel and the peasant] *are seen in profile, facing each other, with the head of a donkey between them in the foreground.*

Linking the two men in the frame, the donkey's head provides a remarkably concise and biting observation on the colonel. As for the priest, he is the moral defender of bourgeois power. Failing to condemn the colonel's treatment of the peasant, he condemns instead Nazarín's Christian judgement on the incident:

> DON NAZARIO: That traveller is a man, not an animal, a son of God just as much as you are . . .
>
> PRIEST *(calming him [the colonel])*: Leave him, Colonel. He is a heretic, probably one of these lunatic preachers from the north.

The priest is revealed to us, moreover, not only as a man devoid of Christian principles but also as someone of unpleasant personal habits:

> *The PRIEST is seen cleaning out his ear with his little finger.*

In effect, he and the colonel are as brutish in their attitudes and manners as the people they condemn, separated from them only by their respective uniforms.[11]

An episode depicting a village struck by an epidemic reveals Nazarín's ineffectiveness in the face of the harsh realities of poverty and illness. As the corpses are laid out at the entrance to the church and a priest sprinkles them with holy water, the irony of the situation speaks for itself. For Nazarín it is, of course, a predicament which demands his Christian intervention and, with the aid of his two disciples, Andara and Beatriz, he busily and ardently sets about his task. In particular, the scene focuses on the dying figure of a young woman, Lucía. Nazarín is concerned above all for her soul:

> Endure your suffering and prepare your soul for the joy of finding yourself in the presence of God.

For Lucía her entry into heaven is of less significance than her departure from this world and her separation from her lover, Juan:

> DON NAZARIO: Set aside the passions of this world, my child. The Lord gives you time to consider your own conscience. . . . Think of the after-life which awaits you.
> *Close-up, from above, of LUCIA. Her brow is furrowed with pain and the resolve to see the man she loves.*
>
> LUCIA: Not the after-life . . . *(She opens her eyes)* . . . Juan!

Indeed, Juan replaces Nazarín at Lucía's side, effectively ousting all that he stands for, and Nazarín's pious words give way to the greater comfort of Juan's last kiss. The priest's irrelevance is signalled too by the arrival of more practical assistance in the form of a carriage, nurses and doctors. The monotonous tolling of the church bells, evocative of the ritual of a religion more concerned with the dead than the living, is transformed with the appearance of these reinforcements into a joyful pealing and the villagers' warm acclaim. Within this context Nazarín's disillusionment is very clear:

DON NAZARIO: There is nothing left for us to do here. *He says the words sadly, with bitterness, clearly resenting his failure. He turns his back on the square and walks away slowly in the foreground . . .*

Often presented ironically by Buñuel, Nazarín is frequently a dignified and sad figure, very different from the other representatives of the cloth who from time to time appear in the film.[12]

In a new episode a shot of a dwarf suspended from a tree by a group of children constitutes a powerful image of the world's inescapable cruelty, filling out the picture of its malice, selfishness and lack of compassion. The introduction of the dwarf provides too, however, a note of tenderness previously absent in the film, for he feels both affection for Andara, the prostitute, and a real concern for her safety. In contrast, Buñuel reintroduces Pinto's passionate, inescapable and brutal passion for Beatriz. Having earlier abandoned her, Pinto resolves to have her for himself again, to subject her to his own ruthless will. Beatriz, confronted by the physical presence of a man who, for all his harshness, has always succeeded in arousing her sexual desires, finds it ominously difficult to sustain and cling to the new kind of life and love she is slowly acquiring with Nazarín even if it is true that her attraction to him is less than wholly spiritual. Indeed, throughout the conversation in which he seeks to persuade her of the virtues of spiritual love, a cow lows repeatedly, asserting the constant reality of animal instincts and desires. Even Andara, we note, feels resentment towards Beatriz, reacting in a very natural and human way to what she regards as Nazarín's preference for the other woman. His own love of God's creation has, of course, no limits, and is reflected as much in his affection for the snail that he allows to crawl on his hand as in his concern for the two women:

DON NAZARIO *(gazing at the snail in his hand)*: Don't be silly, my child. I love both of you equally.

It is a vision of the oneness of mankind whose idealism is placed in a much more realistic perspective by the final shot in which Andara stares resentfully at her fingertips.

The theme of Ujo's love of Andara is developed further in the following sequence in which the dwarf attaches himself to Nazarín's group of followers. Buñuel presents the relationship of the pair without sentimentality but with considerable warmth and humour:

> UJO: ... *(To ANDARA with great affection)* You may be ugly and a whore ... I've never really been fond of anyone before; but as for you, I only have to look at you, and my heart leaps.

It is a warmth, however, which further underlines the viciousness of a world bent on destroying any kind of good or idealism, for as a policeman appears with a warrant for the arrest of Nazarín and Andara, the occasion is one which opens the floodgates to the villagers' prejudice and hypocrisy. Defending themselves in the name of Christianity, they abuse, vilify and assault Nazarín, knocking him to the ground:

> ... *The OLD MAN kicks NAZARIN in the behind and he falls on his face.*

Surrounded by the violent and hostile group, accepting all their insults, Nazarín assumes very clearly the proportions of a Christ-like figure. Andara and Beatriz, the former in particular, react to the world's hostility much more in its own terms, proving the point that in the end they cannot escape its clutches. Nazarín is a lonely voice crying in the wilderness:

> Calm down, Andara! You have behaved very badly! ... Ask forgiveness of the person you have injured, so that God will forgive you.

As he lies on the ground, reviled by his enemies, he is an admirable but simultaneously futile figure on whom the world at large will always trample.

A transition to a village square reveals a column of prisoners chained to each other. When Nazarín is placed in the column next to the Sacrilegist and the Parricide, he is, as it were, Christ flanked by the two criminals. The chains linking the men are as much metaphorical as they are literal, the outward signs of individual and corporate evil, and the general situation is one in which goodness and love are severely tested. Beatriz, confronted once more by Pinto's insatiable and ruthless passion for her, asserts instead her belief in Nazarín. It is a moving statement of her triumph over her own sensuality. Similarly, Andara and Ujo, their love and affection mocked by the villagers, triumph over their mockery. On the other hand, inasmuch as Andara is marched away, she and Ujo separated from each other, their love is already doomed, anticipating the subsequent failure of Beatriz and even of Nazarín himself. As the sequence ends, Ujo is filled with that despair which has already been reflected on Nazarín's face:

> *UJO, seen in medium close-up, sits on the ground. . . . He lowers his eyes sadly.*

As the prisoners march along the road, Beatriz becomes the object of their lust and Nazarín, seeking to protect her, the target of their hatred and resentment. Arriving at her village, Beatriz is subjected too to her mother's scathing accusations of dishonour. But, more importantly, the mother opens the girl's eyes to something she has not seen before, to the fact that her attraction to Nazarín is as sexual as it is spiritual. It is a revelation that shocks and startles Beatriz, bearing in upon her an awareness of the inescapable nature of her sexuality:

> *. . . her eyes are wide open with surprise and with the fear that her mother's words may well be true.*

Her return to the world of the flesh and the end of Nazarín's influence upon her is clearly signposted as Pinto appears and takes her in his arms.

As for Nazarín, he is made progressively aware not only of his own futility in relation to the world at large but, for the first time, of his own far from saintly nature. A sequence set in the prison reveals Nazarín as the victim of the prisoners' unrelenting hatred, subjected to their mockery, their insults and the most terrible physical violence. The Parricide fells him with a mighty blow, kicks him savagely in the stomach and drags him along the floor. In a crucial moment in the film, Nazarín becomes suddenly conscious of his own failure to match the Christian ideal he has set himself and which he would have others strive to follow:

> For the first time in my life I find it difficult to forgive. I will forgive you because it is my Christian duty . . . I forgive you. But I despise you too, and I feel guilt because I cannot separate forgiveness and scorn.

As Beatriz's eyes are opened to the inevitability of her own sexuality, Nazarín is made aware that the gulf between his own feelings of hatred and those of the Parricide is not as great as he would have it.

The ensuing conversation with the Sacrilegist is vitally important. Inasmuch as he saves Nazarín from a worse beating, the Sacrilegist is seen to have some goodness in him. For Nazarín it is a sign of hope:

> Thank you . . . thank you. At heart you are a good man.

The Sacrilegist dismisses Nazarín's words, pointing to his own failure to escape the badness of the world and, more importantly, to the futility of Nazarín's belief that, given the world's essential badness, he can in any way affect it:

> SACRILEGIST: Look at me. I do nothing but bad . . . but what is the point of your life? You are on the side of good and I am on the side of evil . . .
> *Close-up of the priest.*
> SACRILEGIST *(off screen)*: But neither of us serves any useful purpose.

The priest felled

If Nazarín, in his hatred of the Parricide, has begun to doubt himself, the Sacrilegist's words merely confirm his doubts.

The final sequences reveal Nazarín's sense of disillusionment and spiritual isolation. In order to protect themselves from further disgrace, the Church authorities have declared that Nazarín must travel alone with his own un-uniformed guard, separated from the other prisoners. The Church, concerned solely with its image and reputation, offers him nothing. Secondly, Andara, although she wishes to stay with Nazarín, is dragged away from him. And thirdly, as he walks along the road, a cart approaches in which Pinto, accompanied by Beatriz, symbolizes the triumph of the flesh over the spirit and, worst of all, Beatriz's acceptance of that fact:

A closer shot of PINTO and BEATRIZ who looks at him with tenderness. PINTO turns and smiles at her triumphantly. She rests her head on his shoulder and closes her eyes.

Nazarín, confronted by the victory of the world, walks in total despair.

From the ashes of spiritual disillusionment, Nazarín is finally born again into the world, the priest rejected for the man. When a peasant woman offers Nazarín a pineapple, she sees him merely as a weary, thirsty man, and her act of generosity is that of someone moved by the suffering of a fellow human being. Nazarín rejects her charity precisely because he imagines it to be extended to him as a priest, and his rejection of her gift is, in effect, his rejection of his former role. Suddenly conscious of his error, Nazarín accepts the pineapple, treasuring it as the precious offering of one human being to another:

The two of them in medium close-up. NAZARÍN is nearest the camera and he holds the pineapple in his arm like a precious gift.

When the tears roll down his face and his expression reveals both gratitude and hope, they are emotions born of a recognition not of God but of man. In relation to the totally closed ending of *Los olvidados*, the final scene of *Nazarín* indicates a greater optimism on Buñuel's part – an acceptance of the need to embrace and cherish man in all his imperfection.[13]

Nazarín resembles *Los olvidados* in that it has a clear, straightforward story-line. The influence of the picaresque, Cervantes and Galdós makes it the most 'narrative' of the films examined here. But if these literary influences played their part in relation to the general structure of *Nazarín*, the film is in every respect typically Buñuelian. Within its episodic structure, for example, there is hardly an episode that does not add to the development of Buñuel's portrayal of the clash between the spirit and the flesh. The effect of the film's many and varied episodes is to present us with a detailed, multi-faceted picture of the world in all its selfishness. The characters pass before our eyes in a steady stream – Chanfa, the prostitutes, Beatriz, Pinto, the various priests and the different groups of villagers, the colonel and his wife, the foreman and the workmen, Ujo the dwarf, and the criminals, especially the Parricide and the Sacrilegist. In this respect *Nazarín* differs from *Los olvidados*, for there the same characters reappear throughout the film. Its focus is, therefore, limited, while the effect of *Nazarín* is much more panoramic: Nazarín's journey along the highways and byways of life.

The portrayal of the world is, as in the case of *Los olvidados*, ruthlessly unsentimental. The film's violent episodes (and there are many of them) are, for example, presented in an unsensational way, as though they are the normal currency of daily life. When the foreman hits the workman with the butt of his revolver, and is in turn struck with a shovel by another workman, no more prominence is given to the incident than to any other in the film. Equally, when Ujo, the dwarf, is suspended by the children from the tree, the scene is devoid of any false sensationalism. In the experience of the dwarf, the mockery of the world is not, after all, an exceptional event, and it is therefore given in the film no greater weight or value than Ujo himself places upon it. The effect of Buñuel's unsentimental portrayal of the world is precisely to convey its own lack of sentiment.[14]

Because the film is largely concerned with Nazarín's encounter with the world, juxtapositions (reminiscent in some was of *L'Age d'or* and also in anticipation of *Viridiana*) play an important part in it. In the earlier sequences Buñuel's juxtapositions have a humorous effect, notably the presentation of Nazarín's Christian charity and generosity side by side with individuals who are concerned with profiting at his expense. In the episode involving Andara and Nazarín, the priest's concern with the prostitute's moral and spiritual welfare is effectively off-set by her earthy concerns and her total lack of comprehension. In addition, the close-up of Nazarín's hands exposing the flesh of the girl's shoulder and then of the girl in Nazarín's arms are beautifully comic; Buñuel at his delightfully malicious best. Later, of course, the tone of the film is darker, in accordance with Nazarín's growing disillusionment, and juxtaposed shots have a different purpose and effect. In the scene depicting the epidemic, for example, Nazarín attends the dying girl only to be ousted by her lover – the spirit juxtaposed with and banished by the flesh. In another episode Nazarín's Christian compassion is framed by the villagers' hostility and later by the prisoners' bitter resentment of him. The purpose of the juxtapositions is now not so much an ironic one but one of showing Nazarín's growing acceptance of the world and of the way he is, in a sense, slowly cast in its own image. By the end of the film it is not so much a case of contrasting shots reflecting the gap between the world and Nazarín's spirituality but of the gap narrowed progressively to the point where the priest is seen to be aware of his own worldliness.

While *Nazarín* reveals at almost every stage Buñuel's obsession with the theme of religious belief, it is also another fine example of the way in which he exposes the inner life and subconscious desires of his characters. When Beatriz observes Andara and Camella struggling on the floor, their close physical contact arouses in her erotic thoughts of her sexual encounters with Pinto. Buñuel depicts her dreaming in a flash-back which ripples like a reflection on water. Within the daydream the actions of the lovers have an exaggerated form conjured up by a fevered imagination – Pinto buries his face in Beatriz's neck, she kisses him, bites him, and the blood runs from his lips.[15] Not only is the sequence vivid in itself, but the way in which it is triggered by another incident endows the character with true psychological depth. In another sequence Andara sees the laughing Christ, the projection of her own disturbed and confused state of mind. But in addition to these purely cinematic effects, Buñuel, as in all his films, uses objective reality to expose just as surely the thoughts and feelings of his characters. When Nazarín exposes Andara's shoulder, drawing aside the clothing, the close-up of the naked flesh encapsulates the priest's discomfort. And later, as the women's hands touch his body, the shot reveals very clearly the feelings of eroticism which, mingled with religious devotion, dominate them. While *Nazarín* does not possess the overtly sexual motifs of *Viridiana*, it is, like *Los olvidados*, a film in which we are constantly made aware of the inner reality of its characters' lives.

NOTES

[1] Francisco Aranda, *Luis Buñuel* . . . , p. 156, observes that the film is 'a model of interpretative adaptation'. It is a view shared by Tony Richardson: 'It is a mature and beautiful work'. See 'The Films of Luis Buñuel', in *The World of Luis Buñuel*, p. 135.

[2] *Luis Buñuel* . . . , p. 163: 'For the present writer it is a masterwork from

start to finish . . . the action has a feverish lyricism equivalent to the best passages in Emily Brontë'.

[3] See Francisco Aranda, 'The Passion According to Buñuel' in *Luis Buñuel, Modern Film Scripts: The Exterminating Angel, Nazarín, Los olvidados*, London: Lorrimer Publishing, 1972, pp. 108-9.

[4] See *The Cinema of Luis Buñuel*, pp. 87-89.

[5] Carlos Fuentes, 'The Discreet Charm of Luis Buñuel', *The World of Luis Buñuel*, pp. 51-71, quotes Buñuel as saying: 'The critics talk about Goya because they ignore all the rest, Quevedo, St. Theresa of Avila, the Spanish heterodoxes, the Spanish picaresque novel, Galdós, Valle-Inclán . . .' (p. 65). Jean-Claude Carrière, 'The Buñuel Mystery', *The World of Luis Buñuel*, pp. 90-102, observes: 'His true masters, as he acknowledges, are writers, not film-makers. Buñuel has been nourished by many cultural traditions, first the Spanish, particularly the picaresque novels up to the time of Galdós . . .' (p. 98). These articles originally appeared in *The New York Times Magazine*, March 11, 1973, and *Show*, April 1970, respectively.

[6] See Francisco Aranda, 'The Passion According to Buñuel', p. 111, and *Luis Buñuel*, p. 180.

[7] Buñuel transferred the setting of the film from Spain to Mexico. The action takes place during the dictatorship of Porfirio Díaz, who was supported by the powerful landowners, and in its course portrays certain types, notably the colonel and various priests, who give the film a characteristic Buñuelian social dimension.

[8] Francisco Aranda, 'The Passion According to Buñuel', p. 111, draws attention – though not enough, in my opinion – to the humour of the film. Buñuel has himself complained that audiences do not laugh sufficiently at his films.

[9] See Marcel Martin, 'The Priest and the Man', *The World of Luis Buñuel*, pp. 209-213. Martin makes the point that 'all the conformist (or "official") priests in the film are perfectly odious . . .' (p. 210).

[10] Louis Seguin observes of Nazarín that 'he only aggravates those situations into which he intrudes, much like Mother Courage who, by dint of outwitting an abstract war, ends by causing the deaths of her children'. See 'In Three Points', *The World of Luis Buñuel*, pp. 204-209.

[11] The social background of the film, although less prominent than in many of Buñuel's films, is always clearly defined. Freddy Buache makes the very pertinent comment that Buñuel 'uses the example of the ingenuous Nazarín to expose the repugnant Pharisaism of a complacent Christian establishment that gives all the help it can to landlords, judges and colonels'. See *The Cinema of Luis Buñuel*, p. 94.

[12] Marcel Martin, 'The Priest and the Man', p. 211, states that 'if he is ineffective and useless, Nazarín is far from being ridiculous or odious'.

[13] Raymond Durgnat comments that Nazarín's story is 'above all, a *man's*'. See *Luis Buñuel*, p. 111. Marcel Martin, 'The Priest and the Man', makes the same crucial point: 'What is important is that Nazarín is

respectable as a human being. The fact of his priesthood is secondary, since it is when he practically ceases to be a priest that he becomes truly and fully a man. . . . Buñuel ascribes divinity to humanity; he brings his character from mysticism to humanism . . .' pp. 212-213.

[14] We may compare the incident with the equally unsentimental treatment of the legless cripple in *Los olvidados*.

[15] Compare the biting of lips and the appearance of blood in *Un Chien andalou* and *L'Age d'or*.

5
VIRIDIANA

CAST

Viridiana	—	Silvia Pinal
Jorge	—	Francisco Rabal
Lucía	—	Victoria Zinny
Don Jaime	—	Fernando Rey
Ramona	—	Margarita Lozano
Rita	—	Teresa Rabal

Beggars: José Calvo, Joaquín Roa, Luis Heredia, José Manuel Martín, Lola Gaos, Juan García Tiendra, Maruja Isbert, Joaquín Mayol, Palmira Guerra, Sergio Mendizábal, Milagros Tomás, Alicia Jorge Barriga.

Photography	—	José F. Aguayo
Editor	—	Pedro del Rey
Art Director	—	Francisco Canet
Music	—	Selected by Gustavo Pittaluga
Production	—	Gustavo Alatriste for UNINCI
	—	S. A. and Films 59
Script	—	Luis Buñuel
	—	Julio Alejandro
Assistant Director	—	Juan Luis Buñuel
Director	—	Luis Buñuel

Between *Nazarín* and *Viridiana* Buñuel made two films: *La Fièvre monte à El Pao*, a French-Mexican production made in 1959, and *The Young One*, an American-Mexican production shown at the Cannes Festival in 1959. The former has as its principal character a typically Buñuelian figure – Ramón, an official in a small Latin-American republic, a Nazarín-like character whose high ideals lead to disaster. In *The Young One* the characters, especially Miller, the gamewarden of an island somewhere off the southern United States, discover the ambiguity of the attitudes and values they have always accepted, including racial prejudice, and achieve thereby a new understanding of the world. They are films which, together with *Nazarín*, clearly look forward in their themes to *Viridiana*.

In 1960 a group of Spaniards, including the young director, Carlos Saura, impressed upon Buñuel the need for him to make a film in Spain and give a lead to Spanish film-makers who were struggling to give the Spanish cinema a national character. Buñuel was at first reticent but within the space of a few months he was writing to his producers and by December of the same year had taken residence on the seventeenth floor of the Torre de Madrid. Fearing that everything would have changed during his long absence, Buñuel was relieved to find the city much better than he had imagined it, his old haunts still in existence, and his old friends returned from other countries. At the Café Vienna in the Calle Víctor Pradera, Buñuel became the centre of a circle of admirers composed of both the older and the younger generation. Over a period of two months he proceeded with the planning of *Viridiana*, choosing his actors, technical staff and exterior locations. Shooting began on February 4, 1961. For his crew Buñuel chose some of the young technicians who had worked on Carlos Saura's *Los golfos*. For his actors he did not want stars, and the role of Viridiana was given to Silvia Pinal, an actress better known in Mexico for comedy. Buñuel took particular care over the actors who would play the beggars. One of them was a real beggar, another a dwarf who sold lottery tickets. The film was completed smoothly and quickly. It received its première at the Cannes Film Festival on May 17, 1961.[1]

The showing of *Viridiana* provoked a scandal in its way as great as that caused in 1930 by *L'Age d'Or*. The Spanish authorities had, with one or two exceptions, approved the script but did not see the finished film before its showing at the Cannes Film Festival. Buñuel had not in the end made the few important changes suggested by the Spanish censorship: he left intact Don Jaime's suicide, the attempted rape of Viridiana, and the burning of the crown of thorns.[2] The Vatican was scandalized. *L'Osservatore Romano* referred to the film's sacrilege and blasphemy. In Spain General Franco took appropriate measures. There was no reference to the *Palme d'or*, journalists were forbidden to mention the film's existence, copies were seized, José Muñóz-Fontán was sacked, and replaced by one Jesús Sueros. Similar pressures were exerted in other countries. In 1963 the Italian police seized copies of the film in Rome and Milan. In England it was banned in Surrey. For a time it seemed as though *Viridiana* would never be distributed commercially. In the end it was saved by the fact that most of the finance for production had been provided by Gustavo Alatriste, the Mexican husband of Silvia Pinal, and the film thus acquired a Mexican nationality. Subsequently *Viridiana* was shown throughout the world but not, of course, in Spain. In his early films, especially in *L'Age d'Or*, Buñuel had, as Francisco Aranda observes, set out to create scandal. In *Viridiana* he created it without intending to.

Buñuel has observed that, in making *Viridiana*, he had no conscious plan. The film grew out of certain erotic and religious obsessions of his childhood:

> In reality, *Viridiana* is a picture of black humour, without doubt corrosive, but unplanned and spontaneous, in which I express certain erotic and religious obsessions of my childhood. I belong to a very Catholic

> family and from the age of 8 to 15 I was brought up by Jesuits. However, for me, religious education and surrealism have left their marks all through my life.[3]

It was never his intention, he claims, to be blasphemous. Indeed, the film sprang from an image that had long haunted him – the image of a young woman drugged by an old man. Other situations developed quite naturally from this. Because the young woman must be pure, Buñuel made her a novice. He called her Viridiana after a saint who lived in the times of St. Francis of Assisi and because he was attracted by the name. The episode of the beggars suggested itself, for they were the kind of people for whom a former nun would have compassion. It also seemed a good idea to put them in a splendid dining-room and provide them with a feast, and much more striking to accompany their dance with the music of the *Messiah* than with conventional rock and roll. Buñuel's account of the film's birth and development is one which, stressing its natural and spontaneous evolution and his own instinctive feeling for certain associations, juxtapositions and contrasts, underlines the importance he has always given, in his life as well as in his art, to impulse and the expression of the unconscious freed from the constraints of reason and moral dictates. To this extent *Viridiana* is as much a product of surrealism as *Un Chien andalou* and *L'Age d'or*.

On the other hand, Buñuel has spoken of *Viridiana* and of his general aims in a way which points to his social and moral preoccupations:

> We do not live in the best of all possible worlds. I would like to continue to make films which, apart from entertaining the audience, convey to people the absolute certainty of this idea.[4]

It is precisely the aim that he had set himself and brilliantly achieved in *L'Age d'or*. Buñuel has, indeed, often linked the two films, seeing them as the expression of the themes and feelings closest and most dear to him. *L'Age d'or* was, of course, the work of a man of 30, rebellious, provocative, deliberately outrageous. *Viridiana* is the mature, more controlled statement of a man of 61. The manner has changed but the matter is clearly the same.

The opening shot is of the courtyard and the cloister of a convent seen from above. A line of boys two abreast cross the courtyard on the right. In the bottom right-hand corner of the frame a priest and a nun walk away from the camera. In the left-hand corner two nuns approach the camera and a third stands with her back to it. The groups of figures are arranged against the stones of the courtyard which form regular patterns, while the symmetrical doorways and arches of the cloister form the background. Buñuel suggests in his opening shot both the enclosed world and the inflexible ritual and formality of religion. The credits have been accompanied by Handel's *Hallelujah Chorus* which fades as the shot of the convent appears, as though the joyous, expansive spirit of the music has no place in it.

We are introduced almost immediately to Viridiana. The Mother Superior informs her that her uncle, Don Jaime, whom she has not seen for many years, wishes her to stay with him before she takes her vows. Viridiana has no wish to leave the convent but, at the Mother Superior's insistence, agrees to see her uncle. Our first impression of Viridiana is of her lack of true compassion, while the Mother Superior seems less concerned with Don Jaime than with the need to do the right thing.[5] The two women exemplify the meanness of spirit, the well-scrubbed and neatly-ordered piety embodied in the cold formality of the building in which they spend their days.

A transition to a park introduces a close-up of the legs of a little girl, Rita, who is happily skipping. Her legs move quickly backwards and forwards and open and shut like compasses. The little girl's hair is tousled, her breath comes quickly, her eyes shine, her lips are moist, and she bites her lower lip. The legs of a man come into view and the camera reveals Don Jaime, Viridiana's uncle, who is watching with fascination the movement of Rita's legs. The sequence is one in which the theme of religion, with all its austere and joyless overtones, has become the theme of joy and freedom, exemplified in Rita's lack of inhibition. And she introduces too, in an innocent way – in the movement of her legs, the moist lips, the biting of the lower lip (echoes again of *L'Age d'or*) – the theme of sexuality. To this extent Rita anticipates Viridiana, for both of them are sexually immature, and the link between them is clearly established by Viridiana's arrival at this very moment. The little girl's rope, with its unmistakable phallic handles, is important in relation to Don Jaime, for it is the rope with which, after his attempted rape of Viridiana, he hangs himself. The symbol of the child's innocent, uncomplicated pleasure is simultaneously a symbol of the older man's sexual guilt. In typical Surrealist fashion particular objects in the film acquire a multiplicity of fascinating meanings.

A shot of Don Jaime's and Viridiana's legs underlines the contrast with the child. Viridiana, lacking the child's spontaneity and capacity for joy, feels no warmth towards her uncle:

DON JAIME *(downcast)*: Weren't you interested in seeing me?

VIRIDIANA *(smiling, sincere)*: To tell the truth, not really. I can't lie. I respect you . . .

As for him, his life is joyless and empty, like the fields that lie waste, and dark, like the shadow cast by the tree on his house. For the child the fields and the tree are a playground. In relation to Don Jaime they point to his sense of failure and despair.

A new sequence reveals Don Jaime playing the harmonium in his sitting room at night. A close-up of his feet and legs working the pedals provides another variation on the sexual image, in Don Jaime's case connected with the perpetuation through this nightly ritual of his wife's memory. Another shot reveals Viridiana undressing in her bedroom. Her white and beautiful legs embody the challenge posed by the young and lovely girl, physically reminiscent of Elvira, to Don Jaime's almost saintly devotion to his dead wife. As for Viridiana, a close-up of her religious objects – a crucifix, a crown of thorns, a hammer, nails – suggests not merely piety but the harmful, damaging nature of sexual repression. In their different ways Viridiana and her uncle personify the dead weight of convention and tradition that, as in *L'Age d'or*, deadens and destroys instinct and spontaneity.

Viridiana's contact with the world, and especially with the world of Nature, is as much a challenge to her deepest instincts as is her presence to Don Jaime's dead but dutiful devotion. For Viridiana the sight of a cow's udder, of the teat squeezed by a man's hand, and the sensation of the teat in her own hand, are things that disturb her, penetrating the thick shell of her religious upbringing. For Don Jaime (who every night dresses in his wife's clothes in a touching but futile evocation of their love) Viridiana's sleepwalking, and glimpses of her naked flesh, are a terrible and tempting threat to his self-imposed and martyr-like chastity. In a splendidly evocative sequence, rich in meaning and full of implications, Viridiana is the alluring, living form of his erotic fantasies of his dead wife. Her naked thigh is the flesh and blood form of his desire, while her blank, empty expression and the mechanical nature of her movements are the cold hand, the rigor mortis of his guilt. When Viridiana empties ashes – an image of death – beside the orange blossom – symbol of marriage – on Don Jaime's bed, the incident suggests her own emotional coldness and the way in which Don Jaime's awakening sexuality can be achieved only at the expense of a paralysing guilt which will lead in turn to death.

Another sequence marks a new stage in Don Jaime's passion for Viridiana. When he persuades her to wear his

The temptation of Don Jaime

wife's wedding-dress, he begins to clothe his desire, to give it flesh and substance. But its very form is a compromise, a salving of a guilt-torn conscience that, tempted by an image of the present, wraps it in a sacred image of the past. It is a desperate and anguished process, marked at every stage by Don Jaime's crippling obedience to conventional morality.[6] Tempted further, he asks Viridiana to marry him. Shocked by his proposal, she angrily rejects him. He gives her a sleeping draught and, as she lies on the bed in Doña Elvira's wedding dress, he is filled with thoughts of raping her. Again passion is circumscribed by conscience, the ashes that deaden and obliterate the beauty of the orange blossom:

> *Don Jaime now moves from the realm of blind instinct to the realm of conscience . . .*

He has moved from a total devotion to his wife's memory to the first renewed flickerings of passion, to temptation, only to withdraw again, firstly into compromise and then into a terrible sense of failure.

The sequence is accompanied and underlined by many suggestive and revealing images. As Viridiana appears in the wedding dress, the barking of a dog is heard. It is heard once more as Don Jaime gazes at Viridiana on the bed, and again after his final pang of conscience. The sounds of the natural world, with all their associations of instinct and spontaneity, effectively frame the expression of human passion that is full of guilt and inhibition. The complex motives of Don Jaime, an educated bourgeois, are seen too against the background of the simple, unsophisticated world of the servants and the child, Rita. Her dream of the black bull, a clear Freudian image evoking a primitive, age-old world of sexual fantasy and superstition, throws into sharp relief the deep layers of more complex feelings and beliefs which ravage the emotional lives of their bourgeois betters. And if there is a contrast between the child and Don Jaime, there is also one between the child and Viridiana. Witnessing the attempted rape, Rita undergoes a sexual awakening to which the older woman, the object of her uncle's lust, is totally oblivious, her unconsciousness, like her sleepwalking, an effective image of her sexual passivity. Moreover, to observe the scene, the child has climbed the tree, a Freudian symbol of sexual experience and an echo of the newcomer's climbing of the stairs in *Un Chien andalou*. As for Viridiana, all the pointers to her sexual awakening, to her growing contact with the world of feeling of which she is now a part, are also pointers to a continuing exclusion from it. There are clear phallic overtones in a shot of Viridiana peeling fruit:

> *Close-up of a woman's hands peeling fruit. The peel unwinds in a long spiral . . .*

She is seen, too, biting the fruit which her uncle gives her. And when Rita is skipping (her hands grasping the phallic handles of the rope) Viridiana joins her. They are indications of a new awareness which flatter only to deceive.

A new and dramatic sequence contrasts Don Jaime's desperate and anguished pleading with Viridiana's cold and icy prudery. When he goes to her room the next morning, even though she is ignorant of the previous night's events, she quickly covers herself:

> *Viridiana is aware of her exposed body and, ill at ease, covers herself up.*

She would like to force her uncle to leave, but her state of semi-nudity prevents her from getting out of bed. Moreover, as she covers her body, so she insulates her mind and sensibilities against her uncle's revelation of his feelings for her. It is this which drives him to the lie of having raped her while she was asleep, a story which he believes will at least prevent her returning to the convent. Viridiana is horrified and, although Don Jaime then reveals the truth, she is empty of all compassion for his obvious suffering. Her tears are of pity only for herself. Furthermore, her parting words at a moment when her uncle pleads for her forgiveness, strip him of any lingering hope of her he might still have and, more importantly, of any vestiges of self-respect that her compassion might have left intact:

> VIRIDIANA: You disgust me . . . even if what you say is true.
>
> DON JAIME *(more quietly)*: So you won't forgive me?
>
> *The look of the young woman shatters Don Jaime . . . she leaves without even a glance in his direction.*

The cloistered world of the convent and its inappropriateness to the needs of suffering humanity has its eloquent advocate in Viridiana. As for Don Jaime, he is a truly tragic figure – not merely in his anguish but in the sense that it is his misfortune to direct his hopes towards an individual who, while awakening them, simultaneously destroys them, leaving him in the process with a deep awareness of his wickedness. Inasmuch as he is destroyed by Viridiana, Don Jaime is the first example of the havoc that her emergence from the convent unleashes on the world around her.

Two telling shots contrast the ravages of guilt and intolerance in human lives with a joyous embracing of the world. A close-up reveals Don Jaime's body hanging from the tree near his house. He has hanged himself with Rita's skipping rope and his feet can be seen through the foliage. The shot repeats the shots of legs and thighs we have seen before, the images of sexual life and energy, but now the legs are stilled. The different symbols fuse in a single, powerful, evocative image of sexual failure and guilt which lead to death. A second shot, on the other hand, juxtaposed with the shot described above, shows Rita skipping, oblivious to the tragedy. It is identical to the shot in which we first saw her:

> *The same shot of Rita's legs as she skips beneath the big tree as at the film's commencement.*

The repetition of the lively image in the context of Don Jaime's suicide reinforces the theme of the innocent, guiltless, spontaneous enjoyment of life. It is repeated for a third time:

> *... Rita picks up the rope and begins to skip with the same energy. Another shot of her legs.*

The sequence is marked by a great beauty and freshness, a Garden of Eden innocence, in relation to which the spectacle of Don Jaime's lifeless body is one of humanity destroyed by guilt and despair.

Don Jaime's death marks the beginning of another stage in Viridiana's life. A shot of religious images is in many ways a telling variation on the film's beginning. Viridiana and the Mother Superior appear once again. After her uncle's death, Viridiana has moved from her bedroom to another room, the equivalent of her original convent cell:

> *Viridiana's room. A close-up of a black wooden cross and of a crown of thorns which hangs at the end of the bed. The floor of the room is of red brick and the walls are whitewashed.*

Filled with a sense of guilt over her involvement in her uncle's suicide, Viridiana has resolved to undertake the performance of good works:

> I will follow the path that the Lord has shown me. One can also be of service outside a convent...

The Mother Superior, who has come to sympathise with Viridiana over her uncle's death, exemplifies a lack of charity and a meanness of spirit as selfish and self-centred in every respect as Viridiana's piety. In the first place, she has sympathy for Viridiana but none for the dead man:

> You suffered greatly, my child!

Secondly, when she learns of Viridiana's decision not to return to the convent, her sympathy for one of her flock becomes her coldness towards one who has deserted it:

> VIRIDIANA: Mother! . . . Please forgive me if I have offended you.
> MOTHER SUPERIOR: You are forgiven. Goodbye.

The world on which Viridiana seeks to exercise her pious charity is exemplified now in all its unpromising reality in the shape of the beggars who wait for her, perhaps significantly, outside the village church, as though excluded from the ambit of religion. The twelve beggars, in terms of their appearance, evoke the twelve apostles:

> *. . . one is Don Zequiel, an old man of about sixty years of age whose full white beard gives him the appearance of a patriarch . . .*

Buñuel creates an image of saintliness precisely in order to reveal the cracks in it. The pious pleading of the blind Don Amalio is the veneer on a thoroughly nasty nature:

> Kind people! Do not forget an unfortunate blind man.

The old man, Poca, drawing the blind man's attention to Viridiana's arrival, twists the knife cruelly:

> She has the face of an angel. It's such a pity you can't see her.

When the group arrives at Don Jaime's mansion, where they will stay, there is open hostility between Moncho, the servant, and the beggars, and also among the beggars themselves. Don Amalio, angered by Pelón, hits him with his stick, Pelón retaliates, and the others have to separate them. If the image of the Church is one distinguished by its intolerance and narrow mindedness, the image of the world is in its way distinctly similiar. Its essence is caught, perhaps, in the wasteland and the weeds that surround the house:

> *The balcony looks out onto a wasteland: scorched fields, with scrub and weeds . . .*

Viridiana's charity will fall on the stony ground of the company of beggars.

Jorge, Don Jaime's illegitimate son, has arrived now at the house. In relation to the real world in all its unscrupulousness, it is his practical, pragmatic philosophy which stands more chance of success. If the beggars are a facet of the image of the world, Jorge is another, and, like the beggars, he treats it as he finds it:

> *Not given to overimagination or dreaming, he is a practical man, a man of action . . .*

The camera focuses in close-up on Jorge's feet:

> *Close-up of a basin of steaming hot water. In the water are Jorge's feet, and his trousers are rolled up . . .*

The shot links him with the other characters – Don Jaime, Rita, Viridiana – but its earlier sexual associations are now transformed into Jorge's practical activities. He has spent the day walking the estate:

> I have almost walked my legs off today.

On the other hand, Jorge's growing sexual involvement with the women around him is already hinted at. It is something that will test his pragmatism. Lucía, Jorge's mistress, sees his annoyance with Viridiana as evidence of his attraction to her. Ramona, the servant, begins to look at him in a way that is tender and submissive. Between the various characters there are signs of strain and hostility that link them firmly to the beggars. The point is underlined that, in their exposure to the powers of passion and instinct, men are, for all their class and social differences, equal.

A sequence which shows the beggars eating their meal reinforces the theme of men's essential sameness. It parallels a shot of Jorge eating his soup. The beggars, moreover, are dressed more 'respectably', have assumed the outward appearance of their 'betters'. In many respects they echo their 'betters' precisely. Their words, for example, are often full of piety. The Singer observes to Viridiana:

God will reward you.

It is an empty platitude reminiscent of the Mother Superior, and of Viridiana too. Towards her the beggars display a self-interested courtesy. Hobbly opens the door for her and bids her goodnight. It is merely a cover for the viciousness revealed immediately afterwards towards the leper whom he threatens with his stick and, with the help of the others, turns out. At the same time Don Amalio is feeling Enedina's thighs and whispering his lustful desires into her ear. The motif of the thigh, in particular, links him to Don Jaime gazing at Viridiana's thighs. Moreover, Hobbly takes the skipping-rope, another sexual symbol, and ties it around his waist. Through the imaginative interplay of visual images, Buñuel subtly blurs the distinction between the beggars and the other characters.

The image of the world is one which denies at every stage the other worldliness of Viridiana. A shot of her room with its religious objects has its counterpart in Jorge, a man of the world with a cigar between his lips, a mistress, and practical intentions for the improvement of his father's neglected property. They are things from which she cannot now escape, realities – like Jorge's flaunting of his relationship with Lucía and his mocking eyeing of Viridiana's body – which, uncomfortable as they are to her, she must accept. When the camera frames the window that looks outwards from Viridiana's room, the shot is significant. It is the world outside the window, the world of Jorge and Lucía, and of the beggars, which challenges her now and for which her repressive upbringing was so ill-fitted.

A new sequence contains a splendidly ironic contrast. Hobbly is painting a religious scene – of a sick woman lying on a bed, with the Virgin and two angels at her side. The figure of the Virgin has her counterpart in real life in the beggar who poses for the picture, a woman distinguished by her total lack of sentiment and her lack of comprehension of all spiritual values. She can only complain about her lack of comfort;

> Get a move on, I'm cramped all over.

Poca, looking at the painting, is strictly realistic, observing of the invalid:

> She looks like a sick marrow!

His comment on the parentage of Refugio's child is equally unsentimental:

> She has no idea who the child's father was. She told me it was night and she couldn't even see his head.

The sequence closes, as it began, with Hobbly's picture. The religious images frame, in other words, the real picture of the beggars. In the picture on the canvas the Virgin heals the woman. In the real world Viridiana seeks to heal the beggars. But in the real world there are no miracles.

Buñuel's unsentimental portrayal of the world is seen too in relation to a dog. The camera reveals a dog tied by a rope to the axle of a cart which is driven by a peasant. Jorge, for all his practical approach to life, is appalled by the cruel treatment of the animal and buys it from the peasant. Almost immediately, unseen by Jorge, the camera reveals another cart and another dog:

> *The second cart, with another wretched dog tied to its axle, passes before the camera . . .*

The road, it is implied, is endless, the carts and dogs innumerable, and Jorge's charitable gesture as useless as Viridiana's. His remarks to her in relation to the beggars make precisely the point that has escaped him in relation to the dog:

> There's not much point in helping a few of them when there are so many others.

The cruel treatment of the dog has its human counterpart in

the workmen's treatment of the leper, for as the peasant has tied the animal, so the men have tied a can to the leper's waist. Viridiana, taking pity on the beggar, unties the can, a gesture as futile in practice as Jorge's, for the workmen will merely repeat their cruelty. In addition, her bathing of the leper's arm points to the ineffectiveness of Christian principles in a world that is unworthy of them, in which men use God for their own ends. The leper, for example, infected by a woman, puts his arm in the holy water in the church not to heal it but to infect others and thus to avenge himself on them. The priest, devoid of compassion for the wretched man, locks him out of the church. And even Viridiana, extending to the leper her well-intentioned charity, uses him in her own self-interested way.

Another sequence presents Jorge in his father's room at night. He is sitting at a table examining his father's gold watch. Amongst the trinkets he discovers too a small crucifix which has a blade set into its side and which, when opened, converts into a knife, a complex phallic image which underlines the interplay and juxtaposition of religious and erotic sentiment. Lucía, to whom he is indifferent, sits on the edge of the bed in her nightgown. The episode recalls in many ways (notably through the figure of the woman and the religious associations of the crucifix) Don Jaime's nightly worship of his wife's devoted memory. The crucifix that becomes a blade suggests too the destructive nature of the old man's ritual. Jorge, on the other hand, is his father's opposite. When Lucía decides to leave him, he accepts it:

> That's how life is. Some people come together, others separate. What can we do about it if that's the way things happen?

Lucía's emotional and jealous nature is a form of self-indulgence that, like Viridiana's, founders on the cynicism of the world at large.

Jorge and Viridiana's different attitudes are contrasted further in a series of quickly alternating shots. The workmen are seen repairing a storehouse on the estate. Nearby is a ruined building that serves as the beggars' living quarters. Shots of the beggars otherwordly murmurings, as they are led in prayer by Viridiana, are rapidly juxtaposed with shots of cement slapped on a wall, sand being sifted, stones being carried, and wood being sawed. The practical restoration of Don Jaime's property, successfully carried out, has its counterpart in Viridiana's attempted restoration of ruined, delapidated human beings. Jorge's unsentimental view of things is reflected in other ways. He quickly replaces Lucía with the servant, Ramona. They are seen in the attic, sorting out the junk, the debris and the chaos of Don Jaime's life. Jorge's management of his affairs is combined with his realistic, unromantic handling of women:

> *Without more ado, he kisses her on the lips, not bothering to hold her . . .*

Nearby, a cat pounces on an unsuspecting rat. In a world like this Viridiana's charity is futile. While Jorge has quickly acquired another mistress, Viridiana's actions towards the beggars merely force Moncho, the servant, to leave Don Jaime's house after many years of service.[8]

Viridiana's departure for the day begins an extended sequence in which the beggars in all their flawed humanity are revealed to us in close-up. They immediately take advantage of her charity, displaying, like Jorge, an entirely practical attitude to life. As he avails himself of Ramona's presence to indulge his appetites, so the beggars make good use of Viridiana's absence. Hobbly observes:

> We'll have ourselves a couple of lambs. We'll have them roasted.

They embody the morality harshly learned in a cruel and uncharitable world. Ignoring their promise to Viridiana not to enter the house, they are true to their own instincts and to that extent more realistic than Don Jaime, filled with guilt by his attraction to Viridiana, or Viridiana herself, seeking to reform a world she cannot even comprehend. Buñuel's portrayal of the beggars is impressive for its essential truthfulness, and horrifying only to the extent that the truth itself is horrifying.[9]

Between the aristocratic elegance of Don Jaime's mansion and the coarseness of its new inhabitants there is a startling incongruity. As the beggars sit at the long dining-table, the scene becomes a parody of a bourgeois dinner-party, taste and manners completely overturned:

> *The camera reveals an amazing scene. The beggars are sitting at the table; the leper is by himself at a small table nearby. They have finished two roast lambs, the remains of which litter the table. There is a terrible confusion of glasses, plates and bottles . . .*

The faces of the beggars are covered in grease, their dialogue is gross. The rubble of the feast has its counterpart in the figures of Don Zequiel, Amalio, Hobbly, Enedina and Refugio. But for all their coarseness, the beggars remain distinctly human, no worse, indeed, than the bourgeois gathering of *The Exterminating Angel* when, in the course of events, their sophistication has been stripped away.

The spectacle of the beggars' feast is one that is full too of religious associations. Enedina prepares to take a photograph of her companions. They arrange themselves in different poses and as, with her back to the camera, she lewdly lifts her skirt to 'photograph' the group, it is suddenly another version of Leonardo's 'The Last Supper', the central figure of Christ the blind Don Amalio, flanked on either side by his disreputable associates. In this clever and, for many, irreverent sequence, Buñuel deflates the false and sentimental image of the twelve apostles, and of Christ too.[10] The events which follow point, moreover, to man's perpetual unworthiness, to the fact that, if he is made in God's image, the image is a badly flawed and tawdry one. The leper places a record of the *Hallelujah Chorus* on the gramophone. He is pleased merely by the noise it makes. He appears, as did

The last supper

Don Jaime earlier in the film, in Doña Elvira's veil and corset and begins to perform a wild dance to the sounds of Handel's music. If, on the one hand, the scene is a parody of Don Jaime's pointless devotion to his wife's sacred memory, it is also a ruthless exposé of human pervesity in all its worst and most lurid colours. Enedina and Paco make love behind the couch. Their legs stick out in a grotesque repetition of the sexual image seen before. Hobbly hurls a plate of pudding into Don Zequiel's face and the Gardener observes:

> That's just right for you, Don Zequiel! Ecce Homo, that's what I say!

Buñuel's evocation of the defiling of Christ underscores the theme of man's unworthiness. The feast ends with a spectacle of total wreckage as Don Amalio wields his stick:

> *His flaying stick wreaks havoc on the contents of the table: plates, glasses, bottles. Wines, sauces and puddings are spilled. Very quickly the magnificently embroidered tablecloth is like a battlefield.*

It is a scene woven out of the interplay of human selfishness, greed, lust, envy and rage. Wasted on such a world, Viridiana's charity has merely turned the beggars against each other.

The violent climax of the film centres on Hobbly's sexual assault on Viridiana. Jorge, Viridiana and the others return as the beggars begin to leave the house. Hobbly and the leper are concealed in Don Jaime's room. When Jorge enters, Hobbly draws his knife and the leper, coming from behind, hits him with a bottle. Viridiana rushes in to Jorge's aid but, as she tends him, is seized by the drunk and lecherous Hobbly. She appeals to the leper to whom she has shown compassion:

> José, José! For the love of God, stop him . . .

Far from helping her, the leper helps Hobbly by tying Jorge's legs together. Viridiana is saved in the end not by her own appeal to the leper's better nature but by Jorge's practical manipulation of his greed. Recovering his senses, Jorge bribes the leper to dispose of Hobbly:

> I don't want you to untie me. Kill him and I'll let you have the money.

Jorge's pragmatism works in a world which mocks Viridiana's charity. She, indeed, is still encumbered by the crippling weight of her inhibitions which, without Jorge's intervention, would surely have destroyed her:

> *Her clenched fingers grip the rope that the beggar is using as a belt. It is Rita's skipping rope, the same one that Don Jaime used to hang himself. As her fingers touch the handle of the rope, she freezes. Then she lets it go, dropping her arms as if abandoning the struggle.*

The reminder of Viridiana's sexual repression and Don Jaime's suicide is the final evocation of that world of guilt and conscience which, until now, has been her province.

The film's final scenes announce the birth of Viridiana to the world around her. When we see her next, her physical appearance has changed:

> *She is seated a few feet away, sewing. She is wearing a print blouse, which gives her a surprisingly youthful appearance. At last she seems to have become just like any other young woman.*

In contrast to Handel's *Messiah*, jazz accompanies the remainder of the action. Outside the house Viridiana's religious objects – notably the crown of thorns – are thrown onto a fire. The crown of thorns becomes a crown of fire, the symbol of martyrdom the symbol of passion. When Rita pricks her finger on a thorn and sucks it, the gesture has clear phallic implications, pointing to Viridiana's rejection of the religious life and her embracing of the world at large. She seeks now not God's forgiveness but Jorge's:

Viridiana finally looks at him imploringly, as though asking to be understood and forgiven . . .

Her initiation into the convent becomes her initiation into the ways of the world as Jorge teaches her to cut a pack of cards. She, Ramona and Jorge occupy, significantly, Don Jaime's bedroom. The father's crippling conventionality becomes the son's unselfconscious sharing of two young women:

> You sit down too. Come and sit down. All cats are grey in the dark.

As the camera recedes, it is the frenzied, euphoric sound of secular music which celebrates Viridiana's acceptance of the world.

Although *Viridiana* has a clear-cut story-line, it is undoubtedly an extremely complex film.[11] David Robinson has observed that in *Viridiana* 'Buñuel is still the surrealist of 1929' and a study of the film's technique suggests very clearly that in the essentials of his style Buñuel has changed very little in the intervening years.

Here, as elsewhere, Buñuel exposes the inner life, the desires and unconscious urges of his characters. He does so not by a revelation of their dreams, as in *Los olvidados* or *Belle de Jour*, nor by exteriorizing their thoughts and feelings, as in *L Age d'or*, but by exposing their reactions to certain key-objects: legs, the teat of a cow, the handle of a skipping-rope. When the camera focuses, for instance, on Rita's quickly-moving legs, it tells us precisely the nature of Don Jaime's thoughts. Similarly, a shot of the white flesh of Viridiana's thigh exposes his sexual fantasies. The repeated image acquires an obsessive character that reflects Don Jaime's own obsession. The cow's teat and the handle of the skipping-rope, both phallic images, draw different responses from different characters. Rita is young and innocent and takes them for what they are. Viridiana, on the other hand, recoils as she touches them, and Don Jaime gazes with fascination at the handle of the skipping-rope gripped by Rita's hand. They are objects and images that are deeply embedded in the psyche, meaningful too for each and everyone of us. In presenting them on the screen, like the recurring objects of our dreams and fantasies, Buñuel awakens in his audience those very feelings of attraction or repulsion experienced by the characters themselves. It is one of the reasons why *Viridiana* remains a particularly memorable and haunting film, for its symbolic language is deeply ingrained in each of us.

In terms of its social and moral implications, the film revolves around an essential contrast: the clash of the spirit and the flesh. This opposition determines, of course, many of the shots and sequences. Most obvious is the sequence of alternating shots of the beggars praying and the workmen working. When Hobbly paints his picture of the Virgin, the religious figure has her far-from-virtuous human counterpart in the beggar-woman who poses for him. The beggars seated at the dining-table, 'frozen' into an evocation of Leonardo's painting, provide a contrast of association. They contrast too, of course, in their sheer moral and physical coarseness, with the elegance of the mansion setting. The sustained visual contrasts, sometimes abrupt, sometimes subtle, are witty and ironic statements of a more sophisticated kind than the violent juxtapositions that distinguish, for example, *L'Age d'or*. On the other hand, while *Viridiana* is a more mature film in terms of its technique, it retains the simplicity and directness, the 'fast, hard style', of the earlier films.[13] Buñuel presents his images without fuss or ostentation, avoiding gimmicks. He has that instinct for the right shot which has the effect of giving his art the appearance of great naturalness.

While the pictorial qualities of *Viridiana* are themselves remarkable, they are accompanied by an excellent script; another example of Buñuel's literary skills.[14] In the first part of the film the scenes between Viridiana and Don Jaime have a dramatic power that lies as much in the verbal exchanges of the characters as in the pictures of them. The dialogue captures perfectly Don Jaime's growing obsession with Viridiana, his anguish, her coldness and disgust. It has all the qualities of a fine play. In the scenes involving the beggars, where the register is very different, the dialogue finely expresses the changing moods of these complex creatures: their hypocrisy, their deceit, their greed, their lack of sentimentality, their frightening potential for violence. They are, moreover, strongly differentiated one from another, as much individualized by their language as by their physical appearance.

As elsewhere, music is used by Buñuel not as background to or mere adornment to the pictures but as a counterpoint, often ironic in nature. Thus the sounds of Mozart's *Requiem* accompany Don Jaime's drugging of Viridiana and Handel's *Messiah* the beggars' orgy. The latter is, as it happens, the only gramophone record in the house and it is entirely natural that the beggars should use it to accompany their dance. Buñuel's use of music is, to this extent, as economical, as unforced, and yet as pointed as his use of the camera.[15]

NOTES

[1] For the background to the film see Francisco Aranda, *Luis Buñuel*..., pp. 190-198. Aranda provides an illuminating account of a day in the shooting of the film.

[2] Buñuel did, in fact, change the ending of the film in the light of suggestions made by the Spanish authorities. His original plan was merely to have Viridiana go to Jorge's room to give herself up to him. Of the new ending, in which she joins Jorge and Ramona in a game of cards, Buñuel remarked delightedly that it was much better, much more subtle and suggestive.

[3] See Luis Buñuel, 'On *Viridiana*', *The World of Luis Buñuel*, p. 217.

[4] 'On *Viridiana*', p. 216.

[5] Raymond Durgnat, *Luis Buñuel*, p. 120, suggests that the Mother Superior acts 'more, it seems, out of respect for "the done thing". . . .'

[6] See David Robinson, 'Luis Buñuel and *Viridiana*', *The World of Luis Buñuel*, p. 240: 'He is set, as he has always been set, against the soporifics of conventional morality and conventional sentimentality. "I am against conventional morals, traditional phantasms, sentimentalism and all that moral uncleanliness that sentimentalism introduces into society . . . Bourgeois morality is for me immoral, and to be fought. The morality founded on our most unjust social institutions, like religion, patriotism, the family, culture: briefly, what are called the 'pillars of society'".'

[7] Raymond Durgnat, too, sees Don Jaime as a tragic figure: 'In no sense is Don Jaime's posthumous passion merely ludicrous. . . . The erotic transvestite is, basically, seeking to console himself for the loss of a beloved image by becoming it himself. Don Jaime as a lover is here as steadfast, as tragic as Heathcliff plundering Cathy's tomb in *Cumbres borrascosas*' p. 124.

[8] Of Jorge, David Robinson, 'Luis Buñuel and *Viridiana*', p. 239, observes: 'If there is a hero at all, it is Jorge, who lives positively and (as a good surrealist) according to the dictates of desire. Yet one feels that Buñuel does not prefer him to the others. . . .' Raymond Durgnat, pp. 121-122, condemns Jorge quite emphatically: 'The uncle asserted a romantic fidelity-after-death to one woman; the cousin replaces it by an apathetic infidelity. He is in no sense a revolutionary; he's a patcher and botcher. Though he patches Viridiana's life, perhaps he botches it too. His timbers and tools are his "dead things", his fetishes, like Viridiana's nails and crown of thorns, like Don Jaime's dead wife's corsets. . . .'

[9] David Robinson, p. 240, refers to 'the clear gaze of a man who is prepared to recognize the world for what it is. . . .'

[10] See Emilio G. Riera, '*Viridiana*', in *The World of Luis Buñuel*, pp. 218-225, and, in particular, pp. 220-221: '. . . Buñuel does not group the beggars in an arrangement similar to the figures in Da Vinci's "Last Supper" in order to belittle Christ and his apostles by comparing them to some drunkards. What he is doing in this instance is reducing representation of the divine to the human scale. . . .'

[11] Freddy Buache, *The Cinema of Luis Buñuel*, p. 122, draws a comparison with the Spanish picaresque novel, while Francisco Aranda, p. 203, suggests that '. . . Buñuel has given the Spanish cinema the equivalent of Quevedo's *El buscón* and *Los sueños*, of the picaresque, of Galdós. . . .'

[12] 'Luis Buñuel and *Viridiana*', p. 242.

[13] David Robinson puts the point very well: 'Grandly independent of conventional techniques as of conventional ideas, Buñuel seems to have the ability simply to put pictures on the screen with the accuracy and certainty of a good paperhanger sticking up paper' p. 243.

[14] Francisco Aranda, p. 198, refers to the film's 'marvellous dialogue'. It goes without saying, of course, that in this respect much is lost in translation from Spanish.

[15] Emilio G. Riera, 'Viridiana', p. 224, observes that '. . . Buñuel does not conceive of music as a mere adornment, but as an element of counterpoint, to be used integrally rather than as a superfluity.' See, too, Francisco Aranda, p. 200: 'The sound-track uses a lot of music, although Buñuel has not broken with his determination not to use "background" music'.

6

THE EXTERMINATING ANGEL

(El Ángel Exterminador)

CAST

The Valkyrie	—	Silvia Pinal
Doctor	—	Augusto Benedico
Russell	—	Antonio Bravo
Colonel	—	César del Campo
Lucía	—	Lucy Gallardo
Juana Avila	—	Ofelia Guilmaín
Raúl	—	Tito Junco
Eduardo	—	Xavier Massé
Beatriz	—	Ofelia Montesco
Blanca	—	Patricia de Morelos
Nobile	—	Enrique Rambal
Leandro	—	José Baviera
Christian	—	Luis Beristaín
Majordomo	—	Claudio Brook
Silvia	—	Rosa Elena Durgel
Señor Roc	—	Enrique García Alvarez
Ana Maynar	—	Nadia Haro Oliva
Francisco Avila	—	Xavier Loya
Servant	—	Angel Merino
Rita	—	Patricia Morán
Leonora	—	Bertha Moss

Photography	—	Gabriel Figueroa
Editor	—	Carlos Savage Jr.
Art Director	—	Jesús Bracho
Sound	—	José B. Carles
Music	—	Raúl Lavista; Scarlatti; Paradisi
Production	—	Gustavo Alatriste for UNINCI S.A. and Films 59
Script	—	Luis Buñuel Luis Alcoriza
Assistant Director	—	Ignacio Villareal
Director	—	Luis Buñuel

The Exterminating Angel followed quickly on the heels of *Viridiana.* It received its Mexican première on May 8, 1962, and was shown in the same year at the Cannes Film Festival. After the filming of *Viridiana*, its financial backer, Gustavo Alatriste, provided Buñuel with the money to make another film and complete freedom to make the film he wanted. Some years earlier Buñuel and Luis Alcoriza had produced a scenario based on *The Castaways (Los náufragos)*, a short story by the Spanish writer, José Bergamín. They had intended to make the film in 1957, before *Nazarín*, and to entitle it *The Castaways of Providence Street (Los náufragos de la calle Providencia).* It was to this project that Buñuel returned after *Viridiana*, altering certain details and adding others. The title became *The Exterminating Angel (El ángel exterminador)*, the name of a painting by the seventeenth-century Spanish painter, Valdés Leal. When the film was shown at Cannes, it was coolly received, the jury perplexed, perhaps, by what is undoubtedly a complex and difficult film. The International Federation of Film Critics, on the other hand, recognized its merits and awarded it its own prize. Subsequently, *The Exterminating Angel* has often been bracketed with *L'Age d'or* as Buñuel's greatest film.[1]

Buñuel's observations on *The Exterminating Angel* are characteristically tantalizing and often tongue-in-cheek. When, for example, the critics at Cannes asked Buñuel's son, Juan Luis, about the purpose of the film's many repetitions, he had already been instructed by his father to say that without them the film would have been too short. Asked further about the significance of a bear in the bourgeois household, Juan Luis was told to say that his father liked bears.[2] Buñuel, of course, delighted as much in subverting the expectations and preconceptions of the critics as in the film itself he undermines the conventions of the bourgeoisie. His comments on his films in general need to be taken, more often than not, with a substantial pinch of salt.

It is the link with *L'Age d'or* that points most clearly to Buñuel's purpose in *The Exterminating Angel.* In *L'Age d'or* he had brilliantly combined a sustained attack on established social and moral values with an exaltation of man's instincts and passions. They remain, to a greater or lesser extent, the concerns of the films which followed, but Buñuel made them once more the central preoccupation of *The Exterminating Angel.* In its presentation of the bourgeoisie the film is, as Raymond Durgnat has pointed out, an extended version of the drawing-room sequence in *L'Age d'Or.*[3] The new circumstances of the bourgeois guests imprisoned in an elegant mansion, slowly deprived of food and water, thrown back on their own resources, allowed Buñuel to conduct a minute and penetrating examination of their rites, rituals and moral codes, and to do so with a concentrated wit. Juan Luis Buñuel has put the matter well:

> The film, to me, is essentially a comic film, but with a very strong corrosive interior. Corrosive in a social and surrealist sense.[4]

If anything, Buñuel's assault on society's festering institutions is more sustained and more ferocious than that of *L'Age d'or*, though now the broadsword has become a rapier.

The predicament of the bourgeois guests is also one which slowly allows their deepest, most powerful instincts, and even their dreams and fantasies to reveal themselves. To this extent, although in a different sense from the largely sexual preoccupations of *L'Age d'or*, the irrational is to the forefront of *The Exterminating Angel* and some of the film's scenes are amongst Buñuel's most memorable and accomplished cinematic sequences. In conversation with Francisco Aranda, Buñuel has been at pains to emphasize this point:

> I am interested in a life with ambiguities and contradictions.[5]

Beneath the stiff and formal image, the inner life, the ambiguities and contradictions of the elegant company, a permanent source of fascination and a constant fountain of inspiration to Buñuel, are displayed to us in all their rich complexity.

The creative process is also, as is often the case with Buñuel, broadly surrealist. Aranda, describing the shooting of the film, alludes, significantly, to Buñuel's 'psychic automatism', the freedom with which his own imagination allowed him to explore and reveal the subconscious of his characters. Instinct is, to this extent, as much a part of the creative art as of the artist's preoccupations, and Buñuel has underlined the fact in denying for the film both a conscious aim and any one interpretation:

> I have not introduced a single symbol into the film, and those who hope for a thesis work from me, a work with a message, may keep on hoping! It is open to doubt whether *El ángel exterminador* is capable of interpretation. Everyone has the right to interpret it as he wishes . . .[6]

The film grew, it seems, from an image, much as *Viridiana* did, and in the process of its making found in Buñuel's obsessions and memories a constant source of inspiration and invention. In 1957 he had planned a film of William Golding's *Lord of the Flies* and of his own *The Castaways of Providence Street*. The image of a group of people, separated from their fellow men and exposed to their own virtues and weaknesses, was clearly one that took firm root in Buñuel's imagination during these years and, as in the case of so many of his most outstanding films, burst into life as though endowed with its own creative energy. And yet, given that spontaneity so admired by the surrealists and so dear to Buñuel himself, *The Exterminating Angel* impresses for its shapeliness, form, proportion and evident artistry.

The Exterminating Angel begins and ends with a religious image. The credits appear against a shot of a cathedral at night and are accompanied by a *Te Deum*. The camera reveals a boulevard in the town, a street name (Providence Street), and expensive cars moving along the road. Another shot depicts a large wrought-iron gate, the entrance to a private estate, and two servants conversing. The sequence, like the opening of *Viridiana*, suggests the theme of ritual, the religious and social rites that Buñuel is about to present to us in all their elaborate and sanctified forms. The name of the street has a double meaning. Pointing, on the one hand, to the destiny of men and women born to wealth and privilege, it points too to the fateful and ironic joke that Buñuel is about to play on them.

The opening dialogue immediately subverts and undermines the initial sense of order and formality. To the consternation of the butler, one of the servants decides to take a walk in the middle of the preparations for a dinner-party:

> BUTLER: Hey! Where are you going?
> LUCAS: Just for a little walk. . . . I won't be long. . . .
> BUTLER: There are twenty people coming to dinner . . . and you want to take a walk?
> LUCAS (*embarrassed*): I didn't think of that. But I promise I'll be back soon.

Irrational impulses, flooding to the surface, begin to disrupt the accepted order of things, initiating the dominant pattern of the film. Another shot, depicting the drawing room, the dining room, the careful arrangement of candlesticks and glassware, the coming and going of servants, restores the sense of ordered ritual. But this is undermined in turn by the actions of the maids who, like the servant, feel impelled to leave the house, and by the chef's assistant who wants to join them. The second valet abuses the first in quite unexpected terms, his sense of place and position overthrown by a sudden failure to control himself:

> VALET I (*surprised*): Am I supposed to do it?
> VALET II (*interrupting*): Yes, because you're a fool!

In his opening scene Buñuel has merely allowed the unconscious to assert itself in relation to established and accepted patterns of behaviour. It is a process full of rich possibilities.

A new sequence, reminiscent of an episode in *L'Age d'Or*, presents the ritualistic arrival of the guests for the dinner-party. Cars draw up outside the house, Nobile, the host, shows his guests inside and calls in vain for a valet. The shot and the dialogue are then repeated almost identically:

> *... New shot of the front door and repeat of the guests' entrance as it was seen before. NOBILE (seen this time from a somewhat higher angle) advances from the group and looks for a valet.*
>
> NOBILE *(calling out)*: Lucas? *(He goes back to his guests and points to the staircase.)* That's strange! Lucas isn't there. We'll leave our coats upstairs. Come, come with me, please.

Just afterwards, when everyone is seated at the dining-table, Nobile stands up and proposes a toast to Silvia. Almost immediately he repeats the toast:

> *The camera returns to NOBILE, who stands up again with his glass in his hand. He repeats the toast.*

Repetitions of this kind occur some twenty times in the course of the film. They underline the repetitive nature of human lives and actions as a whole, formalized into rites and rituals of the bourgeoisie.[7] Beyond this, they contribute greatly to the film's increasingly disturbing atmosphere. The servants leave on impulse, the guests inexplicably repeat themselves. The ordered nature of life is subjected to the whims of impulse, time and logic. In part it is Buñuel's joke, but the joke has its serious side and, as well as provoking laughter, points to the essential absurdity of human life and action.

The ensuing dialogue is both amusing and disconcerting. It is as if the guests, although speaking to each other, were on a different wavelength, their replies incongruous, illogical, strangely out of accord with our and the listener's expectations. Thus Christian's greeting of Leandro:

CHRISTIAN *(exclaiming)*: Leandro!
LEANDRO *(opening his arms)*: My dear friend! Christian!
CHRISTIAN: How marvellous! I thought you were still in New York!
LEANDRO: Well! As you see, we must have courage in adversity.

The warmth of the two men's meeting is strangely at odds with the coldness of their introduction minutes before:

RAÚL *(to Christian)*: May I present a good friend of mine. He has just arrived in town. Leandro Gómez – Christian Gálvez.
LEANDRO *(rather coldly)*: How do you do?

And even then there was a strange disparity between the cold and formal greeting and the handshake that accompanied it:

The two men shake hands at great length.

The various characters mean one thing but say another: social niceties lapse into embarrassing confidentialities or unintentional suggestiveness. Alicia's reference to her husband illustrates the point:

ALICIA *(almost confidentially)*: Well, when we retired after the concert, he tried once more. I have no complaint on that score – on the contrary, I have to restrain him.
NOBILE: Let him sleep . . . he could try again here.
ALICIA: My God, no! I don't think he would dare here.
NOBILE: No, of course not . . . I expresssed myself rather badly.

The dialogue retains the shape, the pattern and the polished form of typically bourgeois social chit-chat, but at given moments its content is subverted. The wrong word, the inappropriate response is thrown in. Buñuel achieves delightfully humorous effects, but the often bizarre dialogue conveys too the impression of individuals slowly losing their poise and their grip on the kind of normality which has always been confidently theirs.

The point is reinforced by the actions of the characters. The relationship of the doctor and Leonora, conventionally formal, becomes in a moment of impulse her seductive embracing of him. Lucía, the ever correct and solicitous hostess, obligingly fetches Blanca's shawl, encounters the colonel, and they kiss passionately (a pointer to a secret affair hitherto concealed beneath a facade of respectability). Letitia, calmly folding her napkin at the table, picks up an ash tray and hurls it impulsively through the window of the dining-room. As the night wears on and the guests discover that, inexplicably, they cannot leave, conventional requirements begin to vie with pressing private needs. Good manners become incongruously intertwined and juxtaposed with actions of a grosser kind. Leandro removes his tie and jacket and lies on the floor. The lovers, Beatrice and Eduardo, lie down too and Christian, who is on the sofa, takes off his jacket. Lucía is shocked by their undignified behaviour. Nobile, always the good host and anxious not to seem superior to his guests in any way, resolves to join them:

> LUCÍA: I'm sure they'll be ashamed when they remember their behaviour.
>
> NOBILE: I'm sure they will. I'd hate them to feel embarrassed about it. *(He takes off his jacket.)* Let's come down to their level. It will help to mitigate their bad manners.

From its highly formal and ritualistic beginning the scene is slowly transformed. The polite social gathering, still clinging to its own peculiar rites and practices, becomes by the early hours an incongruous spectacle of bodies littering the floor, draped over sofas, and slumped in chairs.

A quick exterior shot reveals that is is dawn. Inside the Nobile mansion the butler is combing his hair in front of a large mirror, fixing his tie and putting on his jacket. In a corner of the drawing room Lucía is arranging her hair in front of a mirror. Silvia, Rita and Ana, conscious of their dishevelled appearance, are concerned with tidying themselves up. From butler to hostess the bourgeois world begins to rise, phoenix-like, from the ashes of the previous night. Lucía, indeed, as conscious of her social obligations as her husband, feels obliged to offer breakfast to her guests. On the other hand, while some of them seek to re-establish their elegant and polished image, others, responding to deeper impulses, reveal a strange attraction to the spectacle of incipient degradation. The darker corners of human minds and passions are tellingly revealed. Juana observes to her brother:

> You are more interesting than ever. It suits you to be dishevelled.

Eduardo says to Beatrice:

> You are more interesting than ever. It suits you to be dishevelled.

If the earlier repetitions of action and speech pointed to the recurring patterns of bourgeois ritual, they pinpoint now obsessive patterns of a deeper nature, stirrings of strong passions which (held in check by a sense of socially accepted standards) will soon unleash themselves. As time passes and Nobile's guests begin to realize that they cannot, for whatever reason, leave the drawing-room, there are signs of despair, helplessness, panic and hysteria. The layers of social refinement are stripped away to reveal powerful currents of primitive emotion.[8]

A new sequence suggests this profound change. It is night. The scene in the drawing room recalls the earlier scene of Blanca's elegant piano recital, but now she is slumped over the piano and her playing reveals her nervousness. Letitia, annoyed by Blanca, angrily slams the piano lid. Previously she and the others had rushed to congratulate her. Now the social graces crumble as the group, previously held together by the bond and necessity of a common vested interest, is splintered into individuals, each increasingly concerned with self-preservation. Francisco, an effeminate, theatrical young man, lapses into despair and then hysteria:

> FRANCISCO: It's hopeless! *(He woefully goes across to his sister, JUANA, and sits by her. LUCÍA is near them, listening attentively.)* We've had it. *(He speaks sharply to his sister.)* Why did you bring me here, dear sister, why? *(He is almost shouting.)* . . .

Mr Roc and Raúl, in particular, begin to threaten Nobile, attributing their plight to him, and, when Letitia takes his part, they turn on her. The traditional courtesies extended to hosts and women cease to function. On the other hand, the mask has not yet slipped completely. Eduardo, conscious of Beatrice's thirst, is gentleman enough to offer her the water from a vase of flowers (having first, of course, removed the flowers) and considerate enough to sweeten the taste with a dash of lemon. Secondly, throughout the scene of growing chaos and confusion, of angry shouts and wild gestures, there are still those who, in the absence of a lavatory, have the decency to relieve themselves, one by one, inside a closet filled with elegant Chinese vases, and to do so, of course, with the utmost discretion:

> *The door of the closet opens. ROC comes out very discreetly, in his shirt sleeves, closing the door behind him . . .*

They are incidents which, in their irony, are typical Buñuel. And so is the increasing emphasis upon the awakening subconscious. In the isolation of the closet the women's fears assume an almost physical dimension:

SILVIA: I raised the lid and I saw a steep precipice, and at the foot of it the clear water of a great torrent.

ANA *(a rather distant look in her eyes)*: Yes, and before I sat down, an eagle flew by below me.

RITA: As for me, the wind swirled a great mass of dead leaves into my face.

Another sequence depicts the drawing room late at night. Most of the guests are sleeping or dozing. The scene echoes the chaos of the first night but there are signs of a further deterioration. In the light of it the characters' clinging to social norms provides Buñuel with further opportunities for irony. Eduardo and Beatrice, for instance, meet discreetly in a closet, concerned that they should not be seen. Their amorous dialogue – 'My love!' 'My death! Oh, my refuge!' – at a moment when the doctor and the colonel are attempting to put Russell's dead body in the closet provides a superbly comic counterpoint. And Buñuel, exploiting a wide range of humorous possibilities, throws in an outrageous Hollywood cliché to frighten Ana out of her wits:

> . . . *her eyes grow wide with fear. The closet door squeaks and opens, and RUSSELL'S lifeless hand flops onto the carpet. ANA chokes back a scream of fear. She tries in vain to awaken LETITIA and collapses in a faint.*

Outside the house, attempts are being made to rescue the incarcerated bourgeoisie. The rescuers are highly organized and filled with a sense of duty towards their masters. A brigade of sappers has attempted to enter the house and failed, for when they reached the gates they lacked the desire to go further. Buñuel parallels his ironic portrayal of the bourgeois guests with a glorious send-up of the social instruments which serve and represent them – the bureaucracy, the police, the army –, as their efforts to serve their benefactors are thwarted and subverted, inexplicably undermined by a lack of will. This paralysis of will exemplified in the instruments of the bourgeoisie is a reflection of the inertia of the bourgeoisie itself, of its own incapacity to free itself from the sickness of conformity embodied in Nobile's decaying household.

It is a few days later, inside the house. Food and water are exhausted and the drawing room and its inhabitants reveal a greater state of physical and emotional disarray. The butler has thrown aside his jacket, his sign of office, and is trying to reach the water-pipe embedded in the wall. He uses an ornamental axe and is aided by Raúl who wields a ball and chain. The emblems of bourgeois wealth and elegance, snatched from the walls, are put to a much more basic purpose; good taste sacrificed in the interests of more pressing needs. The earlier shots of the splendid drawing room now become shots of falling plaster and cement. The former elegance of its inhabitants are replaced by images of naked feet. As the camera moves around the room, it reveals a mound of rubbish in the doorway. The chaos of the room is further echoed in the appearance and the conflicts of the characters. Ana is delirious, Francisco on edge. Raúl unplugs Francisco's electric razor simply to annoy him. Francisco, unnerved by Silvia's combing of her hair, breaks her comb in two. Rita and Christian, otherwise close and affectionate, begin to bicker as Christian hints at her emotional involvement with the priest. It leads in turn to Christian's confrontation with Raúl. Feeings hitherto concealed beneath a social armour of conventional politeness emerge and surface in all their undisguised hostility:

CHRISTIAN *(standing and facing Raúl)*: You are most insulting! And you may be aware that I've had this opinion of you since we arrived.

RAÚL *(shrugging his shoulders)*: What do I care! I've had nothing but contempt for you for far longer than that.

When, as before. Nobile intervenes, Christian and Raúl turn

on him, forcing the colonel to try to calm all three of them. Just after the quarrel, the camera picks out Raúl who is poking at the pile of rubbish. Finding the box of pills which Christian has lost and which he needs for his deteriorating condition, Raúl deliberately throws the box where Christian will never find it. Both moral values and social manners fall away like the crumbling plaster, and as the camera tracks around the room, it reveals in detail the human wreckage. Beatrice is eating paper. Blanca is slumped in a chair, tearing out bunches of hair. Leonora is prostrated on the couch, her face feverish and covered in sweat. The picture is one of physical and moral decay, of a rotting organism initially concealed beneath the façade of bourgeois manners. It is symbolized above all in the stench that begins to fill the room – the smell of Russell's body is also the smell of their own corruption, the growing awareness of their own rottenness and decay.[9]

This complex sequence has exposed the powerful forces that lie beneath the surface of conventional behaviour. The next probes deeper still, exposing the darker areas of the unconscious mind. The glimpse of Russell's hand has had its effect on Ana. The hand, suggestive of putrefaction and sexual anxiety, obsesses her, its white and clammy presence looming ever larger in the dark, chaotic-pattern of her fevered mind. The film becomes, as in parts of *L'Age d'or* and *Los olvidados*, the exteriorization of the configurations of an inner torment. The hand, startlingly white in the darkness of the room, emerges from the closet and slides along the floor towards Ana. Filled with horror and panic, she throws her scarf over the white flesh and strikes it with a bronze statuette. Shortly afterwards, as she sits on the sofa in a state of great anguish, the hand appears again from beneath her scarf and the fingers seize her by the throat. Ana loosens its grip, throws it on the table and, as it prepares to attack again, stabs it with a dagger. The sequence has a magnificent pictorial power and conveys to us in the unique language of the cinema the tangible reality of Ana's nightmare. The images are accompanied too by various terrifying sounds, as though we were inside Ana's head. The ticking of the clock grows louder. Gun shots, the sound of machine-gun fire, and strange creakings fill the room. The evocation of Ana's tormented thoughts, transmitted to us with all the terror that she herself experiences, is one of Buñuel's most powerful scenes. He had suggested the episode of the severed hand for the Hollywood production of *The Beast With Five Fingers*. The same motif is used again in a striking surrealist manner, exposing in no uncertain manner Ana's deep-rooted anxieties.[10]

While Ana is overwhelmed by fear, Mr Roc is tempted to indulge his sexual fantasies. Taking advantage of the darkness, he attempts to kiss Letitia and then to embrace Rita. In the subsequent confusion the colonel is accused by Christian of behaving like a scoundrel, loses the control and self-restraint he has shown throughout, and challenges Christian to a duel. The doctor calms them but the colonel, annoyed further by Alicia, throws her to the floor, much as in *L'Age d'or* Modot sends the blind man flying and, to the horror of the assembled company, slaps Lya's mother across the face. A moment later, when the colonel's anger has subsided, he kneels before Alicia, begging her forgiveness. Even the sanest and most balanced characters begin to lose their self-control, their reason and their common-sense overthrown in a situation where primitive, irrational impulses become the principal motivators. Indeed, when a flock of sheep enters the drawing room, the guests throw themselves upon the helpless animals like a pack of wolves. The sheep, together with a bear, have been introduced into the house much earlier by Lucía with a view to playing a practical joke upon her guests. In the present circumstances sophisticated bourgeois self-indulgence becomes indulgence of a totally savage kind.

Another glimpse of the world outside the house reveals a crowd, armed policemen, children with balloons, and a festive, fair-like atmosphere. The bourgeoisie has become a source of curiosity, an attraction for the masses. In terms of individuals, our attention is drawn to three men: a professor, a policeman and a priest. The professor is marked by his pomposity:

> I will address the newspapers, the public authorities. My voice must be heard. I am certain that I can find the solution to this problem.

The chief of police, ignoring the professor, is the usual Buñuelian dimwit. That he pays attention to the priest indicates a leaning towards superstition, and perhaps an awareness that the Church can generally benefit him more. The priest conveys an impression of humility and Christian charity. He has brought Christian's children to see the house where their father is imprisoned and persuades the little boy to try to enter. When he fails, the priest is annoyed and observes to the crowd:

> Never trust a child!

He has hoped, clearly, to be praised for the child's success, to be seen, perhaps, as a worker of miracles. Buñuel's portrayal of the people outside the house is no more flattering than that of those inside it. Only the innocent child is presented to us with any sympathy.

A transition returns us to the drawing room. A fire has been lit in the middle of the room and the guests are walking around or sitting down, eating greedily. Near the fire is a large pile of broken objects, of wool and stuffing torn from armchairs. The scene is reminiscent of the beggars' feast in *Viridiana*. Like the beggars, Nobile and his bourgeios counterparts have slaughtered the sheep and gnaw greedily at the bones. The cello, a symbol of culture and civilized refinement – we recall the piano of *Un Chien andalou* and the orchestra in *L'Age d'or* –, is smashed for firewood. In the middle of this mounting chaos, Alicia manicures her nails and Letitia puts on her lipstick. They are the token gestures, the tattered remnants of civilized society. Otherwise, links are firmly established between the humans and the animals. Nobile's head, for example, is bandaged. When a sheep is about to be killed, Letitia removes Nobile's bandage and uses it to cover the sheep's eyes. Ana refers deliriously to the shedding of the sheep's blood:

> We must have innocent blood . . . We must wait for the sacrifice of the last sheep.

Almost immediately Francisco's hand is seen to be covered in blood that is seeping from the closet where the lovers, Beatrice and Eduardo, have committed suicide. The various links suggest that the humans, in their actions as well as in their helplessness, are no different from the animals. Indeed, when Francisco suggests pushing Leandro into the room where the bear is prowling around, the joke barely conceals a fierce hostility. When, later, he attempts to carry out his threat, Leandro turns the tables on him, Juana furiously attacks Leandro, throws him to the floor and the two grapple like animals in a fight to the death, the world of primitive instinct, of wolves in men's clothing, is revealed to us in all its savagery. It is a world that points to the futility of social and religious organizations. Christian and Mr Roc, enacting a Masonic ritual in order to avert disaster, are merely absurd, mouthing vocal signs that, in the context of their predicament, is the equivalent of throwing stones at the gods.[11]

This episode, full of suggestive detail, is followed by a brilliant and revealing sequence in which, as in the earlier sequence of Ana's nightmare, we are made aware of the emotional torment of the characters. Voices, which are not the actual voices of the characters but the voices inside their heads, cry out in the darkness, the pattern of sounds mapping out, as it were, the fearful thoughts and dreams of the sleeping guests:

> WOMAN'S VOICE: Help!
> MAN'S VOICE: Quickly, shut the windows!
> UNKNOWN VOICE: Each man for himself!

MAN'S VOICE: In a moment there will be millions and millions of people in the drawing room.

The sounds are accompanied by visual images that are highly suggestive, as they dissolve into each other, of the shifting world of dream. A shot of a cloudy sky appears with a close-up of Raúl superimposed. It becomes a close-up of Letitia on which snow-covered woody mountains are superimposed slowly. The Pope appears on the mountain-top. A close-up of a saw cutting into a tree trunk is transformed into a shot of a saw cutting a hand. The tree becomes in turn a cello, the saw blade slicing through a woman's forehead. In its power to suggest the illogical and terrifying character of nightmare – the secret fears of a threatened bourgeoisie – this is one of Buñuel's most accomplished sequences.

Outside the house the servants are seen returning – the chef and his assistant, the two maids and the two valets. Their reappearance is as unplanned as their departure. Meeting each other unexpectedly, they are surprised and astonished by the remarkable coincidence:

VALET I *(catching his breath)*: The chef and the maids! Did you let them know we were coming?

VALET II: No, I didn't say anything.

VALET I: Well, what are they doing here?

This is a brief but significant episode. Buñuel foreshadows in the servants the way in which the whims and caprices of the irrational are about to effect their masters' release no less than they have marked the period of their incarceration.

In the drawing room a plot is hatched to dispose of Nobile. With the exception of the doctor and the colonel, the men have resolved that only Nobile's death will secure their own release. As the doctor and the colonel resist them – in the name of civilization – a violent struggle ensues. To avoid total disaster, Nobile makes a noble gesture: he will shoot himself. It is a sacrifice as absurd, in Buñuel's presentation of events, as the heroic stand by the colonel and the doctor, or Viridiana's efforts to change the world. In the end the guests are delivered from their fate not by the heroics of Nobile, the colonel and the doctor, nor by any conscious effort of their own, but by a pure element of chance, an absurdly irrational coincidence of circumstances. In the light of the bourgeoisie's frantic efforts to save itself, the simplicity of its release is delightfully ironic.

The camera focuses on Letitia who has made a sudden and startling discovery. The guests, without knowing it, have taken up the positions they were in on the evening of their arrival at Nobile's house. Excited by the discovery and unaware of the motives for their actions, they seek frantically to reconstruct the scene in all its detail:

LETITIA *(anxious about the outcome)*: Who started talking?
(A shot of SILVIA) Make an effort! Try to remember it!
SILVIA *(automatically)*: What a marvellous interpretation!
NOBILE, SILVIA and LETITIA are next to BLANCA.
LETITIA: Answer, Blanca! How did you reply?
BLANCA *(looking at SILVIA)*: Yes, yes . . .

Bit by bit the pieces are put together, the pattern completed. It is as though the experience of the previous days and nights has merely been an awful dream. Led by Letitia, a female Moses leading her people to the promised land, the joyful tribe of the bourgeoisie hurries from the room and out of the house to freedom. The episode is full of subversive humour. It is ironic, firstly, that, for all their efforts to save themselves and their firm belief that they have done so, Nobile and his guests have been saved by the pure chance, the illogical coincidence of their own regrouping. The irrational is to this extent as much their saviour as their scourge. It is ironic, too, that they should find release through the reenactment of those rites and rituals, that stylized mode of behaviour, that is itself the permanent prison of the bourgeoisie. The joke is, of course, Buñuel's and so is the last laugh – or rather, in this particular case, the last laugh but one.

The film's final sequence portrays the cathedral. A *Te Deum* is being sung. The cathedral is full of worshippers and at the altar a priest recites the *Ite missa est.* The camera passes along the front rows of the congregation and reveals Nobile, Lucía, Christian, Rita, Blanca, Letitia, Francisco, Raúl, Ana, the colonel, the doctor, Silvia, Leonora and Leandro. When the service ends the three priests walk towards the vestry door and, somewhat baffled, stop before it. The congregation jostles before the main door of the cathedral but no one leaves:

> *At the entrance of the cathedral, no one goes out.*
> FIRST MAN: We should stay here until they've all gone.
> SECOND MAN: That's what I said . . .
> WOMAN *(going back into the church)*: I've forgotten my missal.
> VOICES *(amid the confusion)*: What's going on? . . . Why don't they leave? . . . Let us through! . . . I can explain! . . . After you! . . . I'm in no hurry . . .

The guests have, of course, escaped only to return to the imprisonment of both social and religious institutions, the enclosed house paralled now by the interior of the cathedral, Nobile's mansion by God's house.[12] Outside shots are heard. In the square demonstrators are rioting and helmeted poilcemen are shooting at the crowd. People fall to the ground. A flock of sheep moves towards the cathedral and begins to enter. In this final episode Buñuel suggests that the bourgeoisie, on the point of extinction in the film, has an enormous capacity to protect and preserve itself. The revolution is bloody, the bourgeoisie has its defenders and its executioners – the police – and, when necessary, a willing supply of sacrificial victims.[13]

Critical opinion has often considered *The Exterminating Angel* to be, together with *L'Age d'or*, Buñuel's greatest film. Francisco Aranda has observed:

> In its language *El ángel exterminador* still remains the most distinctly and completely Surrealist film since *L'Age d'or*, and, in the writer's opinion, is second only to that film in Buñuel's whole *oeuvre*.[14]

The aims of the two films have much in common, for the attack on the bourgeoisie and the revelation of the unconscious are as central to the one as to the other. To this extent there are, inevitably, certain similarities of style, but in *The Exterminating Angel*, thirty two years on and some twenty eight films later, Buñuel's technique is clearly more polished and refined.

In *L'Age d'or* satire of the bourgeoisie – of its image and its values – was often achieved through simple juxtapositions: the dignified ceremony contrasted with wildly embracing lovers, elegant guests with drunken peasants, neat rows of seats with chairs overturned. Contrasts and incongruities of various kinds, an essential part of Buñuel's satiric intent, were created in a bold and direct manner, as in the case of quickly alternating shots. In *The Exterminating Angel* the process is both more subtle and concise. The bourgeois image is subverted not by its juxtaposition with other things, external to itself, but by a kind of self-subversion, by the appearance within the bourgeoisie of all those evils that in *L'Age d'or* seem different and apart from it. In terms of technique two of *L'Age d'or*'s separate images – elegant guest/rough peasant – are now forged into one highly concentrated and expressive shot. The film is full of such succinct incongruities – elegantly clad bodies littering the drawing room floor, dishevelled women trying to arrange their hair, a refined lady eating paper, a gentleman greedily gnawing at sheep's bones. In comparison with the earlier film the visual economy of *The Exterminating Angel* is a source of wonder.

One of the film's most powerful visual impressions is that of mounting chaos and confusion. It derives in part from Buñuel's fascination with concrete objects and from the way in which he uses the camera to present them to us. From the very beginning of *The Exterminating Angel* the camera picks out a whole array of objects – a candelabra, glasses, food, chairs, ornaments, all the insignia of the bourgeoisie. They express the order and the organization of a way of life. In the course of the film these objects are merely arranged differently – the pile of rubble on the floor, the broken furniture, the smashed cello – but presented with the same, almost obsessive sense of detail. The camera travels slowly around the drawing room, as though it were our own eyes, and in that sense constructs bit by bit, object by object, a sense of chaos that has the tangible quality of reality itself.

In purely visual terms the repetitions are important. Nobile and his guests enter the house twice, he repeats his toast, at the end of the film the guests assume once more their earlier positions, and finally they are all imprisoned for a second time. Buñuel uses the repeats for various purposes. They are in part, his joke, his own manipulation, as director, of people who normally manipulate the lives of others. They convey too, of course, in their very stylization, the repetitions and duplications of actions that are the very stuff of everyday life and which, in the peculiarly mannered society of the bourgeoisie, acquire that extra dimension of stiltedness. And above all they suggest the absurdity of individuals who, failing to control their actions, become puppets jerked back and forth in a world ruled by the whims of time and an absence of logic.

The expression of unconscious urges, always Buñuel's special province, is rarely far from the surface of *The Exterminating Angel.* In the earlier part of the film the women describe what they saw in the closet – a raging torrent, an eagle, a whirling mass of leaves. They are at this stage merely verbal images, although very expressive of subconscious feelings. In the increasing delirium that descends upon the household, the verbal images acquire a visual dimension and the language of the film becomes at given moments the graph of human fears and obsessions. The hand, its whiteness heightened by the darkness, is a truly haunting image, reminiscent of the hand in *Un Chien Andalou* and, like it, an association deeply embedded in the human psyche. It is not merely Ana's secret fears but all our fears which Buñuel exposes. The later sequence is, in its cinematic quality, entirely masterly. The series of dissolves – the saw cutting the tree, then the hand, then the forehead – has all the blurred and shifting quality of nightmare, while the accompanying sounds – of the saw, of thunder, of confused voices – are more effective in their evocation of the chaotic, terror-ridden world of dream than any background music. In a sense Buñuel is back in the psychic world of *Un Chien Andalou*, the hand and the mutilated eye re-worked in a variety of ways.

The script of *The Exterminating Angel* is, like that of *Viridiana*, extremely fine, always enhancing Buñuel's pictures. In the early part of the film the dialogue captures perfectly the note of polite sophistication and refined social chit-chat, and simultaneously, as a consequence of Buñuel's timely interventions and subversions, that air of absurdity that he so obviously delights in:

RAÚL: . . . Poor Leonora. *(Pause)* And how is her cancer? Is there any hope?
DOCTOR: None at all. I give her three months before she goes completely bald.
RAÚL: She is certainly in fine shape!

Later, as the masks of refinement fall away, the dialogue expresses equally well both the individual and the collective anguish, the public and the private fears and torments of the imprisoned guests. If Buñuel is the master of the visual image, especially in relation to its representation of the inner life, he reveals too an unusual ability to express the latter in the spoken word.

NOTES

[1] See Francisco Aranda, *Luis Buñuel . . .*, p. 210.

[2] See Aranda, p. 212.

[3] *Luis Buñuel*, p. 126.

[4] See 'A Letter on *The Exterminating Angel*', in *The World of Luis Buñuel*, p. 254.

[5] *Luis Buñuel . . .*, p. 212.

[6] See Aranda, pp. 211-12.

[7] Of the repetitions Buñuel's son has written: 'As to the repetition of events . . . there are some twenty identical repetitions . . . [It] is just an idea he had. He says, 'In everyday life we repeat ourselves every day. Every morning we get up, we brush our teeth with the same brush and with the same hand and movements, we sit at the same breakfast table, we go to the same office, meet the same people . . . and how many times has it happened in a party where we say hello to someone and an hour later we again shake hands, say hello, and then exclaim. "Oh, what are we doing, we just said hello a minute ago" . . .' See 'A Letter on *The Exterminating Angel*', *The World of Luis Buñuel*, p. 255.

[8] Joan Mellen observes: 'Their hastening incapacity causes them now to treat each other in ways once reserved for their victims. Buñuel uses the narrative device of their entrapment in one room to reveal the character and qualities they ordinarily take great pains to conceal'. See 'An Overview of Buñuel's Career', in *The World of Luis Buñuel*, p. 12.

[9] See Michel Estève, '*The Exterminating Angel*: No Exit From the Human Condition', in *The World of Luis Buñuel*, pp. 247-48: 'As the hours pass, and day follows night in a rigorous, implacable monotony, the masks fall, one by one, reduced to ashes in the fire of truth. And this, man's truth as it is presented by Buñuel, reveals, little by little, its fundamental ferocity. By a violence as subtle as it is insistent, *The Exterminating Angel* underscores the conflict between the essence of the individual and his mask. Abandoning their coats, shedding their gowns, the guests – prisoners in their own hell – cast off their façades. Seen in this perspective, Buñuel's film is the antithesis to his *Robinson Crusoe*. As opposed to the sound man "in a state of nature", the "social" man, elegant, sophisticated, distinguished in diplomatic or military circles, becomes, in the face of peril, "a wolf of a man" '. Estève's essay, published originally

in *Etudes Cinématographiques*, pp. 22-3 (Spring 1963), examines the points of contact between *The Exterminating Angel* and Sartre's *No Exit*.

[10] *The Beast With Five Fingers* was made in 1945. The director, Robert Florey, had asked Buñuel for his ideas on the dream-sequence. In the finished version only the episode of the severed hand was retained, but it is interesting to note that it was this that captured the attention both of some of the French film critics and of the Surrealists themselves.

[11] See Ado Kyro, 'Surrealism in *The Exterminating Angel*', in *Modern Film Scripts: The Exterminating Angel, Nazarín* and *Los olvidados*, London: Lorrimer Publishing, 1972, p. 10: 'All rituals, all religious antics, all idealisms are shown to be powerless. The yellow flag is the sole, humiliating sign which applies to all the slaves alike'.

[12] Michele Estève, '*The Exterminating Angel* . . .', p. 249, observes: 'The guests leave the salon at last, but they can only understand the Te Deum as a new call to the old social structure, and they quickly don their masks of respectability and go on as before'.

[13] In relation to the revolution Joan Mellen makes a very perceptive comment: 'As the rioters are gunned down, the scene discloses that those servants who first escaped from the house at the beginning of the film will have the following choices: returning like sheep to the side of their masters; being shot in cold blood if they protest ineffectively; or preparing a fight to the finish. Those who reject the last of these alternatives will share the doom reserved for their "betters"'. See 'An Overview of Buñuel's Career', p. 12.

[14] *Luis Buñuel* . . . , p. 210.

7
BELLE DE JOUR

CAST

Séverine	—	Catherine Deneuve
Husson	—	Michel Piccoli
Hippolyte	—	Francisco Rabal
Charlotte	—	Françoise Fabian
M. Adolphe	—	Francis Blanche
The Professor	—	François Maistre
Pallas	—	Muni
Pierre	—	Jean Sorel
Anais	—	Geneviève Page
Marcel	—	Pierre Clementi
Mathilde	—	Maria Latour
The Duke	—	Georges Marchal
Renée	—	Macha Meril
Catherine	—	Dominique Dandrieux

Photography	—	Sacha Vierney
Editor	—	Louisette Hautecoeur
Art Director	—	Robert Clavel
Sound	—	René Longuet
Production	—	Paris Film Production,
		Robert and Raymond Hakim
Director of Production	—	Henri Baum
Script	—	Luis Buñuel
		Jean-Claude Carrière
Assistant Directors	—	Pierre Lary
		Jacques Fraenkel
Director	—	Luis Buñuel

In the four years that separate *The Exterminating Angel* and *Belle de Jour* Buñuel considered various projects and made two films: *Le Journal d'une femme de chambre*, a French-Italian production of 1963, and *Simón del desierto*, a Mexican production of 1965. The first of these two films is an adaptation of Octave Mirbeau's book of the same name, of which Jean Renoir had already made a film in 1946. The setting of a bourgeois country house allowed Buñuel to develop, through the characters who live in it, his favourite themes of perverted bourgeois sexuality, while servants and neighbours reflect different brands of left and right-wing political ideology. The film has a strong political atmosphere, for Buñuel set the action in the years preceding the Second World War, but it has, above all, a range of characters – from the grandfather with his collection of dirty pictures and ladies' boots to the sex-murderer servant – who provide a constant and rich source of fascination. *Simón del desierto*, on the other hand, returns to Buñuel's preoccupation with religion. Simón is a holy man from the beginning of the Christian era who, dedicated to the ascetic life, has spent the last fourteen years perched on top of a pillar in the desert. He addresses the watching people, many of whom ignore him. In the film's epilogue he is transported to a night-club in modern New York, attempts to drive Satan away, but fails. Simón is, in effect, another Nazarín, and in him Buñuel embodied once again the theme of the futility of Christian ideals in a world impervious to change.

Work on *Belle de Jour* began in 1966 after the failure of Buñuel's plan to make a film based on Matthew Gregory Lewis's *The Monk*. The French producers, Robert and Raymond Hakim, approached Buñuel with a view to making a film adapted from Joseph Kessel's novel, *Belle de Jour*, written in 1929, and in the course of a mere five weeks he and Jean-Claude Carrière had completed the script. Shooting began in the summer of 1966, scheduled to take ten weeks, but in the event requiring only eight. Submitted as the French entry at the Venice Film Festival, *Belle de Jour* won the Golden Lion of St. Mark and a prize awarded by a group of independent journalists. In general, however, the critical reaction to the film was and has remained somewhat mixed. In Venice the public response was not unanimously favourable. In France, on the other hand, and afterwards in Britain, the public were enthusiastic. The French press proved to be divided, ranging from the polite coolness of *Paris Match* to the rhapsodic praises of *L'Express*. Joseph Kessel, the author of the book, observed that 'Buñuel's genius has surpassed all that I could have hoped. It [the film] is at one and the same time the book and not the book. We are in another dimension: that of the subconscious, of dreams and secret instincts suddenly laid bare. And what formal beauty in the images! And beneath the severity, the most contained and most moving pit'.[1] In contrast, Francisco Aranda's opinion that '*Belle de Jour* is something less than we might have looked for from Buñuel's maturity' reflects the doubts that many critics continue to have about the film.[2]

Of Kessel's novel Buñuel himself stated: 'The book does not please me in the least'.[3] In outline there are, though, close similarities between the novel and the film. In both the beautiful Séverine, married to the handsome surgeon, Pierre Sérizy, yet discontented with her unexciting bourgeois lot, becomes obsessed by the thought of working in a brothel. Kessel's, no less than Buñuel's heroine, responds to masochistic impulses, longs to be dominated sexually in a way that she is not by her husband, and finds in Marcel, a young gangster, the kind of aggressive lover who satisfies her needs. In novel and film the ending, too, is for the most part similar. Marcel attempts to kill a friend of Pierre's who is about to disclose the truth about Séverine, the plan misfires and Pierre is seriously injured. He is subsequently paralyzed and confined to a wheelchair. Séverine, overwhelmed by guilt, confesses to Pierre, and he refuses to speak to her again. In Buñuel's film the ending is different in the sense that it is Pierre's friend, Husson, who reveals the truth to him. Pierre, moreover, far from rejecting Séverine, seems to accept her for what she is and for what she has done to him, while she indulges in a daydream of a happy future.

Buñuel's *Belle de Jour* has, clearly, the narrative line of Kessel's book, much as *Nazarín* retains the framework of Galdós's novel. On the other hand, Buñuel seized on the surrealist threads, the sexual and psychological implications of the novel, and proceeded to weave them into one of his richest and most complex tapestries. Before making the film, he drew attention to the source of his real interest in the story:

> This novel of the twenties, of the period of Paul Morand, done in a realistic style, is about the masochistic impulses of a woman who, fearing that she is frigid, ends by working in brothels. I hope I can save such a stale subject by mixing indiscriminately and without warning in the montage the things that actually happen to the heroine, and the fantasies and morbid impulses which she imagines. As the film proceeds, I am going to increase the frequency of these interpolations, and at the end, in the final sequence, the audience will not be able to know if what is happening to her is actual or the heroine's subjective world – reality or nightmare.[4]

The finished film is not, in effect, as puzzling or disconcerting in its distinction between external and internal reality as Buñuel implied in this interview, but in terms of its emphasis upon the revelation of the subconscious it is certainly Buñuel's most consistently surrealist film since *Un Chien andalou* and *L'Age d'or*. Elliot Stern has observed that *Belle de Jour* 'is close in spirit to his first great film, *L'Age d'or*. Indeed, one of the things in *Belle de Jour* which seems to have bothered people is its fidelity to what can only be called the true spirit of surrealism: ... the invigorating, positive, liberating surrealism which marked *L'Age d'or*, caused riots when that film was first shown, and resulted in its being banned for a generation. The result is more mellow, less overtly aggressive than *L'Age d'or*, even calm. But it is all there'.[5] The triumph of Buñuel's film lies undoubtedly in its evocation of the passions that boil beneath that calm, aristocratic, untouchable image conveyed by Séverine. In giving herself to them, Séverine takes up again the cause of Gaston Modot and Lya Lys against a bourgeois society whose values and morality she, the cool, expensive, conservative, emotionally stunted woman, reflects. For all its glittering façade, its plush and elegant surface, *Belle de Jour* is as corrosive and subversive as any of Buñuel's earlier films.

The credits appear against a shot of a secluded track in the Bois de Bologne. An open landau drawn by two horses, with liveried coachman and footman, comes towards the camera, and in the landau are Pierre and Séverine. The landau passes by to the sound of a jingling harness and is then seen in another shot approaching along a more deserted track. In the first conversation of the film, Pierre speaks of Séverine's coldness towards him and she, annoyed by the remark, refers to his failure to arouse her. Pierre's manner towards his wife suddenly changes from tenderness to roughness, he instructs the coachman to stop, they tie Séverine to a tree, Pierre rips the clothes from her back, instructs the servants to beat her with whips and, when they have carried out his orders to his satisfaction, allows them to make love to her. Séverine's reaction to these events is seen to consist of a mixture of repugnance and pleasure. When the footman touches her bare shoulders she is fearful but expectant. When the coachman kisses her naked back she closes her eyes in horror and in ecstasy.

This is one of Buñuel's most powerful and suggestive sequences. Typically Freudian in its associations (the rope that ties Séverine, the phallic tree and the whips, the gag in her mouth), it exteriorizes Séverine's sexual obsessions. Moreover, the links between the unconscious and reality are firmly and convincingly established. The opening scene is

Severine's fantasy

Séverine's daydream as she lies in bed waiting for Pierre. When he gets in beside her, he kisses her with the tenderness which in the daydream has been the basis of her accusation against him. Similarly, when he leans towards her, she reacts to his advances with the coldness already witnessed before. In the world of fantasy Pierre has, of course, become a different man – the dominating, sexually aggressive figure that Séverine would like him to be towards her. In the reality of their bedroom, on the other hand, he merely accepts her coldness with resignation as he turns away from her and puts out the light:

> SÉVERINE: Please forgive me. You are so kind . . . and so understanding, but I . . .
> *(The camera pans to PIERRE, who says brusquely)*
> PIERRE: Never mind. Go to sleep. *(He turns away from her).*

Here, as elsewhere, the obsessions of Buñuel's characters are firmly and inexorably rooted in the reality of their own lives.

A new sequence is set in a winter sports resort. Images of bars and shops and of bronzed and elegant people establish the essentially bourgeois setting of the film. In particular we are introduced to Henri Husson, an ageing playboy and inveterate womanizer. His conversation with his mistress, Renée, is a stylized and empty game of words and gestures; a ritual they have enacted many times before. When Pierre and Séverine appear, it presents Husson with another opportunity to display his cynical worldliness. In some respects Husson reminds us of the bourgeois gentlemen of *L'Age d'or* who react with total indifference to the servant's suffering and pay scant attention even to the shooting of the gamekeeper's son. He is, in short, an empty man, but if he is incapable of any kind of passionate commitment, he is in this respect not so much different from Pierre and Séverine as an older, emptier form of them. Inasmuch as they are emotional cripples, isolated within themselves and from each other by feelings and attitudes largely conditioned by the society in which they live, they, no less than Husson, are its spokesmen.

Séverine and Renée, Husson's mistress, are seen in the back of a Paris taxi. Renée observes that Henriette, a mutual friend, is given to working in a brothel. Séverine's reaction to this information is at first indifference, but, as Renée continues, becomes a mixture of that attraction and revulsion that distinguished her behaviour in the day-dream:

> *While RENÉE has been speaking SÉVERINE'S expression has completely changed. She has become very interested, but subsequently she seems to share RENÉE'S revulsion.*

The taxi driver's account of his own experience of taking customers to brothels deepens her curiosity. When the taxi stops before the apartment house where Séverine lives, a shot of the building underlines its comfortable bourgeois character and provides a telling contrast to the dark world of sexuality that lies outside her social and emotional experience but to which she now increasingly responds. In its portrayal of a woman awakened to the world, *Belle de Jour* has an affinity with *Viridiana* and Séverine is as much the repressed victim of her social environment as is Viridiana of her convent education.[6]

A shot of Séverine's elegantly furnished drawing room with its expensive and tasteful furniture sustains the bourgeois image. The setting is, on the other hand, a frame for the expression of sexual longings and memories both dark and revealing. When Séverine drops a vase of flowers and, shortly afterwards, knocks over a bottle of perfume, it is clear that her thoughts are concentrated still on the conversation in the taxi. This, moreover, is firmly linked now to an episode from her past, revealed to us in a second daydream. The camera reveals the legs of a little girl – reminiscent of *Viridiana* – and the knees of a workman who is kneeling on the floor. In another shot the man is seen to have his arms around the girl and, when he kisses her, she closes her eyes and holds her breath. In terms of her adult life the incident explains both Séverine's sexual coldness towards her husband and her barely admitted-to but growing fascination with the secretive sexual exploits of Henriette and the other prostitutes. Between the reaction of the young Séverine to the advances of the rough workman and the feelings of attraction and repulsion experienced by the adult woman in her obsessive dream of sexual violation there is a firm and clear parallel. It is evident too that Séverine the child, overwhelmed by feelings of fear and guilt, had never spoken to her mother of the sexual assault. From her childhood she is seen to be, like many of Buñuel's characters, a person inhibited by a constricting sense of conventional morality, yet someone who is simultaneously attracted, in a very human way, by the very things that cause her guilt.

If Séverine's childhood plays its part in her sexual development, so does her essentially sterile bourgeois marriage. A sequence set in Pierre's study contains some revealing symbols, notably his books which, as in *Un Chien andalou* and *L'Age d'or*, point to the inhibiting and deadening influence of culture. Séverine's embroidery is also an activity that, practised every night, suggests the lifeless, self-perpetuating ritual of bourgeois existence:

> *It is as though PIERRE and SÉVERINE meet here every evening and occupy the same places.*

But crucial too in its effect upon her is Pierre's attitude to women. Revealing to Séverine that, before his marriage to her, he regularly frequented brothels, Pierre suggests too that for him there are two different mutually exclusive kinds of women: those on whom he can expend his lust – the prostitutes – and those, like Séverine, who decorate his life like ornaments. It is an attitude as damaging to her as to himself, and explains in part his failure to arouse her. In addition, Pierre's chauvinism has a hint of cynicism evocative of Husson's and, for all the difference between them, identifies them both as bourgeois cousins.[7]

An encounter with Husson at a tennis club confirms his sexual cynicism and accelerates Séverine's awakening. Husson's account of his own experience of brothels, intended to impress her with his worldliness, touches a particular chord in Séverine. His allusion to the prostitutes as women who are 'completely enslaved' is one which, matching Séverine's dream image of herself bound and gagged and subjected to male sexual domination, conjures up an increasingly fascinating vision. It is significant that Séverine ignores the advances of the calculating but emotionally empty Husson. The ageing philanderer, scratching at the surface of passion, cannot meet her needs any more effectively than can her husband.

The commencement of Séverine's journey of self-discovery is predictably difficult and faltering, the shedding of the masks of many years a slow and painful process. In a new sequence she is seen in the street mentioned earlier by Husson, her own inhibitions contrasting with the prostitute who passes her with a careless swinging of the hips. As Séverine climbs the stairs (we recall this Freudian motif in *Un Chien andalou*) to Madame Anais's establishment, her conscience presents her with another inhibiting, guilt-ridden childhood memory. It is her first communion. When the priest offers her the wafer, commending her soul to our Lord Jesus Christ, Séverine stubbornly keeps her mouth closed, rejecting the body of Christ despite the priest's insistent, accusing words – 'Séverine, Séverine, what's wrong with you?' The incident has haunted her ever since, interwoven with the childhood sexual assault in a close-knit pattern of religious and sexual guilt. Throughout her first encounter with Madame Anais, Séverine continues to be assailed by doubts, but in agreeing to work for her from two until five each afternoon she begins to free herself from the constraints of her past existence.

Séverine's second visit to Madame Anais's is marked,

significantly, by images of a more overtly sexual nature, pointers to her sexual awakening. A shot of Séverine's feet as she climbs the stairs links with the earlier shot of the little girl's legs – and it is also, of course, reminiscent of the predominant sexual motifs of *Viridiana.* A little later the camera focuses on Madame Anais's hands:

> *A close-up of the drinks trolley. We see ANAIS'S hands as she ladles cherries in brandy from a jar . . .*

We are reminded, perhaps, of a shot in *L'Age d'or* of the servant's hands on a caraffe of wine, an explicit phallic symbol. It is, in any case, evocative of the earlier shot of the priest's hands:

> *. . . medium close-up of his hands as he dips a wafer in the golden chalice . . .*

In shifting the emphasis from religious to wordly associations, Buñuel suggests very clearly Séverine's growing response to the world of the senses. When she shakes her hair loose, she lets it down in more than a literal sense. And when each afternoon between two and five she assumes the name of Belle de Jour, she acquires with that name a new identity.

A first glimpse of the prostitutes and of one of the customers introduces a note of gaiety. Monsieur Adolphe is a small, paunchy, vulgar and rather silly middle-aged man, but, for all his vulgarity, he is full of zest, given to verbal and practical joking and pinching the girls' bottoms. As he stands with his arms around the two girls, Charlotte and Mathilde, he pronounces his simple philosophy of life:

> Here's to fun. . . . That's the way I am. I enjoy living. And I want everyone else to laugh.

Monsieur Adolphe's sexual activities, embodying his fun-loving attitude to things, are expressed in the practical joke in which a long snake (with, perhaps, phallic implications) leaps from a box into Mathilde's face, reducing the company to helpless laughter. If Buñuel disapproves of this vulgar little man, he is at least free from Séverine's inhibitions. She is, of course, unsettled by such vulgar jollity. She has attempted to leave even before Monsieur Adolphe's appearance. As he hugs Charlotte, kisses her breasts and slaps her behind, Séverine watches uncertainly. When they all drink her health, she experiences feelings of amazement and fear. Just as in the setting of Madame Anais's establishment Séverine's elegant and expensive dress is out of place, so her conventional attitudes continue to inhibit her. There are, on the other hand, moments which expose very clearly her longing, expressed already in her daydreams, for sexual domination. When, obedient to her bourgeois attitudes, Séverine resists Monsieur Adolphe, Madame Anais treats her with an unexpected forcefulness:

> *SÉVERINE stands with a strange expression on her face, as though her fear and desire to escape had suddenly left her. It is as though she expected to be treated like this, as though she wanted it.*

Alone with Monsieur Adolphe, Séverine is overcome by horror and repulsion, but when he seizes her and throws her on the bed, she willingly succumbs:

> *Then he leans over her and the camera tilts down. He falls on top of her, kissing her roughly. She does not resist him any longer.*

Séverine's dream of sexual domination, has, in effect, become reality, albeit an imperfect one in the figure of Monsieur Adolphe.

A transition takes us to Séverine's flat, later the same day. She is taking a shower and rubbing herself vigorously, while a subsequent shot reveals her burning her underclothes and stockings. It is a ritual in which, dominated by her guilty conscience, Séverine attempts to cleanse herself – physically, and in other senses too – of the experience of the afternoon. A daydream, introduced by the sound of cow-bells, powerfully illustrates the continuing hold of guilt upon her.[8] The scene is set in the Camargue, a herd of wild bulls gallops past, and Pierre and Husson are seen in conversation. The tolling of a church bell, together with the men's allusions to religion, indicate the predominant trend of Séverine's subconscious thoughts. Her daydream is a variation on the obsessive daydream of the film's beginning, for Séverine's hands are again tied, but in other respects longing has given way to guilt. She wears a long, white sleeveless robe, symbolic of the purity to which she should aspire. The coachman and the footman have become Pierre and Husson who pelt her with mud and hurl abuse at her. They embody both the degradation to which she has submitted and the accusing voice of her own conscience. Séverine's guilt, no less than her desire, is expressed by Buñuel in a consistently vivid and convincing manner.

For all her reservations, Séverine's sexual longing increasingly asserts itself, and a week later she is back at Madame Anais's. Her second customer, a professor of gynaecology, provides Buñuel with the opportunity for some splendidly and often hilariously funny situations relating to bourgeois sexuality in all its variations. However, the scene also has a striking psychological truthfulness. When the professor emerges from the bathroom he is dressed as a servant and his manner is entirely submissive. In the sense that he is someone who seeks domination, he is Séverine's counterpart, but since he is also the opposite of the kind of man she wants, Séverine cannot meet his needs and Charlotte takes her place. Observing Charlotte's expert domination of the professor, Séverine is fascinated and repelled, for she identifies with him and shares his experience. The scene is the equivalent of her dream and she, as in the dream, is an observer – if not of herself, of someone very like herself. For all its humour, the incident is revealing in relation to Séverine's inner life.

This fantasy experience becomes reality with the appearance of a powerfully built oriental gentleman.

Séverine is fascinated by his impressively muscled body and responds to him with a warmth we have not seen in her before. It is a very different woman who flings her arms around his neck and who, at the end of the sequence, is seen to be flushed, happy and calm: a woman newly born to her sexuality. It is significant too that the oriental gentleman speaks only his own language, for the lack of verbal communication highlights the physical and emotional rapport which he establishes with Séverine. Buñuel underlines the importance of the moment in two apparently bizarre but otherwise clearly meaningful details. Firstly, the oriental gentleman carries a mysterious box whose contents, if any, are never revealed to us. Although the box makes a buzzing sound, it is otherwise strongly reminiscent of the box in *Un Chien andalou* which, in Freudian terms, symbolizes the vagina and therefore anticipates here the oriental's sexual possession of Séverine. Secondly, the oriental holds a little bell in his left hand which he shakes. The sound of the bell evokes Séverine's sexual fantasies, but, inasmuch as the oriental is a real man of flesh and blood, those fantasies have taken on an actual significance. The sequence as a whole is one which marks a decisive step in Séverine's sexual self-discovery.

Another extended dream sequence is introduced by the sound of bells. The landau of the opening scene appears once again in the Bois de Boulogne with the same coachman and footman, but now Pierre's place is taken by an older man, a smartly dressed individual of aristocratic appearance. Stopping at an open-air café where he sees Séverine, the Duke persuades her to accompany him to his country château where he proceeds to enact a ritual in which closely interwoven images of sex, religion and death evoke Séverine's confused state of mind: desire and guilt mingled with thoughts of death. Séverine, otherwise naked, is made by the Duke's servant to wear a long black veil attached to a crown of flowers and is taken by him to a chapel where the Duke has just attended Mass. She lies in a coffin, her hands crossed as if dead, and the Duke places lilies on her body, weeping, addressing her gently, and expressing his guilt for his involvement in her death. Almost without warning, though, his mood changes, he laughs grimly, disappears beneath the coffin and, as the thunder rolls, it begins to rock. A startled Séverine looks over the side of the coffin and is both disgusted and interested by what she sees. The Duke's tenderness towards her is, perhaps, an echo of Pierre. The religious associations link with Séverine's shameful memory of the communion service. Inasmuch as the Duke's tenderness becomes sexual aggression, it accords with Séverine's secret longings. He embodies, in effect, what she wants Pierre to be – a man who sets aside a fatherly tenderness in favour of a passion that will fulfill her. At the end of the sequence Séverine is seized by the servant and thrown out into the pouring rain:

> *He takes her arm and pulls her roughly towards the open door. . . . With a brutal push he turns her out into the pouring rain, picks up her coat and throws it after her. . . .*

The brutality of the incident is reminiscent of both the behaviour of the coachman and the footman in the first dream sequence and of Pierre and Husson throwing mud at Séverine. It is an episode which, in its intermingling and interweaving of various obsessive strands, exposes in a completely convincing manner the confused and shifting world of the unconscious.[9]

A brief transition to Séverine's bedroom suggests that in her relationship with Pierre there is a new warmth, a shedding of the sexual coldness to which he has referred. She reveals the eagerness displayed at Madame Anais's in the encounter with the oriental gentleman, and if the scene in the bedroom is superficially reminiscent of earlier episodes, it also presents Séverine as a different woman:

> . . . More and more I want to be alone with you. I'm not afraid of you any more. I seem to understand you

> better and to be closer to you . . . I love you more each day . . .

As Séverine has, between two and five, flowered into Belle de Jour, so Belle de Jour lives increasingly in Séverine.

The appearance of Husson, who is still absorbed by Séverine, anticipates his role in the film's conclusion. Séverine refuses to see him, but his arrival at her house occasions another daydream, set in the winter sports resort seen earlier in the film. Husson's attraction to Séverine is interwoven now with incidents from the dream involving the Duke, reality and dream become confused and blurred, overlapping in another fantasy. Séverine and Husson, in a clear repetition of the Duke's disappearance beneath the coffin, crawl beneath the table, and shortly afterwards the table begins to rock. It is Renée now who peers beneath the table to observe the scene. She sees Husson holding a packet of lily seeds – a detail reminiscent of the Duke placing lilies on Séverine. The sequence, like the previous dream, defies logical explanation. As the film unfolds, Buñuel's exposure of Séverine's inner life traces an increasingly complicated pattern, mapping out an intricate series of responses to what has become for her a richer, more varied and more complex experience of living.

A new sequence introduces Marcel, who is to affect Séverine profoundly. He is engaged with Hippolyte, a much older man, in a robbery, after which they make their way to Madame Anais's. Hippolyte is an old and garrulous customer. Marcel, a newcomer to the establishment, says little, but already he is seen to have an authority which impresses itself on Séverine. When Hippolyte shows an inclination to have Séverine for himself, Marcel merely reaches out and puts his cane – a phallic symbol – between them. He is the strong, dominant figure to whom Séverine is increasingly attracted, and when they go into the bedroom it is she, uncharacteristically, who takes the initiative:

> *She throws them* [*boots*] *aside and embraces him. They kiss.*

For her Marcel has an arrogance, a directness, a sheer physical presence which she finds irresistible. His gold teeth, replacing those knocked out in a fight, and the scar which Séverine fingers on his shoulder blade, are the insignia of a man very different from Pierre; a man of action who wears his battle wounds like medals.[10] The end of the sequence reveals Marcel and Séverine entwined on the bed. In this violent, assertive youth – the embodiment of the sexual brutality she longs for – she has found both her ideal lover and her true self.

Séverine's awakening to her husband, suggested in an earlier sequence, is, of course, affected by her meeting with Marcel. A shot of a long, deserted beach in the south of France, in autumn or winter, is the frame for a scene which presents Pierre and Séverine's dejection. He is convinced that she is hiding something from him, while she is bored by her absence from Paris and Marcel. When Pierre refers once more to the coldness that seems to distinguish her attitude towards him, Séverine draws a distinction between physical and spiritual love:

> There are so many things that I want to understand . . . things about myself. . . . My feelings for you have nothing to do with pleasure. . . . There's much more to it than that. . . . You probably won't believe me, but I've never felt so close to you. . . .

If her experience has revealed to her the existence of different kinds and levels of love, it has in another sense, through the physical nature of her feelings for Marcel, confirmed the more platonic nature of her marital relationship. Furthermore, however much Pierre seeks to transform their sexless relationship, the possibility of such a transformation is now denied to him.

Marcel is seen again in a shady bar in a Paris street, engaged with Hippolyte in a drugs transaction with two other men. It is an episode which underlines once more Marcel's aggression, for a comment directed at him leads him to whip out a knife and he is forcibly restrained by Hippolyte. But the main emphasis of the episode is on his fascination with Séverine. If the cool, elegant bourgeois woman has found her ideal lover in this physical and violent youth, he paradoxically has discovered in her a constant fascination. News of her return to Paris sends him rushing off to Madame Anais's:

> . . . *MARCEL'S face lights up. He grabs the second ear-piece wildly and puts it to his other ear.*
> MARCEL: Since when? It's a fact? . . . I'm coming over.

In their eager pursuit of passion Marcel and Séverine resemble another Gaston Modot and his longed-for Lya thirty-five years on.

A sequence at Madame Anais's presents a violent conflict between Marcel and Séverine, in the course of which, angered by her absence from Paris, Marcel threatens her with his leather belt. Séverine, reacting spiritedly, reveals an unaccustomed anger and resolve, her eyes blazing:

> If you do that again, I'll leave . . . and you won't see me ever again.

Subsequently, anger and frustration give way to a passion of equal intensity as the lovers fall on the bed. With Marcel, Séverine has learned to feel, to experience and express true, powerful emotion. When he asks her about her feelings towards himself and towards her husband, Séverine's reply is significant:

> They are two quite separate things.

It is clear that, in terms of true sexuality, Pierre and Séverine are doomed. When, indeed, in a brief episode at the hospital where he works, an empty wheelchair disturbs Pierre, there is already an ominous foreboding of the cripple he is soon to become.

Husson's unexpected appearance as a customer at

Madame Anais's throws Séverine into a state of total panic. In a highly emotional moment she reveals her detestation of him, an attitude which sharpens his sense of resentment and of delight in his newly-acquired power over her:

> . . . You enjoy being humiliated . . . I do not . . . I will say nothing to Pierre. . . . But my friends will be delighted to know you are here. I could send you some customers.

As the film approaches its conclusion, Séverine is, in a sense, a tragic figure. It is Husson who initially mentioned Madame Anais's, he who discovers her there, and he who can now expose her. The bourgeois philanderer to whom true passion is a closed book stalks Séverine throughout the film; the embodiment, perhaps, of a bourgeois cynicism which, insensitive to deep emotional needs, reduces them to its own debased image. At all events, Séverine's fear of Husson affects her deeply and is revealed in a significantly changed version of the first daydream of the film. The camera reveals the landau in the Bois de Boulogne, while another carriage is seen approaching. Pierre descends from the first, Husson from the second, and they prepare to fight a duel. As Pierre turns, raises his pistol and shoots, he suddenly catches sight of Séverine. She wears the clothes she wore in the first sequence of the film, she is tied to the same tree, but now she is dead, struck in the temple by a bullet. Séverine's erotic daydream of physical pleasure with the servants has been transformed by her meeting with Husson into a terrible vision of social disgrace and the vengeance of a wronged husband. In Freudian language guns are as much sexual symbols as whips but for Séverine they are now associated more with sexual guilt than pleasure.

Séverine, as a consequence of her fear of Husson, has ceased to work at Madame Anais's. In a new sequence Marcel, anxious to know the cause of her disappearance, is seen arriving at her apartment. He is his old, insolent, casual self, while Séverine, overcome by fear of Pierre's return, is once again the plaything of her conscience:

Her fear increases steadily through the scene, and MARCEL'S apparent indifference only makes her more fearful still.

Now, however, things change suddenly and decisively. Not long after she has persuaded Marcel to leave, Séverine hears three gunshots in the street. Marcel is seen driving furiously away, while the body of a man lies on the pavement. Marcel's car, out of control, crashes into another, he tries to escape, shoots at a policeman, and is shot dead in the subsequent exchanges.

A short scene in the hospital reveals that the man shot by Marcel is Pierre. He has little hope of complete recovery, and when we next see Pierre and Séverine together in their apartment he is in a wheelchair, completely paralysed, blind, and unable to speak. Séverine is calm, at peace, and treats Pierre with kindness. She makes a significant observation:

It's funny, since ... *She hesitates* ... your accident ... I haven't had any dreams ...

Her experience with Marcel of true passion has, in effect, exorcised her sexual fantasies and made her fully aware of her own sexuality. Through him, even though he is dead, she has (like many of Buñuel's leading characters) been born again, both to a deeper understanding of the world and of herself. When Husson visits Pierre and tells him the truth about Séverine, the tears that run down Pierre's cheeks may express not merely his grief but his acceptance of things – both past and present – for what they are. In the light of man's understanding of his imperfections, the malice of a man like Husson can achieve nothing.

The sound of cow-bells and the thunder of hooves introduces Séverine's final daydream. Pierre rises from his wheelchair, walks briskly to the drinks trolley, suggests a holiday in the mountains and embraces Séverine. She looks through the window and the landau of the opening sequence is seen again, with the coachman and the footman but without Pierre and Séverine. Her observation that her erotic dreams no longer trouble her is seen to be confirmed. Her final dream (in which she and Pierre are finally happy) is, despite its harsh constrast with the grim reality of a life with a crippled husband, a pointer to the fact that she has ceased to equate love with sexual brutality.[11]

Of the film's formal qualities Francisco Aranda has made the following observation:

> From a formal point of view, it was the best-made film of his [Buñuel's] career to date (it was the one for which he had most means), even though stylistically there are elements which trace directly back to *Un Chien andalou*.[12]

The comment is interesting inasmuch as it draws attention to the visual beauty of *Belle de Jour*, made with all the sophisticated resources, financial and technical, of the modern film industry, yet links it to the silent, black and white *Un Chien andalou* made three and a half decades earlier. For Aranda, the earlier film is the better one. The later film is, for all its elegance, 'the work of an old master who is in total control, avoids all dangers, maintains his youthful vigour and sustains his themes, but is somewhat tired in face of the commercial impositions of the producers'.[13]

The cool elegance of much of *Belle de Jour*, represented above all in the figure of Séverine herself, reflects the formal elegance of the bourgeois world to which she belongs. Buñuel, ever the artist of detail, be it of the slums of Mexico City or the lavish houses of wealthy families, constructs his elegant picture piece by piece. Thus, a shot of Séverine's apartment:

> *General shot of the beautifully furnished drawing room in SÉVERINE'S and PIERRE'S apartment. A vase of red roses stands on a low table placed between two mustard-coloured sofas.*

Later a shot of Pierre's study with its desk, its bookcase, its reading lamps, its armchairs, in one of which Séverine, dressed in a pink dressing gown, is seated, underlines the impression of wealth and comfort. When Séverine is seen sitting on the sofa in the drawing room reading a magazine, the shot has all the cool formality of a typical bourgeois activity. Throughout the film shots of the rooms and furniture of Séverine's apartment, from the drawing room to the bedroom to the bathroom, from the paintings to the ornaments to the drinks trolley, build up an image of an essentially stylized, ritualized way of life. The surface appearance conveyed by the film, enhanced greatly by colour, is all-important, for it establishes the elegant frame within which Buñuel can display all the more effectively the inner, unconscious, far from cool and elegant needs and desires of his central characters, and of Séverine in particular.

The dream sequences and daydreams are not only more numerous in *Belle de Jour* than in any other Buñuel film between 1929 and 1966; they are also very similar to those of Buñuel's first film. In the first daydream, for example, the emotions of the characters (the desire of the coachman and the footman, the fear and the anticipation of Séverine) are conveyed in a visual manner. There is some dialogue but the technique is otherwise that of the earlier silent film, in which the facial expressions of the characters, and the close-ups which reveal their feelings, play an important part:

> *A low angle medium close-up of the COACHMAN . . . with an expression of lustful pleasure on his face.*
> *A low angle close-up of SÉVERINE. Her face reveals a mixture of pleasure and repugnance . . . The COACHMAN kisses her in the small of her back and she throws her head back, closing her eyes.*

The same is true of many of the other episodes. In Séverine's recollection of the childhood assault, it is the girl's reaction, expressed in her closed eyes and her holding of her breath, which is important. In the episode in which Pierre and Husson pelt her with mud, close-ups of her face emphasize her guilt:

> *Close-up of SÉVERINE, now covered with mud. She stands motionless as more mud hits her, and her voice is heard crying (although her lips do not move)* . . .

The cinematic language of the film is very reminiscent of the heightened emotional states revealed in *Un Chien andalou*, and indeed in *L'Age d'or*.

Buñuel pinpoints the sexual awakening of Séverine in other ways too. When, for example, Marcel is sitting on the bed with Séverine, the camera reveals his back in close-up and Séverine's fingers exploring the scar over his shoulder-blade. Later, in another episode of love-making, the camera moves along the lovers' bodies to focus on Marcel's foot rubbing Séverine's leg. Buñuel avoids shots of explicit love-making. However his selective shots are highly erotic, their power residing precisely in the fact that they not only pinpoint very clearly the passions of the characters at a given moment, but also convey to the audience private experiences with which it is familiar and to which it can itself respond. Furthermore, *Belle de Jour* is distinguished by the sexual imagery, notably of legs and feet, that we have seen in Buñuel's earlier films, in particular *Viridiana*. When Séverine visits Madame Anais's establishment on the second occasion, the occasion on which she has her first customer, the camera focuses on her feet as she climbs the stairs. In a scene involving Marcel and Séverine, her legs are seen in the foreground of the frame. In the same sequence the camera shows his boots in close-up, and in a later episode his foot rubbing her leg. Hands too, as in *Un Chien andalou*, are an important sexual motif. In particular, the shot of Séverine's hand caressing the scar on Marcel's back is highly erotic. Earlier, the shot of Madame Anais's hands ladling cherries in brandy, and echoing the shot of the priest's hands extending the wafer to Séverine, has transformed a religious initiation into a sexual one. The cinematic language of the film is, in short, highly purposeful. Andrew Sarris has observed:

> Instead of indulging in Kessel's sentimental psychology by staring into Catherine Deneuve's eyes, Buñuel fragments Deneuve's body into its erotic constituents. His shots of feet, hands, legs, shoes, stockings, undergarments, etc., are the shots not only of a fetishist, but of a cubist, a director concerned simultaneously with the parts and their effect on the whole. Buñuel's graceful camera movements convey Deneuve to her sensual destiny through her patent-leather shoes, and to her final reverie through her ringed fingers feeling their way along the furniture with the tactile tenderness of a mystical sensuality . . .[14]

Belle de Jour has often been maligned, partly by those who find Séverine's indulgence in prostitution distasteful, unbecoming of her, and partly by those who see Buñuel's film as the elegant but tired work of an ageing master. These are however the reactions of people who fail to grasp Buñuel's intentions and fail to see beneath and beyond the film's exterior.

NOTES

[1] See Francisco Aranda, *Luis Buñuel . . .*, pp. 228-229.

[2] *Luis Buñuel . . .*, p. 229

[3] Buñuel's opinion is quoted by Elliott Stein. See 'Buñuel's Golden Bowl', in *The World of Luis Buñuel*, p. 279. The article first appeared in *Belle de Jour, Modern Film Scripts*, London: Lorrimer Publishing, 1971.

[4] Quoted by Aranda, *Luis Buñuel . . .*, pp. 226-228.

[5] 'Buñuel's Golden Bowl', p. 280.

[6] Joan Mellen, 'An Overview of Buñuel's Career', *The World of Luis Buñuel*, pp. 3-27, discusses the portrayal of the vicitimized woman in Buñuel's films. See, in particular, pp. 14-17: 'In *Viridiana, Belle de Jour,* and *Tristana,* Buñuel condemns the victimization of women by the bourgeois patriarchy centered in Spain and France. Lacking self-

confidence and any sense of their value as human beings, Buñuel's women become simultaneously frigid and callous . . .' p. 14.

[7] Andrew Sarris, 'The Beauty of *Belle de Jour*', *The World of Luis Buñuel*, pp. 289-296, draws a distinction between the Pierre of the novel and the film: 'Pierre emerges through Jean Sorel as a much duller character than in the book, but it is difficult to see what any director can do with the character of the Noble Husband in such a grotesque context' p. 292.

[8] The sound of bells also announces daydreams in *L'Age d'or*.

[9] See Freddy Buache, *The Cinema of Luis Buñuel*, p. 173: 'The careless spectator might assume Buñuel's talents as a director to be merely those of a rich man's Jean Delannoy; but when observed attentively the film reveals countless overlapping elements . . .'

[10] Raymond Durgnat, *Luis Buñuel*, p. 143, observes that 'Marcel is the anti-gentleman. Not only is he a thug, with a concealed blade in his walking stick, but it is stressed that he utterly rejects not only honour among thieves but the most primitive duties of friendship. He is as outside any possible law as Jaibo in *Los olvidados*, whom he physically resembles; he too dies like a dog. He also defiantly parodies the gentleman, with his gold-riddled upper gums, his dandy affectations . . .'

[11] The ending of the film has been a source of endless trouble to the critics. Buñuel had himself stated that 'in the final sequence, the audience will not be able to know if what is happening to her is actual or the heroine's subjective world – reality or nightmare'. That it is the latter is, however, suggested by the sound of bells which introduces the episode. The actual interpretation of the incident, notably Pierre's recovery, has run the gamut of critical opinion. Elliott Stein, 'Buñuel's Golden Bowl', p. 281, describes the film's conclusion as 'the most astonishing "open ending" in the history of the cinema'. Andrew Sarris, 'The Beauty of *Belle de Jour*', suggests that 'Buñuel is ultimately ambiguous so as not to moralize about his subject. He wishes neither to punish Séverine nor to reward her. He prefers to contemplate the grace with which she accepts her fate . . .' My own view is that Pierre's 'recovery' takes place in Séverine's imagination and suggests at the same time the beginning of a new relationship between them.

[12] *Luis Buñuel* . . . , p. 229.

[13] *Luis Buñuel* . . . , p. 230.

[14] 'The Beauty of *Belle de Jour*', p. 292.

8
TRISTANA

CAST

Tristana	—	Catherine Deneuve
Horacio	—	Franco Nero
Saturna	—	Lola Gaos
Don Cosme	—	Antonio Casas
Don Lope	—	Fernando Rey
Saturno	—	Jesús Fernández
Don Ambrosio	—	Vicente Solder

and: José Calvo, Fernando Cabrián, Cándida Losada
María Paz Pondal, Juan José Menéndez,
Sergio Mendizábal, Antonio Ferrándis,
José María Caffarel, Joaquím Pamplona.

Photography	—	José F. Aguayo
Editor	—	Pedro del Rey
Art Director		Enrique Alarcón
Sound	—	José Noguiera
Production	—	Epoca Films and Talía (Madrid) Films Corona (Paris) Selenia Cinematografica (Rome)
Script	—	Luis Buñuel Julio Alejandro (from the novel by Benito Pérez Galdós)
Assistant Directors	—	José Puyol Pierre Lary
Director	—	Luis Buñuel

The commercial success of *Belle de Jour* gave Buñuel the opportunity to choose his own subject for his next film, *The Milky Way (La Voie Lactée)*, which he completed in 1969. He had long been interested in making a film with a religious subject and, before making *Belle de Jour*, had written a script based on Matthew Gregory Lewis's *The Monk*. Buñuel's plans did not materialize in relation to this particular subject, and the film of *The Monk* was eventually made by Ado Kyrou in 1972. However, with *The Milky Way* Buñuel both achieved his ambition and made a remarkable film. Employing a narrative structure which can best be described as picaresque, Buñuel presents the story of two beggars on a pilgrimage to the shrine of Santiago de Compostela, and through them develops in six sketches or scenes the central theme of the film: the heresies connected with the six principal dogmas of the Catholic Church. The sketches have a surrealist quality in the sense that their action moves freely through time and space, but they also share a striking unity of theme and vision. Buñuel, as is always the case when he deals with religion, shows its effects upon men, notably the extent of man's inhumanity to man throughout the ages in defence of some dogmatic point or article of faith. Francisco Aranda has drawn attention to the historical importance of *The Milky Way*, seeing it as a film which 'opens up the way to a speculative, essayist cinema'.[1] For all its seriousness of subject it has that characteristic humour that is part and parcel of Buñuel's portrayal of mankind.

Plans for the making of *Tristana* go back to 1962 when, after completing *The Exterminating Angel*, Buñuel had been looking for another subject. After considering various possibilities, including Dostoievski's *The Everlasting Husband*, he had been persuaded to make a film of Galdós's novel, and plans had gone ahead for shooting to commence in Madrid. Buñuel prepared the scenario with Julio Alejando, his co-writer on *Viridiana*, the studios were hired, locations chosen, and the censorship seemed satisfied. At the last minute, however, the censorship intervened, mindful no doubt of *Viridiana*, on the grounds that the new code of censorship prohibited incitement to a duel. The script, of course, contained a duel, plans for the film fell through, and it was another eight years before Buñuel would return to it.

By 1970 Buñuel had lost interest in the subject. As Francisco Aranda has noted, he had originally seen *Tristana* as a film which would allow him to continue working in the Spanish cinema and which would to some extent heal the damage done by *Viridiana*.[2] Since 1962 he had, moreover, enhanced his reputation with some highly personal films, and it could be risky to embark again on the old subject. In the end he seems to have been persuaded to go ahead not through any enthusiasm of his own but because so much money and effort had already gone into the planning of the film. Buñuel arrived in Madrid in the Spring of 1969. When filming began, after some delay, in the Autumn, things went smoothly enough. He had assembled one of the best film crews available in Spain and shooting was completed in less than two months. As far as his actors were concerned, Buñuel took particular care over Fernando Rey's portrayal of Don Lope, Tristana's uncle, and was immensely pleased by the work of an actor who had served him well in *Viridiana* and who would do so again in both *The Discreet Charm of the Bourgeoisie* and in *That Obscure Object of Desire.*

Tristana, like *Nazarín*, is based on a novel by Benito Pérez Galdós. In many respects the novel and the film are very similar. Galdós depicts the uncle, Don Juan, as a generous and sympathetic Madrid 'gentleman' or 'hidalgo' who has seen better times. He takes the orphaned Tristana into his care and she later becomes his mistress. Her affair with a young painter takes up more space in the novel than the film, but in both Tristana finally returns to her uncle. Subsequent events are, however, very different. Galdós's ending is the happier one, for Tristana marries Don Juan, settles for her lot and contents herself with making puddings for a highly delighted husband. Buñuel's ending is a total contrast.

Tristana's illness, the amputation of her leg and the bitterness of her relationship with Don Lope reflect Buñuel's central concern with the theme of a bourgeois society which cripples and destroys human relationships. Indeed, if there is a single phrase which encapsulates the meaning of Buñuel's film, it is Don Lope's highly conservative viewpoint: 'A woman of honour, a crippled leg, and in the house'. It is a phrase which does not exist in the novel. In the film, moreover, Galdós's Madrid becomes Toledo, a city, in Buñuel's view, much more evocative than cosmopolitan Madrid of the oppressive weight of Spanish social and moral values.

Critical opinion of *Tristana*, as is almost inevitable in relation to any Buñuel film, has been somewhat divided. Pilar de Cuadra, for example, writing in the *Diario de Barcelona*, considers Buñuel to have betrayed Galdós's novel by transforming the idealistic Tristana into a hard and disillusioned woman.[3] It is the view of someone (and it is not uncharacteristic) who does not understand Buñuel. Others, in complete contrast, see *Tristana* as Buñuel's best film. César Santos Fontenla, writing in the Spanish film magazine, *Nuestro Cine*, has observed:

> . . . and if I am not bold enough to say that *Tristana* is Buñuel's best film, I do believe that it is the one which comes closest to it . . .[4]

Its particular virtues lie for many not in its connection with or fidelity to Galdós's novel but in Buñuel's transformation of the novel into a personal and highly corrosive representation of twentieth-century Spanish society. Louis Marcorelles, writing in *Le Monde*, concludes that *Tristana* is the 'most powerful denunciation of the bourgeoisie to have appeared on our screens for a very long time'.[5] In this respect *Tristana* is, like several of Buñuel's later films, highly deceptive. Its manner is somewhat muted and restrained and yet, beneath the surface there lurks, as in the case of the scorpions of *L'Age d'or*, a savage sting.

The credits appear on the screen over a shot of Toledo. It is, however, a Toledo deliberately differentiated from El Greco's famous painting of the city, presented instead as a typical provincial Spanish capital. The opening sequence is designed in every detail to convey the dullness, the clinging to tradition, and the crippling claustrophobia of provincial Spanish life. The rooftops with their red tiles stretch away into the background, the river winds slowly, and the bells of a nearby church toll monotonously over the city. On the outskirts two women are seen approaching, both of them dressed in the traditional black of mourning. One of them is Saturna, the forty-year old servant, already older looking than her years, her name symbolic of her melancholy. The other is the young and beautiful Tristana, her youth and beauty muted by her dark clothing:

> *. . . her black dress, which is somewhat shabby, spoils her graceful shape, and a small veil covers her fair hair . . .*

Tristana's name, with its evocation of sadness, is especially appropriate to the oppressive ambience of the environment in which she lives, a town on which the weight of social and religious conventions hangs heavily.[6]

The introduction of a group of deaf mutes announces the important themes of a crippled and mutilated humanity. As the boys play their game of football in total silence, struggling to express themselves in bold and vigorous gestures, the spectacle is unnerving and strangely ominous, a metaphor for humanity at large locked in its own incommunicable suffering. One of the boys, Saturno, is Saturna's deaf-mute son, and a link is immediately established between him and Tristana, a pointer to her own subsequent mutilation. He, for example, is drawn to her, responsive to her beauty, while she attempts to communicate with him and offers him an apple as a token of her friendship. They are in many ways kindred spirits, both exposed in their youthful vulnerability to the world at large. Saturno, indeed, is about to leave the etablishment in which he has lived for many years and has been found a job by Don Lope, Tristana's uncle. The boy, no less than Tristana, is about to embark on a journey in the course of which his dependence on his fellow men is absolute.

In the scenes which follow, Don Lope's essentially bourgeois character is steadily developed. He is seen in the street flirting with a young and attractive serving girl, expressing himself uninhibitedly with a person of a lower class. When, on the other hand, an older bourgeois lady appears, Don Lope quickly reverts to a dignified and formal attitude appropriate to his social standing. Similarly, conventional attitudes colour his initial relationship with Tristana. Since her mother's recent death, Don Lope has assumed the role of guardian to the girl. He feels a genuine compassion for her and treats her kindly, but always with the authority inherent in and expected of his newly acquired role. For her part Tristana is respectfully submissive, obedient to her uncle's wishes, desirous only to please him:

> *DON LOPE looks at TRISTANA and she lowers her eyes, hurrying to remove the handkerchief from her head and to put on her shawl, anxious to leave, so that DON LOPE will not scold her.*

His anger when he finds her cleaning his study emanates from a strictly hierarchical view of society, while the study itself, with its massive desk, its bookshelves, its solid furniture and heavily framed pictures, is the image of bourgeois conformity.

For all his conventional attitudes Don Lope is, nevertheless, a somewhat ambiguous character, even a rebel against the society of which he is a solid bastion. Far from accepting traditional religious values, Don Lope rejects them, promising to rid Tristana of her 'superstitions' once she is under his roof. Furthermore, when the police appear in pursuit of a thief who has escaped with a lady's purse, Don Lope delights in sending them the wrong way and proclaims himself defender of the weak. To an extent he embodies a liberal and rebellious spirit. However, Don Lope's rebellion, conducted within a society whose ideals he largely champions, smacks of a certain self-indulgence, of a posture easily assumed and easily discarded. Needless to say, it is not Don Lope who finds the freedom he claims to champion but others who, more exposed than he to the painful process of living, learn the true meaning of liberty.[7]

A new sequence, set in the bell tower of the cathedral, introduces the sexual theme. When, for example, Saturno puts his arm around Tristana's waist, she reacts with indignation and chases him up the stairs. In the boy's audacity and the girl's confusion Buñuel evokes awakening sexuality and adolescent curiosity, as well as the happy innocence of youth. The theme is developed further when, as they climb to the bell tower itself, Saturno attempts, much to Tristana's apparent annoyance, to look up her skirt. The motif of the girl's legs, as important in this as in any of Buñuel's films, encapsulates erotic desire, however innocent. The introduction of one of the great bells is also significant, for the bell-clapper has an evident phallic association. Tristana reaches out to touch it. As she does so, subconscious sexual fears, connected with Don Lope, flood to the surface:

> *. . . a sudden expression of surprise, quickly transformed into terror, is reflected in her face: inside the great bell, the clapper has become the severed head of Don Lope, his eyes fixed, staring, chilling . . .*

In the sequence as a whole, from the sexual frolicking of adolescence to the revelation of deeply hidden phobias, Buñuel progressively lays bare, in true surrealist fashion, his characters' lives. And the next episode also fills out the picture in relation to Don Lope. Rushing to Tristana's bedroom as she wakes up screaming from a nightmare, Don Lope is disturbed by his niece's evident physical maturity:

> *Because her nightdress is loose, the neck-line is somewhat revealing. DON LOPE pulls up the edge of*

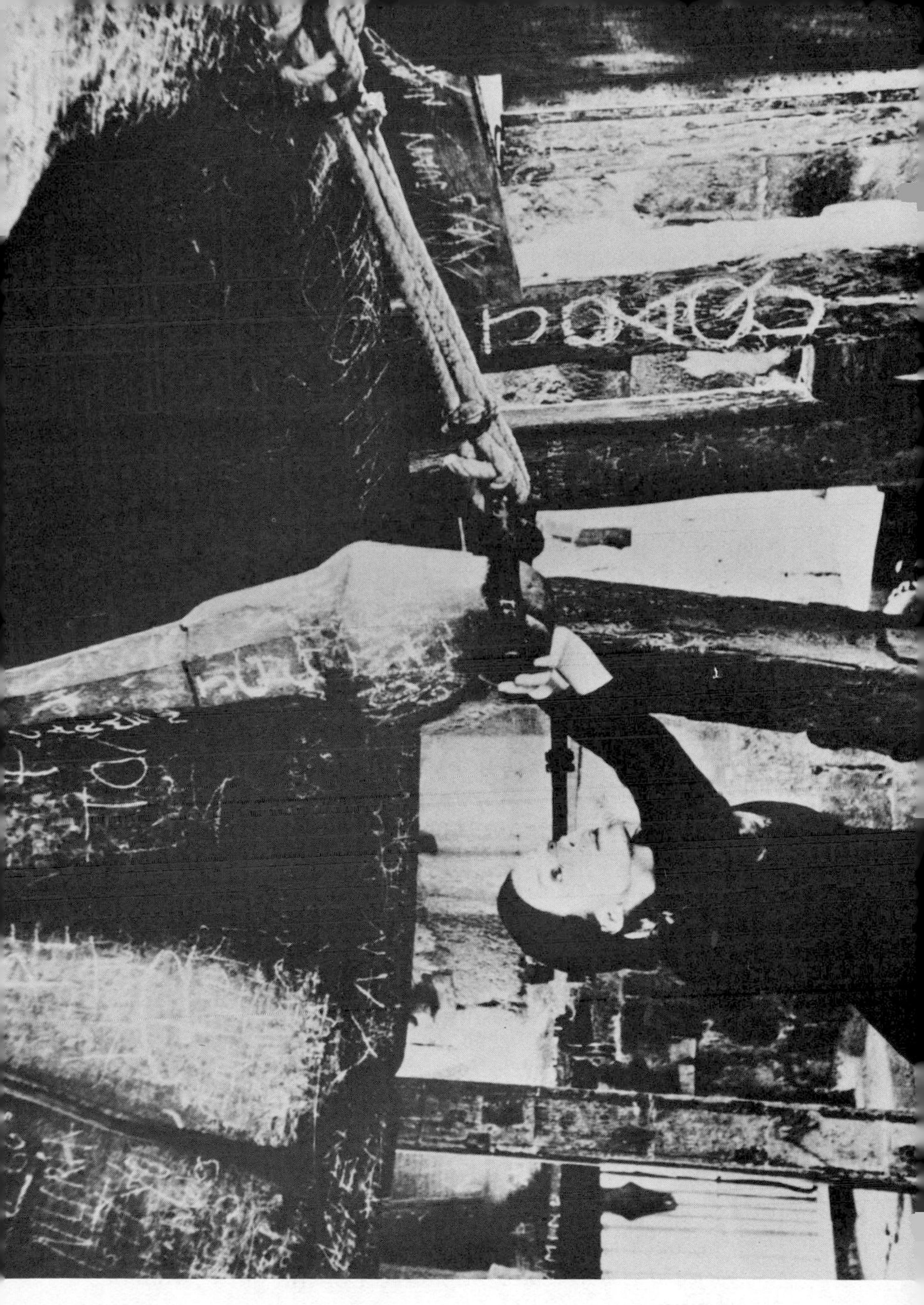

Tristana touches the bell clapper

the sheet in order to cover her. His expression has changed: it has become more serious, even disturbed.

He is, in a sense, another version of Viridiana's uncle, Don Jaime, increasingly absorbed by the physical proximity of his niece's beauty. Here, as in the earlier film, it is Buñuel's particular achievement to communicate to us at every stage the emotional and mental landscapes of his characters' existence. But in *Tristana*, as in *Belle de Jour*, he sets them firmly within another kind of landscape – the solid, unchanging, apparently unruffled landscape of Spanish provincial bourgeois life.

The contradictions of Don Lope's character continue to display themselves. An episode set in a café presents the bourgeois ritual, with Don Lope at its centre, of daily encounters and conversations: the whole a stylized performance. In another episode, set in his house, his highly conservative view of a woman's role in life – be she servant or family – is seen when Tristana brings his slippers and, kneeling before him, puts them on his feet. When he orders her to eat an egg, he will not be denied.

Against this, Don Lope orders Tristana to cast aside the traditional black of mourning, deeming it the custom of barbarians. When he reads the newspaper he vents his spleen on the corrupt nature of Spanish institutions. In another episode involving the valuation of some of his household effects, he bitterly attacks the commercialism of the modern world. Resembling Don Jaime in his sexual attraction to his niece, Don Lope is very much his opposite in many of his social attitudes.

A sequence set in a dress shop pinpoints both Don Lope's increasing sexual interest in Tristana and, even more importantly, her growing awareness of her attractiveness as a woman. The dress which Don Lope buys for his niece confirms her physical maturity:

The neck-line of the dress is revealing and allows one to form a very clear impression of the girl's feminine charms.

When Don Lope puts his arm around her waist, the action reminds us of Tristana and Saturno in the bell tower and transposes adolescent into adult sexuality. As for Tristana, she is transfixed by her own image in the mirror, aware of her emergence as a woman:

> I feel so strange . . . I seem like someone else.

It is the first stage of Don Lope's liberating influence upon his niece.

Two subsequent episodes develop the pattern further. In the first of these, Tristana and her uncle are walking arm in arm outside a church. His unconventional views on love and marriage, totally at odds with the society in which they live, provide her with a perspective which she would not otherwise have, freeing her from the bonds of conventional attitudes:

> . . . Passion must be free. It is the natural law. No chains, no signatures, no blessings.

A shot of Tristana, poised to kiss a religious statue on the lips, is revealing both of her new sexual awareness and of her casting off of the Church's hold upon her. As for Don Lope, Buñuel presents him with sympathy and dignity. Three times older than his niece, he is redeemed by love, transformed from a potentially ridiculous and absurd figure into someone quite touching in his delight at Tristana's favourable response to him. She, in turn, loses her submissiveness, and in another scene a few days later is seen undressing in Don Lope's bedroom with all the self-assurance of an experienced woman. However it is already clear that, in freeing Tristana, Don Lope has freed within her impulses which, given his years, he cannot continue to satisfy. He has created the circumstances of his own tragedy.

When we next see Tristana and Don Lope, some time has passed and both have changed significantly. Don Lope has aged and his health is poor. The sprightly, dignified man of a few years earlier is now, in dressing-gown and night-cap, a decrepit and even repulsive figure. Tristana is more mature, less dependent on her uncle, and, after the first flush of freedom, increasingly weary of him. Her brusqueness is perfectly natural, and Buñuel, far from condemning her, presents it as an inevitable fact of life; the spontaneous reaction to her circumstances of a young and largely unfulfilled woman. The end of the sequence is clearly symbolic in relation to the ending of the film. Tristana, in the course of eating her meal, separates two peas on her plate, studies them, takes one and eats it. Inasmuch as the peas represent Don Lope and herself, Tristana is evidently the survivor.

A new sequence, tracing the pattern of Tristana's growing restlessness, reintroduces the symbol of the bell-clapper. She has begun to dream again of the bell-clapper transformed into Don Lope's severed head, a dream which, if it originally expressed her adolescent sexual fear of him, reveals now a castration wish and a longing for his death. Her sexual feelings begin to focus, instead, on Horacio, a young and handsome painter whom she meets, significantly, on the patio of an abandoned convent. This crumbling symbol of the Church is both an ironic setting for the beginnings of an extra-marital relationship and (like Tristana's kissing of the religious statue) a pointer to her shaking off of guilt for the sake of passion. But the lovers' encounter has as its counterpoint an incident in which a stray dog, suspected of attacking a child, is ruthlessly hounded by a crowd of people and finally shot by a self-satisfied policeman. Erring women, no less than straying dogs, risk the vengeance of a society quick to pounce on unacceptable behaviour.

The tension of social image and inner feelings lies at the heart of another finely observed scene. Don Lope and Tristana walking out together are the very epitome of bourgeois respectability. Don Lope, smartly dressed, stomach pulled in, cane in hand, projects a carefully rehearsed public image.[8] His accustations against Tristana, contradicting his earlier views on love and marriage, are precisely those of a hide-bound intolerant society:

> . . . And don't forget that I have two further obligations towards you: I am your guardian and your husband.

Anger, moreover, is contained, the mask not allowed to slip in public:

> *DON LOPE struggles not to let his anger show nor to attract the attention of others.*

For her part, Tristana answers Don Lope's accusations by confronting him with his own arguments:

> I am free, aren't I? I am answerable only to myself. I am following your advice, don't you see?

Beneath the image, Don Lope's tragedy is movingly revealed. He is a man who, rebelling in some respects against the society in which he lives, conforming in others to its precepts, is ultimately the victim of his own lack of total commitment, of his own double standards.

A scene in Horacio's studio presents both the force and power of passion and the insidious and inescapable hold of social convention. Tristana has hidden from Horacio the nature of her relationship with Don Lope. When she reveals the truth to him, she observes, true to her belief in her own freedom, that she is free to love him:

> I know I am dishonoured . . . , but free to love you.

Horacio, for all his youth, passion and apparent bohemian unconventionality, is overwhelmed, partly by surprise, but partly too by the fear of involvement in an affair involving honour. In the end he sweeps aside his doubts and the scene ends with the lovers' passionate embrace, but, like so many of the film's other episodes, it sustains the image of passion vainly striving to free itself from the stranglehold of traditional moral and social values.

The spectacle of youthful passion is transformed immediately into the ageing, dishevelled figure of Don Lope in singlet and braces, alone in the house. If the earlier sequence of Don Lope walking with Tristana displayed his dignified public image, Buñuel reveals again the pathetic reality beneath the image. This is the private sadness, even the tragedy, beneath the facade of conventional Spanish life in which appearance has always been all-important. Indeed, no sooner have we seen Don Lope as he is than we observe him assume, with powder, dye and brush, the mask designed for public view:

> *He is in his shirt-sleeves and he is putting the finishing touches to his moustache and beard with a little brush that has been dipped in black dye . . .*

The camera focuses for a moment on the image in the mirror, underlining both its ritual character and its lack of substance. The sequence ends with a display of Tristana's defiance of Don Lope (she throws his slippers into the rubbish-bin) reasserting the painful reality behind the image.

Tristana, for all her statements about freedom, is, like Don Lope himself, a contradictory and ambiguous figure. In following her instincts and taking a lover, she subverts the fundamental precepts both of the Catholic faith and the Spanish code of honour. Adopting an attitude of disrespect towards Don Lope and flying in the face of all his admonitions, she also abandons woman's traditional, submissive role. She practises, in effect, Don Lope's subversive preaching. On the other hand, she, like Don Lope, cannot escape the influence of attitudes and modes of thought that are deeply, unconsciously ingrained in her. When, for example, Horacio suggests she go away with him, Tristana's desire for freedom runs counter to a very conventional caution and fear of the consequences:

> Let me think about it. It is not as easy as you think.

It emerges too when Horacio clashes with a passer-by. The latter, a typical bourgeois, objects to the lovers' kissing in the street. When Horacio threatens him and the bourgeois mentions the police, Tristana, thinking of her honour, begs Horacio not to involve her in a scandal:

> Horacio, don't get me involved! . . .

In the last resort she cannot, any more than Don Lope himself, shake off the moral and social habits of a lifetime.

Buñuel's view of his characters caught in the intricate web of sexual desire and social pressures, the one exclusive of the other, is both consistently realistic and compassionate. Don Lope, for instance, is presented to us as a man who, having enjoyed Tristana, feels her imminent loss all the more keenly. When in the course of pleading with her, he draws her to him and his hands begin to squeeze her waist, the incident reveals both clearly and touchingly the painful reality of the old man's sexual needs. Moreover, her rejection of him in favour of another man drives him to consider his name and reputation; to embrace the ideals of a society he has condemned so often. The champion of sexual liberty, the critic of Spanish institutions, Don Lope is the victim of both. In his role as the affronted male he is in many ways a comic figure; the spokesman of a society ruthlessly mocked by Buñuel. In an incident in which he seeks out Horacio and, much to the young man's astonishment, slaps his face and challenges him to a duel, the image of honour is one reduced to its ultimate, anachronistic absurdity.[9] On the other hand, while mocking the stereotype, Buñuel never loses sight of the old man's capacity to arouse our sympathy. The absurdity of the encounter becomes a final image of Don Lope's sadness:

> *. . . each of them goes his own way. DON LOPE does so sadly, bowed, shoulders hunched, as he is slowly lost in the darkness.*

When we next see Don Lope two years have passed and the situation has changed once more. His fortunes have improved and he, although two years older, has all the vigour and aplomb of years gone by. In a conversation with a friend, Don Cosme, in the course of which they discuss the recent death of Don Lope's sister, the former utters conventional platitudes of sympathy. Don Lope, on the other hand, is his old irreverent self, shocking his friend with a series of outrageous observations:

> . . . Listen, Cosme. If our parents could take everything with them when they die, we children would be left with nothing.

For all this, it is the reassertion of Don Lope's bourgeois status that is most significant, exemplified in the now impressive dining-room with its silver, china and expensive furniture:

> *Some changes can be seen to have taken place: some of the older and more delapidated furniture has disappeared and given way to pieces that are much finer and in better condition. The dinner service and the silver on the sideboard, as well as other items in general, indicate clearly that prosperity has entered this household.*

It is the bourgeois background into which Tristana is about to be sucked.

While Don Lope's fortunes have improved, Tristana's have deteriorated. Saturna informs Don Lope of the fact that Tristana is seriously ill and has, on that account, returned with Horacio to Toledo. Don Lope, proceeding quickly to the hotel where they are staying, learns from Horacio that Tristana is suffering from a tumour in her leg, believes that she is dying and wishes to end her days in Don Lope's house. He is, of course, shocked by the news of Tristana's illness, but his sense of shock is mingled, significantly, with feelings of triumph and elation:

> *A close-up of Don Lope who can hardly contain his feelings: joy because she is still free, sadness on account of her illness.*

In the course of his discussion with Horacio, Don Lope has discovered that Tristana has, true to her ideal of freedom, repeatedly refused to marry him. In the light of this revelation, Don Lope agrees eagerly to have her back, and in a subsequent remark to Saturna, reveals his intention never again to set her free:

> Now, Saturna, she will not escape! If she enters my house, she will never leave it!

Don Lope's motives are, of course, complex. Tristana's return is for him a victory over a younger and more handsome man. It satisfies too his feelings of vindictiveness towards Tristana. But on another, and equally important level, it is all to do with the restitution of his honour. Tristana's departure with Horacio has undermined not only Don Lope's self-respect but also his public image. Her return to a man who will take her back, through kindness and compassion, effectively restores that image. Buñuel, in sharply underlining Don Lope's real motives, reveals once more with a keen and penetrating gaze, the hypocrisy that passes for honour, the hollowness of bourgeois morality.

In a new sequence some removal men are seen placing a piano in the drawing-room of Don Lope's house, while a doctor is writing a prescription for Tristana. A shot of Tristana in her bedroom reveals that Don Lope has had it specially prepared and decorated for her:

> *. . . curtains and expensive carpets, new and cheerful furniture which is very feminine, a screen, lamps, china, jars . . .*

He, it is clear, will keep Tristana in the traditional Spanish manner, fulfilling literally his earlier words – 'A woman of honour, a crippled leg, and in the house'. They are, indeed, words which acquire now a particularly sharp and cruel sense of irony as Tristana's condition worsens and the doctor concludes that only amputation of the leg will save her life. The motif of the cripple, present already in the figure of Saturno, assumes deeper and stronger resonances. Don Lope, shocked by the doctor's course of action, reacts with horror to Tristana's mutilation:

> Poor creature! To mutilate her so horribly!

He does not grasp the fact, of course, that mutilation can be more than physical or that, in a very real sense, Tristana's fate will be little different from that of the majority of Spanish women. Emotionally damaged, locked very often in loveless marriages which deny their individuality, exposed to the crippling influences of arid religious and social conventions and institutions, they, like Tristana, are less than whole. Furthermore, however much Don Lope may lament Tristana's fate, it is he (the conservative, bourgeois part of him) and others like him, who are responsible for it. Tristana represents Spanish woman, Don Lope in many ways Spanish man. To the extent that he professes liberal ideals, he is, in Buñuel's view, like so many liberals in the years preceding the Spanish Civil War, essentially conservative, guardian of a country crippled by the narrowmindedness of centuries.[10]

In a brief but important encounter with Horacio, Don Lope suggests, much to Horacio's surprise, that he visit Tristana daily. It is, to all appearances, a kind and generous offer. Don Lope, however, makes no reference to the amputation. He calculates, no doubt, that Horacio's visits, far from inflaming the young man's passion for her, will have the opposite effect, and his campaign, purporting to reveal the kindness of his heart, is motivated in reality only by cold and cynical calculation. The scene is distinguished by its sustained and gentlemanly politeness. Its surface, like the film in general, conceals the hypocrisy of bourgeois society.

Tristana has recovered after the amputation of her leg and is next seen seated at the piano in the drawing-room. She is playing a sonata and the camera focuses on her hands as they traverse the keyboard, moves slowly down to reveal her leg amputated at the knee, and back to her hands again. The close-ups evoke the contrast between the creative

Close-up of Tristana's amputated leg

act of music making and the ugliness of her deformity, revealing how the world at large will see Tristana. For the majority she is now a useless cripple, to be pitied or looked upon with horror. In Tristana her deformity has already accentuated a fiercely independent spirit. She is still beautiful, denying her mutilation and, in a clash with Horacio, she asserts in no uncertain fashion the importance of her existence:

But I am still alive!

Buñuel's emphasis on Tristana's legs – reminiscent of the foot and leg motifs in many of his films – also gives a new dimension to the sexual theme. Inasmuch as she has ceased to be an object of sexual desire, she has effectively freed herself, as much from Horacio as from Don Lope, even if in some perverse way the latter finds the amputee even more attractive. And, having done so, her worth and value as a person in her own right, free from sexual connotations, is correspondingly heightened. Tristana's physical mutilation is thus, paradoxically, the gateway to a new kind of liberty. There are already indications that her thoughts lie elsewhere, beyond the limitations of the room and the society of which she is, physically, the prisoner:

TRISTANA looks into the distance, without seeing, as though she is far away, while DON LOPE takes the crutches.

It is a few years later when we next see Tristana and Don Lope. He looks much older and Tristana, in the intervening years, has acquired a severity both of expression and manner:

Her face is extremely pale and reveals an expression of unusual harshness.

Their roles have changed and it is she who, far from being dominated, dominates Don Lope. Like Lorca's Bernarda Alba, Tristana bangs her stick on the floor to reinforce her orders. Don Lope is intimidated by the forceful expression of a woman he fully expected to keep in quiet seclusion.[11]

The scene is set in the garden of a country house. In a conversation with Tristana the priest urges her to marry Don Lope to give a greater respectability to the fact of their living together under the same roof. Tristana, on the other hand, has no wish to marry Don Lope, such is her dislike of him. It is clear that her mind is occupied by other things. When we see her a little later, seated before the mirror in her bedroom, Saturno enters, locks the door, and indicates his desire to go to bed with her. Tristana reacts angrily because Saturno presumes too much. Relationships must now, clearly, be conducted on her own terms, a truth underlined in another scene a few days later when Saturno appears beneath Tristana's window. She is naked beneath her dressing-gown and, when she goes to the window, Saturno makes excited gestures, urging her to reveal herself to him. Tristana, high above him on the balcony, opens her dressing-gown wide, allowing him to feast his eyes on her naked body. Like some high-priestess with her worshipper at her feet, Tristana boldly asserts her sexual independence. However, one cannot fail to note that her exploitation of her sexuality is coloured now by elements of cruelty and perversion.

The shot of the naked Tristana becomes, in a typically ironic juxtaposition, a shot of the statue of the Virgin in a church. Tristana's wedding to Don Lope is taking place. Later Don Lope is seen preparing himself for bed and his new wife. Much to his consternation, Tristana goes to her own bedroom. For her, marriage to Don Lope is merely an official sanction which she can use to express more freely her independence. She has finally learned how to use the hypocrisy of bourgeois institutions to her own advantage. Don Lope, in contrast, is now a typical bourgeois, having abandoned his earlier unorthodoxy. Not only has he married (contravening his earlier observations to Tristana) but he is now in the habit of keeping company with priests. The episode in which he and three priests drink their chocolate and eat their biscuits has a cosy conventionality which is disturbed, significantly, only by the dragging sound of Tristana's crutches as she restlessly paces the corridor outside. Don Lope is, clearly, a man who has settled for his comfortable lot:[12]

> After all, my friends, life is not as bad as many people believe . . . It is snowing outside, but here we are nice and warm.

Tristana is seen to be obsessed still by the dream of the bell-clapper transformed into Don Lope's severed head. But if previously it suggested her wish for Don Lope's castration and destruction, it now announces his death. He is taken ill in the night and calls out to Tristana to help him. When she appears she reveals no emotion. Don Lope begs her to call the doctor. Tristana goes into the next room, pretends to make the phone call, and, finding Don Lope almost unconscious, opens the window to let the bitterly cold wind blow in on his half-covered body. It is a final, defiant assertion of her freedom, but one that is marked too by a bitter vindictiveness.[13] Tristana has achieved her liberty only at the expense of her innocence.

In contrast to many of Buñuel's films *Tristana* is most striking for its ordinariness. Many of the films discussed here, from *Los olvidados* to *Nazarín*, are distinguished by their vivid and closely observed presentation of the real world. Francisco Aranda has said of *Tristana* that the film 'has not a single scene of brilliance', and he refers to its 'quiet, discreet tone . . .'[14] In this film, more than anywhere, Buñuel concentrates on creating, slowly and unostentatiously, the atmosphere of Toledo in which the characters are placed and to which they are subservient.

The opening shot is, in many ways, characteristic of the film as a whole. The camera presents us with a general view of Toledo which brings to mind El Greco's famous and dramatic painting but which, in contrast, dwells only on the rather drab, ordinary and unexciting nature of the place. From this panoramic shot the camera moves gradually to pick up Saturna and Tristana until they are shown in close-up. In other words, the two women, themselves the embodiment of an age-old custom in their mourning black, are seen in relation to and firmly placed within a physical setting which, in its dullness and conventionality, has hardly changed for centuries. In the course of the film, shot by shot, almost imperceptibly, the physical presence of Toledo is made familiar to us. Tristana meets Horacio in the patio of a crumbling, abandoned convent. On another occasion Tristana and Don Lope walk through the arcade of one of the city's squares. Without fuss or bother Buñuel builds up a detailed picture of squares, churches, convents, streets and facades whose very solidity is a statement of the staid, conventional and oppressive values of a provincial Spanish town.[15] And the same is true, of course, of the film's interior sequences, notably in relation to Don Lope's house. In the early part of the film the camera picks out the heavy, typically bourgeois furniture of Don Lope's study: the massive desk, the bookcases, the framed pictures on the walls. Later a shot of the dining-room reveals the silver coffee service on the table and expensive china on the sideboard. Every unobtrusive detail adds to the picture of a conservative and largely bourgeois society.

In conjunction with such settings, Buñuel pinpoints too human activities that, acted out day by day in Spanish society (and in others too) heighten the film's stifling evocation of convention. A sequence in a café reveals the men sitting in groups, smoking and talking, and in a corner the table where Don Lope meets his friends daily. Daily life assumes the character of ritual. Later, when we see Don Lope walking arm in arm with Tristana – his posture stiff, his step jaunty – he is participating in another social rite whose formality is further underlined by the regular columns of the arcade that forms the background. Later in the bathroom

Don Lope carefully dyes his beard and moustache, preparing himself for another public performance. In the last scene of the film old age prevents him from going to the café, but the ritual continues in his own house. Buñuel, more than in any other of his Spanish films, seeks to create and communicate to us the dull, endless routine of a society which does not look beyond itself.

In paying due attention to *Tristana's* evocation of external reality, it would be wrong, however, to ignore its portrayal of the characters' inner lives, for they too are effectively revealed to us.[16] In this sense the film has, however, only one strictly surrealist element: the transformation of the bell-clapper into Don Lope's severed head. It is, in effect, one of Buñuel's most concise, suggestive and startling images, as memorable in its way as the bleeding piece of meat in *Los olvidados*, for it reveals in a flash the complex processes at work in Tristana's youthful mind. The bell itself evokes her narrow and largely religious upbringing. The clapper, with its phallic shape, points to the stirrings of sexual curiosity. And its transformation into Don Lope's head reveals firstly her sexual fear of him, and later her desire for his castration and death. It is an image that is used very sparingly, for only in the film's last scene is it seen again when Tristana has a nightmare. But its sparing use is, of course, the source of its effectiveness, for within the dull monotony of the physical world of the film the sudden revelation of the unconscious is like a flash of lightning.

Otherwise, Buñuel exposes the inner lives of his characters in less dramatic ways. When, early in the film, the young Tristana climbs to the bell-tower and Saturno peers up her skirt, the shot of Tristana's thighs, revealing them to us from Saturno's viewpoint, expresses very clearly his sexual feelings. Later, when in the church we see Tristana poised to kiss the lips of the religious statue, the shot suggests her awakening sexuality. After the amputation of Tristana's leg, both the stump and her artificial limb are shown in close-ups:

... the right leg has been amputated at the knee and a bandage covers the stump; the left leg is covered by a thick silk stocking ...

There is, clearly, an enormous contrast between the youthful beauty of Tristana's legs early in the film and the ugliness of her mutilation which suggests, in turn, the horror inflicted on her mind. Again, when Tristana stands on the balcony and exposes herself to Saturno, Buñuel captures the eroticism of the moment not in a shot of Tristana's body, which is concealed from our prying eyes, but in the astonishment written on Saturno's face. For all its concentration on external reality, *Tristana* has, very clearly, all the familiar hallmarks. It still contains all the concern for human beings that distinguishes Buñuel's films.

NOTES

[1] *Luis Buñuel* ..., p. 230.
[2] *Luis Buñuel* ..., p. 238.
[3] *Diario de Barcelona*, 9 April, 1970.
[4] *Nuestro cine*, n. 96, Madrid, April 1970. The translation is my own.
[5] *Le Monde*, Paris, May 1970. The translation is my own.
[6] See Freddy Buache, *The Cinema of Luis Buñuel*, p. 176: 'Buñuel evokes the unruffled calm of a small country town – the silent streets, the cosy interiors, the Sunday walks, the housework, the café after Mass, the women busy in the kitchens ...'
[7] Freddy Buache, pp. 177-8, has some interesting comments on Don Lope: 'In several other spheres, Don Lope always displays a keen sense of non-conformism, and particularly concerning anything to do with religion. He is also a typical example of a large number of Spaniards on whom their Catholic education has left a profound stamp and who, in order to prove that they still have some desire to emancipate themselves during the period from the end of their adolescence up until the beginning of their old age, are all too willing to adopt a swashbuckling attitude and to stop being practising Catholics, while remaining, in secret, superstitiously attached to their religion ...' p. 177.
[8] Buñuel, though he had many human examples of such behaviour on which to model Don Lope, may well have in mind here the third chapter of *Lazarillo de Tormes* in which the 'gentleman' walks down the street

'with a measured step and an upright stance'. This chapter is, in any case, as Buñuel would well know, one of the most delightful send-ups of honour and respectability in the whole of Spanish literature.

[9] Aranda, *Luis Buñuel* . . . , p. 243, notes that duelling was 'a custom extremely comic to the Surrealist, and so fascinating as to make him into a collector of pistols'.

[10] Joan Mellen, in *Tristana, The World of Luis Buñuel*, pp. 297-305, makes some pertinent comments on this aspect of the film: '*Tristana* reflects as well Buñuel's preoccupation with the decay of Spain. He explores its obsession with the old order, represented by Don Lope and his cronies who meet every day in a café filled with indolent former aristocrats. It is a world defined by norms and relationships which have outlived their time and have now become dangerous. *Tristana* takes place in the twenties after the fall of the first republic which presaged the invasion of the fascists in the next decade. It conveys the image of a Spain that is already amputated. The crippled Tristana represents in her person the generation to be maimed by the Civil War, embodying as she does the frequent image in Franco's Spain of the amputee' p. 300. See too Robert G. Havard, 'The Seventh Art of Luis Buñuel: *Tristana* and the Rites of Freedom', *Quinquereme*, (1982), (forthcoming).

[11] There are, as well, clear similarities between *Tristana* and *La casa de Bernarda Alba (The House of Bernarda Alba)* in the sense that the latter, written in 1936, reflects precisely the evils of Spanish provincial society – especially its narrowmindedness – that are Buñuel's concern.

[12] See Aranda, *Luis Buñuel* . . . , p. 243: 'As to the final scenes of Don Lope offering refreshments in his home to a group of priest friends, it is a demonstration of what can frequently happen to such Spanish gentlemen in their old age . . .'

[13] Joan Mellen, *Tristana*, p. 305, sees the ending as reflecting 'the hopelessness Buñuel feels, both toward Spain and toward its victims'.

[14] *Luis Buñuel* . . . , p. 241.

[15] Joan Mellen observes that 'Toledo's narrow winding medieval streets provide a real labyrinth to echo Tristana's unconscious imprisonment' p. 299.

[16] See Freddy Buache, *The Cinema of Luis Buñuel*, p. 176: 'The surreal can be sensed lurking beneath the surface, although it never completely shows its face: with wonderful simplicity, Buñuel uses its implied presence to inject powerful tension into every scene.'

9

THE DISCREET CHARM OF THE BOURGEOISIE

CAST

Ambassador	—	Fernando Rey
Simone Thévenot	—	Delphine Seyrig
Thévenot	—	Paul Frankeur
Alice Sénéchal	—	Stéphane Audran
Sénéchal	—	Jean-Pierre Cassel
Florence	—	Bulle Ogier
Colonel	—	Claude Piéplu
Bishop	—	Julien Bertheau
Peasant	—	Muni
Minister	—	Michel Piccoli

Photography	—	Edmond Richard
Editor	—	Hélène Plemiannikov
Art Director	—	Pierre Guffroy
Production	—	Greenwich Productions
Script	—	Luis Buñuel Jean-Claude Carrière
Director	—	Luis Buñuel

In 1972 Buñuel returned to Madrid with the script of *The Discreet Charm of the Bourgeoisie*, claiming that he would make no more films and that the script was merely the outcome of his boredom in Mexico. At all events he was on his way to Paris a month later to discuss the script with his friend and producer, Serge Silberman, who liked it sufficiently to allow Buñuel to start filming at once. Shooting began on 15 May, 1972 and was completed in less than six weeks at a cost of 800,000 dollars. Throughout the process of filming Buñuel was in good humour, sustained no doubt by the complete freedom to improvise that the script allowed him, and, apart from the threat of a labour dispute, the film was completed without problems.

Critical reaction to *The Discreet Charm* was highly favourable and the film won many prizes. Jonathan Rosenbaum, writing in *Sight and Sound*, considered it to be 'the funniest Buñuel film since *L'Age d'or*, probably the most relaxed and controlled film he has ever made, and arguably the first global masterpiece to have come from France in the seventies . . .'[1] Jean de Baroncelli, in *Le Monde*, saw it as a highly original creation in a clearly defined artistic development:

> Firm as a rock in relation to his old rebellions and his creative trajectory, Buñuel has covered his claws with a glove of sweetness in order to be able to scratch better. What he offers us here – this surprising and penetrating mixture of comedy-lampoon, surrealist vaudeville and oniric poem – is very much himself. Only he could put together these ingredients. Woven out of dreams, decorated with the tinsel of the imagination, this new film belongs quite naturally to a long line: there is no problem of continuity in Buñuel's work.[2]

Manuel Alcalá, in the Spanish magazine *Reseña*, regarded *The Discreet Charm* both as the culmination of Buñuel's career and as a new point of departure:

> We are in the presence of a masterpiece, disconcerting

in its implications, paradoxical in its twists and turns, ferocious in its social-political and religious criticism, and enchanting in its fluid cinematic qualities. Buñuel, who at 73 is still producing hits, has made a film that is both tough and youthful. On the one hand he has produced a film that encapsulates all his earlier work, while on the other he has given us something truly new in terms of cinematographic style.[3]

In relation to the earlier films, *The Discreet Charm's* greatest debt is clearly to *L'Age d'or* and *The Exterminating Angel.* In both films the bourgeois guests come together in a large and elegant house, cars draw up ceremoniously, impressive entrances are made, and the dialogue has all the stylization of social ritual. The interruptions that distinguish *The Discreet Charm* from beginning to end are anticipated to a certain extent in *L'Age d'or.* Furthermore, in *L'Age d'or* the stiff formality of bourgeois life is constantly assaulted too by uninhibited passion in the persons of Gaston Modot and Lya Lys. When in *The Discreet Charm* the Sénéchals submit to erotic impulses, climb through the window and rush to make love in the garden, keeping their guests waiting in the drawing-room, it is a clear echo of the earlier film. As far as *The Exterminating Angel* is concerned, its numerous and deliberate repetitions are reflected to some extent, if in a rather different way, in *The Discreet Charm.* Both films contain horrific dreams which terrify the characters, and the terrible apparition of the murdered Chief of Police is in the same tradition of and has a similar effect to the severed hand of *The Exterminating Angel.*

In comparision with the earlier films, the tone of *The Discreet Charm* is, however, different. Buñuel's open and often violent aggression has become a mocking, more objective irony. Indeed, *The Discreet Charm* is full of the most delightful and hilarious episodes. It would be wrong, however, to assume that, because Buñuel's manner has changed and developed, the sharpness of his satire of the bourgeoisie is in any way blunted. Francisco Aranda has made the observation:

> *Le Charme* is for the writer a good film, well integrated into an historic moment, the present. It is not a landmark, as *El ángel exterminador* was.[4]

It would be more accurate to say that *The Discreet Charm* is a different landmark.

The opening shots of *The Discreet Charm* are highly reminiscent of the beginning of *The Exterminating Angel*. The camera depicts firstly the streets of a city at night and then a residential area in the suburbs: the province of the bourgeoisie. Indeed, as in the earlier film, a car draws up outside an elegant mansion and its bourgeois occupants alight in ritualistic manner – the Ambassador, elegantly dressed; Monsieur Thévenot, a businessman; his wife, an attractive woman with a superior air; and her younger sister, Florence. The similarity with the opening sequence of the earlier film is suggested too by subsequent events. Whereas Nobile's guests entered the house to find the servants gone, here they find no fire in the house, nor is the table laid for dinner. Madame Sénéchal, the perplexed and embarrassed hostess, informs the new arrivals that they are a day too early. While they point out excitedly that they have already made arrangements for the next evening. Buñuel undermines with relish the company's bourgeois poise and then throws in a delightful touch of irony, for the hostess, unable to provide a meal, is whisked away by her impatient guests to eat with them in a nearby restaurant. Both the incongruous reversal of the normal situation and the bourgeoisie's almost unseemly craving for food establish the film's deliciously subversive irony.

In a new sequence the group is seen alighting from the car outside a restaurant. The shot repeats very clearly their earlier arrival at the Sénéchal household.[5] Moreover, there are pointers to their further consternation when they learn that the restaurant, praised by Thévenot for its excellent food, is now under different ownership. And, when they finally go inside, they are confronted by the disturbing fact that the tables are as unprepared for dinner as was the dining-room in Madame Sénéchal's. Buñuel, manipulating the situation, delights in its absurdity, and through the introduction of a series of incongruities, makes it even more ridiculous. When, for example, the group is engaged in a solemn discussion of the wine-list, the waiter takes two lighted tapers into an adjoining room. Soon afterwards, as they discuss the menu, muffled sobs punctuate their conversation. The three women, overwhelmed by curiosity, leave the table in the direction of the sounds while the two men strive to preserve a semblance of bourgeois manners.

AMBASSADOR *(off screen)*: Where are you going? . . . Come, stay here!
THÉVENOT *(off screen)*: Don't be indiscreet!

A shot of the interior of the room reveals that it is being used as a mortuary. The corpse of a man is laid out ceremoniously, surrounded by candles, and a woman is seated nearby weeping. As an accompaniment to the solemn scene, Thévenot's voice is heard off-screen ordering the meal, the ritual of death wittily juxtaposed with the ritual of eating. For the three women it is all too much and they quickly leave the restaurant, accompanied by the protesting men. If on the first occasion a confusion of dates had prevented them from eating, it is chance (in the form of the restaurant owner's inconvenient death) which now intervenes. Buñuel, as in the case of *The Exterminating Angel*, delights in subjecting the ordered ritual of bourgeois life to the subversive whims and caprices of the irrational.

A new scene reveals the Ambassador working at his desk. It is the following day and Thévenot and Monsieur Sénéchal are ushered into his presence. The conversation, which centres on the confusion of the previous evening, underlines the essential stylization of quite ordinary aspects of bourgeois activity, a point emphasized too by ceremonious handshakes and the careful consultation of diaries in order to arrange another date for lunch. In the middle of the ritualistic scene the Ambassador takes a rifle from a cupboard, opens the window and shoots at the toys displayed by a female street vendor who, in turn, makes off in a waiting car. The Ambassador informs his astonished companions that she is one of a group of terrorists who plan to kill or kidnap him. For all its rigid self-sufficiency the bourgeoisie is always threatened by external forces, a theme which occurs in many of Buñuel's films.[6] The remainder of the sequence reveals the Ambassador, Thévenot and Sénéchal to be involved in drug-smuggling on a large scale. They, in short, are as much engaged in criminal activities as the terrorists themselves. Buñuel strips away the masks to reveal the true essence of bourgeois morality.

A transition reveals the suburbs of the city in the daytime. The Ambassador, Thévenot, Madame Thévenot and Florence arrive once more at the Sénéchal household in what is, apart from the time of day, a repeat of the film's beginning. Their positions in the car are exactly the same as on the first occasion, and when they alight the driver and the Ambassador exchange identical words. Buñuel transforms the repetitive nature of bourgeois activity into joke and, if ends parallel beginnings, we sense already that the distinguished company is doomed to miss another meal. The hosts, dressing to meet their guests, suddenly become the victims of uncontrollable erotic impulses, undress instead of dressing, and the guests are made to wait downstairs while Monsieur and Madame Sénéchal make wild and passionate love:

> *Meanwhile, in the Sénéchal's bedroom, the couple are still in bed, locked in a passionate embrace.*

But if passion disrupts the tidy ritual of bourgeois life, it is also subject to the demands of bourgeois propriety, and

Sénéchal, conscious of the embarrassment caused to himself and his guests by his wife's ecstatic cries, is forced to restrain himself. If meals are interrupted, sexual appetite is inevitably thwarted.

The remainder of the episode is full of the most delightful humour. The guests, still awaiting their hosts, are served drinks in the drawing-room, and Thévenot launches into a long, detailed and pretentious account of the merits of different drinks, correct room temperatures, and appropriate glasses. Buñuel endows the set-pieces of bourgeois life, from the ordering of meals to the choosing of wines, with all the pomp and ceremonious cliché of religious rites. Meanwhile, in close juxtaposition with Thévenot's tedious exposition, the Sénéchals are seen climbing down from the bedroom window, their solicitude as hosts cast aside, like their clothing, in the ardent pursuit of passion. Like Lya Lys and Gaston Modot in the garden-scene of *L'Age d'or*, they rush into the bushes to the joyful accompaniment of chirping birds. When the news of their disappearance is announced to the waiting guests, they are totally bewildered. Not only have they missed another meal, but for the Ambassador and Thévenot the disappearance of their companion can only mean that the police are on their tracks.

As the car whisks the group away, a bishop approaches in the opposite direction. Buñuel presents this man of the cloth as a true self-advertisement of piety and virtue:

MAID: Have you come on foot?
BISHOP: Yes. I had a car. But I sold it to help the poor.
MAID: Would you like a drink?
BISHOP: Thank you, I don't drink.

Informed by the maid that the Sénéchals are not at home, the bishop enters the gardener's shed, puts on the gardener's clothes and tries out his tools – a prelude to a delightfully comic sequence. The Sénéchals have now returned from their amorous adventures in the garden and are seen smoothing out their clothes, striving as hosts to assume once more an appropriate sense of dignity. The maid informs them of their guests' rapid and frightened departure, and the Sénéchals, astounded by the news, are themselves strangely disquieted. At every step Buñuel spreads consternation amongst his bourgeois victims. When the bishop appears, dressed as the gardener, they throw him out as someone of inferior class only to be further baffled and embarrassed when he enters again in his bishop's robes. The stock situation of misunderstanding and mistaken identity is employed by Buñuel to splendid comic effect, heightened further all the time by Sénéchal's concern to remove blades of grass from his wife's hair and clothing. It transpires, moreover (to the Sénéchals' further amazement) that the bishop is seeking the position of gardener, for, in his own words, he considers himself to be, if not a worker-priest, then at least a worker-bishop. Buñuel develops the incongruous situation with a total solemnity that is the source of its fine humour. The sequence closes with the Sénéchals and the bishop engrossed in the serious negotiation of his wages, which he insists, as a Christian and a good trade-unionist, must not exceed the going rate.

A brief episode depicts the Sénéchals, the Thévenots, the Ambassador and Florence walking along an empty road that crosses a vast plain. The road has no signs, nor do we know where the characters are going. Within the earlier realistic settings of the film, the episode has a symbolic, even dream-like quality, as though the six characters in search of a meal are doomed to journey together forever.

A new sequence has as its setting an elegant tea-room with three-piece orchestra and white-coated waiters. When Madame Sénéchal, Madame Thévenot and Florence enter, take their seats and order some tea, the promise of their further frustration is already teasingly set before us. From the outset there are signs of unease, for Florence, submitting to unconscious impulses, cannot bear to look at the ageing viola player and feels obliged to change her seat. It is not long, moreover, before the waiter returns to inform the women that all the tea has gone, such has been the demand for it.[7] While they wait for coffee (and already we feel they wait in vain) they are, in addition, subjected to the attentions and then to the harrowing tale of a young lieutenant who insists on recounting his tragic childhood. Buñuel allows us to see the events in flashback. We are shown the drawing-room of a large house in a provincial town in which a little boy – the lieutenant – is being fitted out for military school. His mother is dead and there follows a brief farewell between the boy and his father which is distinguished by its coldness and formality. It is a largely realistic episode which becomes, in turn, markedly surrealist. The boy is seen entering his mother's bedroom at night. Her voice calls to him and two white, almost fleshless arms emerge from amongst the clothes hanging in the wardrobe. The voice informs the boy that the man he believes to be his father is not his real father. The latter is revealed to the boy in vivid close-up – a young man with a bullet-hole through the centre of one eye, shot in a duel by the boy's 'father'. Later that night, the boy, following his mother's whispered instructions, poisons his 'father's' drink and he dies in agony to the accompaniment of flashing lightning and rolling thunder, at which point the lieutenant ends his story. It is a piece of outrageous 'grand guignol' – extremely fine in itself, but splendidly incongruous in the staid and formal setting of the tea-room. The story's Oedipal associations, its nightmarish images are delightfully at odds with the tasteful room and the sophisticated company. The women's consternation coincides with the waiter's return and the information that there is no coffee. The bourgeoisie continues to be assaulted by the unexpected.

In the next episode the Ambassador is seen in his elegant flat. He is engaged in the ritual of preparing himself for the arrival of Madame Thévenot and, like Don Lope in *Tristana*, fastidiously sprays his mouth. Buñuel's ironic portrayal of these bourgeois rites contrasts splendidly with subsequent events, for in the presence of the lady herself all formality,

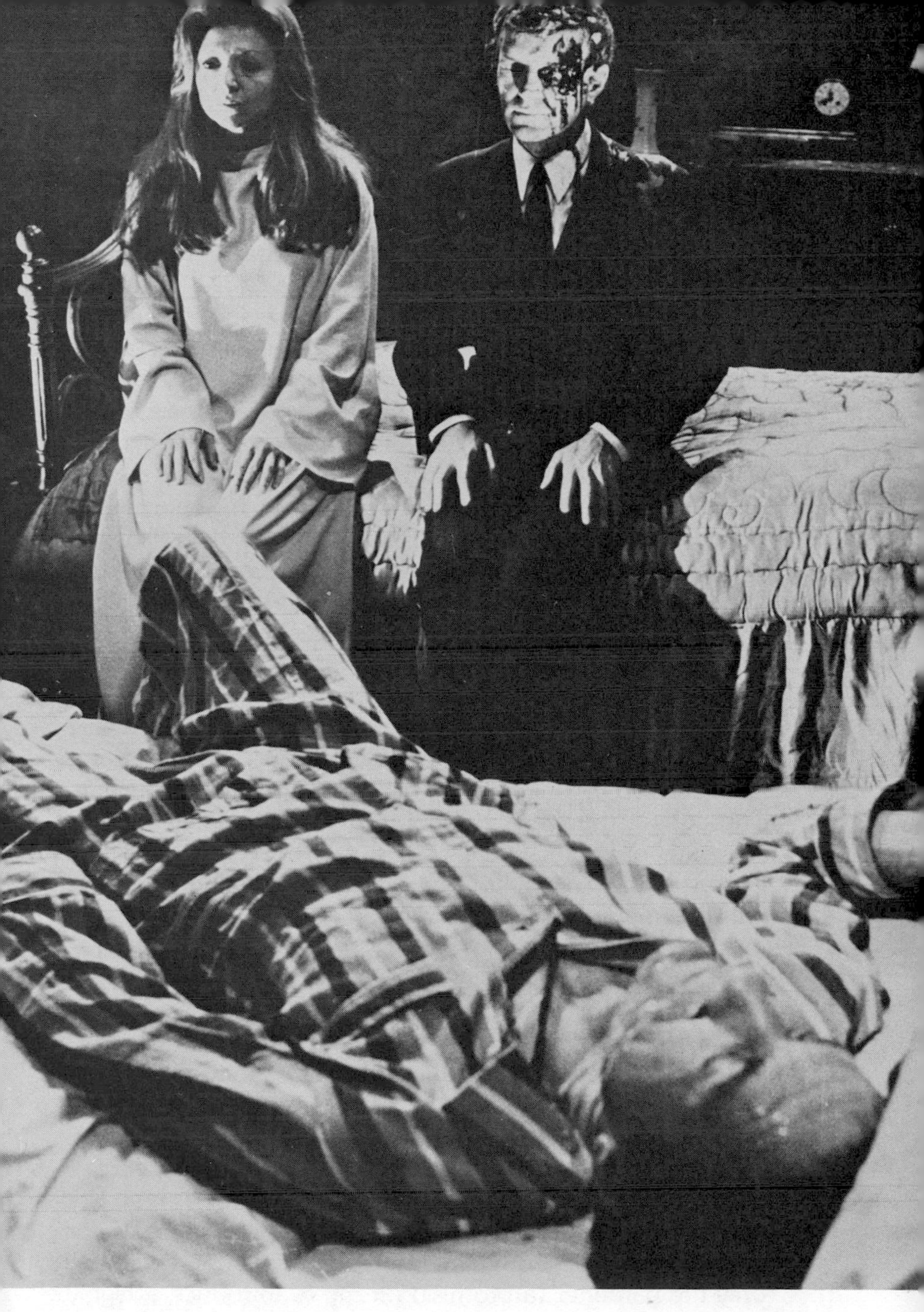

The lieutenant's tale

including the Ambassador's dressing-gown, is unceremoniously cast aside in the pursuit of a desperate passion. But if Buñuel delights in taking the food from his characters' mouths, so he maliciously frustrates their sexual hunger, as he does too in *That Obscure Object of Desire.* Urged to take her clothes off, Madame Thévenot replies that she is not yet sufficiently at ease, and almost simultaneously the door-bell rings to announce the arrival of her husband with an invitation from the Sénéchals to yet another dinner. It is again a stock situation which Buñuel exploits in his own way. There is the irony, for instance, that the Ambassador's sexual appetite is frustrated by a dinner invitation. And when, having explained her presence in his flat, the Ambassador, lusting still for Madame Thévenot, persuades her husband to wait in the street while he shows his wife his 'sourciques', Buñuel gives to an old cliché a perfectly outrageous twist.[8] The Ambassador, however, continues to be frustrated, and after Madame Thévenot's departure the focus of the sequence switches once more to the female terrorist of an earlier episode. She attempts to surprise the Ambassador in the flat but is in turn outwitted by him. Throughout the scene Buñuel underlines, notably through close-ups of hands, feet and legs, the Ambassador's sexual interest in the girl who for him is merely a possible substitute for Madame Thévenot:

> *A close-up of THE AMBASSADOR, followed by a shot of his hand which rests on the girl's knee, moves up and presses her thigh.*

But it ends with his betrayal of her. He cannot interest her and pretends to let her go, only to deliver her into the hands of the waiting police. If the sequence begins on a comic note, it ends with a condemnation of the Ambassador's hypocrisy.

Madame and Monsieur Thévenot, Florence and the Ambassador are next seen arriving at the Sénéchals for dinner, accompanied by the bishop even though he is now only the gardener (a promising irony to introduce a highly amusing episode). The maid's announcement that dinner is served seems to point at last to the group's attainment of its long-desired and steadfastly pursued objective. But even as they are serving themselves – and before they have taken the first mouthful of food – the doorbell rings and they freeze at what is by now for them an ominous and fateful sound. It announces the totally incongruous appearance of some fifteen soldiers whom Sénéchal has agreed to billet in his house the next day but who, by some confusion, have arrived too early. Once more the intervention of chance upsets the well-laid plans of the bourgeoisie. There is now the further irony that they begin to wait upon the soldiers, for Madame Sénéchal provides them with food. Thévenot – always the expert – plies them with drinks, and the bishop hurries to bring more chairs. The development of the episode is full of amusing touches, notably the discussion of the Colonel's smoking of marihuana, but it also allows Buñuel to criticize the bourgeoisie. The Ambassador, for instance, refuses a cigarette, and he and Thévenot, both high class pushers of drugs, hypocritically condemn their use:

> THÉVENOT ... It is the first step towards more serious abuses ... Drug addicts horrify me!

But for all its social criticism, the emphasis of the scene is largely comic, and Buñuel, having perpetrated on the guests one frustration, proceeds to subject them to two more. Firstly, no sooner have they sat down again than the Sergeant arrives with an urgent message for the Colonel which advises the soldiers to depart immediately. And secondly, before their departure, the Sergeant further delays the guests' dinner by insisting on describing to them one of his recent dreams. Knives and forks are set aside in readiness for another journey into the unconscious.

The Sergeant's dream is shown to us in flash-back. He is seen in a dark and deserted street while a bell tolls monotonously in the background. As the Sergeant walks along the street, he encounters a young man with a white face who smells of earth and who informs him that he has lived in the street for six years and will continue to do so for ever. When the youth leaves the Sergeant and enters a dark shop, another young man appears, even paler than the first, and tells him that the latter, called Ramírez, has been dead for six years. Almost immediately the Sergeant meets a young woman emerging from another shop. They engage in conversation, in the course of which the Sergeant, who clearly knows the woman, refers to her rejection of him:

> . . . Whenever I wanted to speak to you, you went away from me, you rejected me. Do you remember?

They embrace, and a fleeting shot reveals the Sergeant leaning over a dead body. He enters the shop to look for Ramírez and finds only a flickering light and a wreath of dead flowers. Meanwhile, the second young man and the young woman have disappeared from the street. The Sergeant looks for them in vain and tears stream down his face as he calls into the darkness:

> Where are you, mother? I am looking for you in the shadows . . . Mother!

It is an episode in which Buñuel evokes with his customary sure touch the shifting, mysterious world of dream, the power of unconscious motives and relationships, and here, above all, the fear of death and ultimate loneliness.

The guests have listened with fascination to this Freudian horror story, forgetting all about their stomachs and made conscious, no doubt, of their own inner lives. Buñuel uses the dreams as mirrors as well as jokes, but if the bourgeois company sees its reflection at all it does so only fleetingly, and when the soldiers have finally departed the ritual of the meal becomes once more the focus of attention. But hardly have the guests resumed their seats than the Colonel reappears to inform them that, much as he regrets it, army manoeuvres will continue while they eat, to commence with a session of shelling and to continue with a cavalry attack. Sénéchal observes:

> . . . It is all perfectly normal.

His remark is, of course, the epitome of bourgeois courtesy and quite absurd in the context. But it also points, perhaps, to the fact that Sénéchal and his companions, subjected constantly to the intrusion of the irrational, begin to accept it as normal. The sequence ends when the Colonel invites his hosts to dine with him on the following Friday.

The Colonel's words overlap the beginning of an episode in which two cars – the Ambassador's and Thévenot's – draw up outside the Colonel's house. The group alights in the usual manner, enacting yet again the ritual of earlier arrivals. The action in which they are now involved has become, in every sense a piece of theatre. In the Colonel's house the guests are surrounded by costumes and props – military uniforms, weapons and hats, one of which Sénéchal puts on the bishop's head, as though he were an actor. The wine which they drink is, moreover, the coloured water of the theatre, and when a servant stumbles and drops two roasted chickens they bounce across the floor and are revealed to be made of cardboard. Above all, as the guests are seated at the table, the curtain behind them suddenly goes up and they find themselves looking at and being looked at by a large and noisy theatre audience. The characters, with the exception of the bishop, are disconcerted by being in the public gaze and flee from the stage. They attempt, in short, to escape the roles imposed upon them when, in reality, the essence of their lives is role and ritual, public performance, and their every act and word has the character of stage performance.

At the end of the sequence Sénéchal wakes up. The experience in the theatre has been a dream, a nightmare. Buñuel's purpose is to suggest the extent to which bourgeois life has all the artificiality of theatre and, secondly, to indicate the bourgeoisie's blindness to their own absurdity. The very

top, The march of the bourgeoisie p.263
bottom, The bourgeoisie on stage p. 255

next scene seems designed to underline both points. Sénéchal has dreamt his dream immediately prior to his visit to the Colonel's and the camera now reveals the Colonel's drawing-room in which the characters are arranged in stylized groups and poses and their dialogue has all the character of carefully rehearsed lines. The Colonel's wife, moving from group to group, performs her role of hostess:

> COLONEL'S WIFE (*well into her role as mistress of the house*): My dear friend, another port?

The ending of the episode has a totally theatrical air. The Colonel quarrels with the Ambassador and slaps him across the face, and the latter, in reply, draws his pistol and shoots the Colonel. If most of the sequence is distinguished by its stylized formality, the ending is a piece of pure melodrama. The reality of bourgeois life is, it seems, even more theatrical than the theatre itself. Buñuel makes the point tellingly, but in the process he also perpetrates a splendid joke. Sénéchal's dream of the experience in the theatre was not, after all, Sénéchal's, but Thévenot's, who has dreamt, firstly, that Sénéchal has dreamt that they were all in a theatre, and, secondly, that they have all been guests at the Colonel's house. If Buñuel disconcerts his bourgeois group by means of the strange and unpredictable workings of reality, he subjects them too to the unnerving experience of their own dreams. And, to an extent, he also mystifies us, his audience, in the sense that our perception of the distinction between reality and dream is at this particular point no clearer than Thévenot's.

In another short sequence the six characters are again seen walking along the road. It stretches into the far distance and in the surrounding landscape there is no sign of life, no buildings, no sign-posts, no advertising-hoardings. As in the case of the earlier sequence, the shot creates a sense of the characters' suspension in space and time, of their universality, and also of their bewilderment and isolation.

A new sequence begins in the garden of the Sénéchal

household where the bishop is assiduously cultivating his garden. When a peasant woman appears in search of a priest to attend a dying old man, the bishop discards his gardening clothes, assumes his robes and eagerly answers the call of duty. The development of the episodes is both witty and cutting. In the process of confession the old man reveals that he has murdered his former employers, for whom he worked as a gardener, and when he shows the bishop a photograph of his victims and their little boy, the bishop recognizes them as his parents and himself. Buñuel has placed his bishop in the incongruous position of absolving his parents' murderer – and of hearing at first hand the perils attendant on the profession of gardener! But the bizarre humour of the incident is not allowed to conceal Buñuel's criticism of the Church. The bishop absolves the old man of his sins:

> . . . *THE BISHOP raises his right hand and makes the sign of the cross.*
> BISHOP: And now, peace be with you.

Then he calmly shoots the old man before departing in his 'customary tranquil manner'. It is a withering juxtaposition of incidents.[9] A parallel might also be drawn with the ending of *L'Age d'or* when, after the girl's shriek is heard from within the castle, the Duke of Blangis, dressed as Christ, emerges with an expression of great piety.

In the Sénéchal household the Ambassador, the Thévenots and Florence have now arrived for lunch. They are, in Thévenot's words, dying of hunger, and the maid quickly brings the food. As they are about to eat – and with an inevitability that is by now like some preposterous and bad joke – the doorbell rings, and the maid opens the door to reveal on this occasion the imposing spectacle of a Chief of Police, four inspectors, and several deputy inspectors who proceed to arrest the Ambassador. When Sénéchal intervenes on the Ambassador's behalf, protesting his innocence, he too is quickly arrested, and Thévenot, seeking to help Sénéchal, is clapped in handcuffs. And finally the women, complaining of police insensitivity, are unceremoniously dragged away. One of the predominant features of this amusing episode is its sense of ritual, but of a ritual played now against the bourgeoisie. The Chief of Police, no less than the elegant company, has his own stylized, ritualistic phrases:

In the name of the Law, I arrest you.

In the course of the scene he repeats it three times, a magical incantation which enslaves one by one the bourgeois occupants of the room. And there is irony too in the spectacle of bourgeois fastidiousness, triumphant to the last, as the women are led away:

MADAME THÉVENOT (*protesting*): Oh, don't touch me! Don't touch me, I tell you!

The camera reveals the cells of a police-station where the company has been locked up. Two agents are engaged in conversation, one of them a newcomer, and the other man begins to tell him the story of the former Chief of Police, whose portrait decorates the wall, and who, it is revealed, was assassinated on the 14th July. The story of the Chief of Police, a brutal man, unfolds before our eyes, epitomized in a violent and sadistic interrogation. He is questioning a young long-haired man, whom he clearly dislikes, about a recent bomb-attack. He punches the youth in the face, and then, in a bizarre incident, has him placed inside a grand piano whose wires are connected to an electric circuit. The narrator of the story reveals, moreover, that the Chief of Police's ghost returns to the police-station every year on the night of July 14th. The two men leave quickly and a distant clock strikes twelve. The lights suddenly go out, footsteps are heard approaching, a door squeaks, there are horrendous shouts off-screen, and the ghastly, bloodstained figure of the Chief of Police appears, stumbling along the corridor. Inside their cells the bourgeois prisoners observe the scene with terror, especially the women as the terrible apparition approaches their cell. It is another preposterous piece of 'grand guignol', played by Buñuel for all it is worth. Another delightful touch involves the current Chief of Police. Sleeping in an armchair he is tormented by a terrible nightmare, from which he wakes only to find its fearful protagonist standing before him. The sequence ends when, on the instructions of the Minister of the Interior, the Ambassador and his friends are released.

A new episode reveals the Sénéchal household. Once more the table is set for dinner. The Sénéchals, the Thévenots, the Ambassador and Florence are seated at the table, and their manner and conversation, superbly structured by Buñuel, has all the stylization of a typical bourgeois dinner-party. Suddenly there is a sound of breaking glass, the group is immediately disconcerted, and three armed men – gangsters or revolutionaries – enter the room. The bourgeois party is lined up against the wall and, when Sénéchal protests, cut down by a burst of machine-gun fire. The once elegant figures lie on the floor, ripped apart, blood spilling from the bullet holes. In the very moment of eating their meal, the bourgeois company have, ironically, seen their food – and now their lives – snatched away. The Ambassador, however, is still alive, for, unseen by the intruders, he has concealed himself beneath the table. In a bizarre and extremely amusing moment he is seen reaching out for a piece of roast meat and then, before they shoot him, crouched beneath the table, ravenously tearing at it. It is not, ironically, his crimes which overtake him finally but his voracious hunger. And there is another, even more delightful irony to come. The slaughter of the bourgeoisie has, after all, been only a dream from which the Ambassador now wakes up, his jaws still champing at an imagined roast. Buñuel has subjected his bourgeois victim to a final, terrible fright – and has fooled us too with his ingenuity. But when the Ambassador goes to the kitchen, helps himself from the fridge, and begins to eat heartily, it is as though nothing that has happened has really shaken him. Here Buñuel suggests, as he does in other films, that the bourgeoisie, although threatened by external forces – terrorists and revolutionaries – and assaulted by its own private fears, has an infinite capacity for self-preservation.[10]

It is a point which the film's concluding sequence seems to underline. The six characters are seen once more walking along the interminable road. They are now quite sprightly and alert. Whatever the other implications of the shot, it suggests that the bourgeoisie marches on forever.

The preceding analysis of *The Discreet Charm of the Bourgeoisie* reveals the extent to which it brings together elements from Buñuel's earlier work. The farcical moments of *L'Age d'or*, its withering sarcasm, and the magnificent dream sequences that distinguish so many of Buñuel's films, are fused together here in an apparently effortless manner, with a total ease and cinematic mastery to which many critics have called attention.[11] *The Discreet Charm* is possibly Buñuel's most accomplished film in a technical sense, but it is important to understand that Buñuel's technique, for all its virtuosity, is always the servant of his satiric purpose.

The comic and biting moments of *L'Age d'or* are often achieved by incongruous juxtapositions. Thus in the middle of the bourgeois dinner party a rustic cart lumbers through the drawing-room, and the governor's solemn laying of a foundation stone is accompanied by the wild sexual groping of Gaston Modot and Lya Lys. Such contrasts account for much of the delightful humour of *The Discreet Charm*. When, for example, the frustrated guests enter a restaurant and discuss the menu, Buñuel has as a counterpoint to their solemn and pompous ritual the laying-out of the restaurant owner's corpse in the adjoining room. Later, as the guests arrive for lunch at the Sénéchals, are provided with drinks in the drawing-room, and indulge in typical bourgeois pleasantries, Buñuel reveals the Sénéchals locked in amorous embraces, climbing through the window and rushing frantically into the bushes to consummate their erotic impulses. The film is full of equally effective incongruities, be it the dinner party in the midst of military operations or the bishop's shooting of the man he has just absolved. Buñuel's barbed humour has, if anything, grown sharper with the passing of the years, and is all the more effective for its cooler, more ironic tone.

If *The Discreet Charm* is surrealist in its attack upon the bourgeoisie, it is clearly so in relation to its revelation of the subconscious. The first episode of this kind consists of the lieutenant's account of his mother-fixation and his father's murder. Buñuel invests the sequence with highly graphic images – the mother's white, outstretched arms, the lover's bloodstained face with its one eye, the father's death agonies to the accompaniment of thunder and lightning. It is the horror of the Gothic, with all its Romantic extravagance, transferred to the screen. Later in the film the Sergeant recounts his dream of death, another episode which is full of waxen faces and suitably lugubrious backgrounds. And later still there is the splendidly horrific, dream-like sequence involving the appearance of the Chief of Police's ghost. This is an incident decked-out by Buñuel with all the traditional tricks of conventional horror films – creaking doors, dragging feet, a hideously bloodstained figure – but achieved with great aplomb. In his earlier films Buñuel employs dream sequences almost entirely to expose the unconscious thoughts of his characters – Pedro's mother-fixation in *Los olvidados*, Séverine's sexual fantasies in *Belle de Jour*, Tristana's sexual fear of her uncle. In *The Discreet Charm*, on the other hand, dreams are used to frighten the bourgeoisie out of its tidy mind. Buñuel piles outrageous horror on outrageous horror, and does so, moreover, in the polite, genteel setting of a tea-room for the Lieutenant's tale, or the aristocratic setting of the Sénéchal's dining-room for the Sergeant's. More than in any other Buñuel film, surrealism becomes expressed through humour.[12]

Finally, *The Discreet Charm* is distinguished by a quite outstanding script. The dialogue of many of Buñuel's films is, as we have seen, extremely fine, ranging from the earthy exchanges of the beggars in *Viridiana* to the bourgeois trivialities of *The Exterminating Angel*. In *The Discreet Charm* Buñuel, aided, of course, by Jean-Claude Carrière, constructs whole passages (the discussion of a menu, of a wine-list, of astrology) in which the trivia of bourgeois mentality, elevated into an elaborate ritual, become a superb self-parody. It is an aspect of the film which illustrates once more that Buñuel's mastery of words as well as pictures has created some of the most fascinating and literate films in modern world cinema.

NOTES

1 *Sight and Sound* (Winter 1972-73).

2 *Le Monde*, 16 September, 1972. The translation is my own.

3 *Reseña*, No. 66, June, 1973.

4 *Luis Buñuel . . .*, p. 248.

5 Repeated actions are important, as we have seen, in *The Exterminating Angel*, creating there a sense of absurdity and of the bourgeois guests' growing loss of control of their situation. In *The Discreet Charm* the repeated episodes convey much more a sense of the ritualistic activities of bourgeois society.

6 In *The Diary of a Chambermaid* the bourgeoisie, enclosed in the great house and absorbed by its own fetishes, attempts to isolate itself from the forces of chaos and revolution that increasingly threaten it. Similarly, in *That Obscure Object of Desire*, the protagonist's sexual obsession, the sole concern of all his activities, is set in a world of violence – terrorist explosions open and close the film – to which he is oblivious.

7 Some of the articles on *The Discreet Charm* are remarkable for their absurdity. See, for example, John Simon, 'Why is the Co-Eatus Always Interruptus?', and Charles Thomas Samuels, 'Tampering with Reality', both in *The World of Luis Buñuel*. In the former, for instance, Simon's observation on the lack of tea is characteristic of the article as a whole: '. . . they go, of an afternoon, to a fashionable café-restaurant in Paris and, successively ordering tea, coffee and hot chocolate, are told by the returning waiter that the place is out of each. So they leave.

Where is the joke or satire in that? No decent restaurant is ever out of all beverages, so the scene does not correspond to some ludicrous reality . . .'

[8] The word 'sourciques' is, of course, a nonsense word, invented by the Ambassador, and contributes further to the sheer hilarity of the situation. Raymond Durgnat, *'The Discreet Charm of the Bourgeoisie'*, in *The World of Luis Buñuel*, p. 379, makes the point that Thévenot, 'rather than face a fact which would require (or allow) for some sort of decision (or resolution), and because he's too ashamed to confess that he doesn't know what a "sourcique" is, allows his suspicions to be quickly lulled, thus allowing his wife and her lover time for another high-speed coupling . . .'

[9] A great deal has been made of the humour of the film, and Francisco Aranda suggests, *Luis Buñuel . . .*, pp. 247-48, that 'there is less urge to disturb'. This scene certainly belies the statement.

[10] In *The Exterminating Angel* the bourgeoisie survive their ordeal and, even if at the end of the film they are trapped once more, there is no suggestion that they will be defeated.

[11] Jonathan Rosenbaum, *Sight and Sound* (Winter 1972-73), observes that Buñuel 'has arrived at a form that covers his full range, permits him to say anything . . . its remarkable achievement is to weld together an assortment of his favourite themes, images and parlour tricks into a discourse that is essentially new . . .'

[12] In the light of Buñuel's masterly fusion of the elements of his earlier films, Francisco Aranda's view that *The Discreet Charm* 'is not a landmark' (see note 4) seems less than justified.

CONCLUSION

A close study of Buñuel's films – including those not studied here in any detail – reveals both their consistency and unity of vision and the remarkable power with which Buñuel communicates that vision. *Un chien andalou* commences with the famous and still disturbing assault upon the eye. *That Obscure Object of Desire* ends with a mighty terrorist explosion. Buñuel's entry into the world of film is thus linked to what is probably his departure from it by a characteristic act of subversion, assault and attack upon complacency, be it social, moral or artistic. The sense of shock is one that echoes through most of Buñuel's films in one form or another: in *L'Age d'or* the outrageous behaviour of the lovers; in *Viridiana* the irreverent transformation of the beggars into Christ and his disciples; in *Tristana* the heroine's final exposure of her dying husband to the icy wind. But if such incidents form a constant thread through Buñuel's cinema, they remain with us not merely because they are variations upon a theme that we come to recognize, but also because they are, in the hands of a master of the language of film, highly memorable images. The style is very much the man, the form and the content totally interdependent.

For Buñuel, the bourgeoisie – which for him always signifies those who hold the reins of power – is the embodiment of all complacency, the principal target for his spirited assaults, and thus to a greater or lesser degree the subject of all his films. In those studied here, *L'Age d'or*, *The Exterminating Angel*, *Belle de Jour*, *Tristana* and *The Discreet Charm of the Bourgeoisie* present a detailed, even microscopic scrutiny of the rich and powerful: both of their appearance and the reality that lies beneath the surface. As to the first point, Buñuel captures in Séverine's cool, unruffled face the very image of bourgeois poise. Throughout the films mentioned above the image is developed in a multiplicity of ways: in shots of splendid houses and elegant interiors; of richly-dressed women and dinner-jacketed men; of formally arranged groups engaged in formal conversation; of polite gestures and social gatherings – in short, of a way of life distinguished by its clinging to unchanging rites and rituals. Moreover, the mannered surface of bourgeois life is the outer manifestation of other forms of rigidity: social, sexual and religious inhibitions; intolerance of any deviation from established norms; the damaging and often self-destructive consequences of a leech-like clinging to them. Séverine's cool exterior is thus the visible form of her frigidity. In *Tristana* Don Lope projects to the world an elegant image of himself, a facade composed of appearance and manner, but is beneath it an empty man, a hyprocrite who behind closed doors preys upon his niece and, when she seeks her freedom, makes every effort to deny it to her. The bourgeoisie, in short, clinging to its values, destroys both others and threatens to destroy itself. Among its victims are Lya Lys and Gaston Modot, dragged from their rapturous embraces by an outraged public and constantly thwarted in their pursuit of passion; Nazarín, the priest, cast out by the Church in his efforts to spread the Christian faith; and Viridiana's uncle, Don Jaime, driven to suicide by a sense of guilt prompted by his desire to seduce the girl but nurtured in the end by a life-long exposure to the social and religious values of the world in which he lives. As for that world, it is also the source of its own decay. No film expresses better than *The Exterminating Angel* the idea of a society trapped within itself, paralyzed, inert and decomposing, elegant clothes and manners falling away, and the fragrance of perfumed bodies transformed into the sickly stench of a rotting corpse.

Buñuel's heroes and heroines are, of course, the rebels, or at least those who strive to achieve freedom. The theme of sexual liberty takes on many forms. In *L'Age d'or* it is celebration and rebellion, Modot the scourge of the bourgeoisie, the violator not merely of their prudery but of their property, leaving in his path a trail of overturned chairs and devastated drawing-rooms. Viridiana, in contrast, is less a rebel than someone who, through a long and often anguished process in which she is more a passive than an active figure is slowly converted from her pious rejection of the world and the flesh to an acceptance of it. Séverine, more active than Viridiana, forges her own conversion and salvation, lives out her fantasies and in so doing frees herself both from her own frigidity and from the cold materialism of her bourgeois world. For Tristana, on the other hand, freedom is achieved in the end at a harsh and bitter price and her triumph, though complete, leaves its mark as much upon her spirit as on her crippled body. In the end in many cases the victory is less than total and the questions posed are at least as important as the answers. The passion ardently pursued by Gaston Modot is finally denied him and he is left to rage in vain as Lya returns to the bourgeois fold, mindful of her aberrations. In *The Exterminating Angel* the bourgeoisie, on the very brink of extinction, rises again from the ashes, and in *The Discreet Charm of the Bourgeoisie* its various representatives, though shaken by nightmares of their own destruction, survive to contine their march along an eternal road. Who, then, enjoys the real victory? Buñuel has often acknowledged that the forms of repression change but the fact does not. The clear implication of his films is therefore that rebellion against the *status quo* is, however essential and admirable, always difficult, often damaging, and usually doomed. The shot of the Ambassador eating heartily at the end of *The Discreet Charm*, already forgetful of his nightmares, points to the bourgeoisie's capacity to insulate itself against all threats to its survival.

Buñuel's concern with freedom cannot be divorced from his preoccupation with Surrealism in the widest sense. His deep fascination with the instinctive and the irrational, evident before his involvement with the official Paris Surrealist group and a constant feature of his work after his departure from it, is a complex matter – attributable in part to temperament, in part to cultural background – but it is easily explained by Buñuel's beliefs that in the process of dreaming or responding to unconscious and instinctive impulses man is relatively, if not entirely, free, and in his 'truest' state. To this extent even the bourgeois characters acquire in the magnificent dream-sequences of the films a liberty denied them in the daily living of their lives, albeit at times a liberty distinguished by horror and nightmare. On the other hand, Buñuel's paradoxical statement that Surrealism taught him that man is never free points to his awareness of the limitations of both the conscious and the unconscious life. When, for example, Séverine dreams of her childhood, of the sexual assault upon her and her refusal of communion, the dream reveals the capacity of traditional moral values – for Buñuel bourgeois values – to extend their vice-like hold beyond the boundaries of the waking world, to haunt and imprison man with spectres of guilt and fear even in his sleeping state. In another sense too Buñuel discovered at an early stage that in practical terms Surrealism promised more than it could give. The Paris Surrealist group proved to be, for all its advocacy of freedom, an intolerant clique from which Buñuel found it necessary to break away – an equivalent in that sense of the very institutions it sought to undermine. The contradictions, ironies and ambiguities inherent in the quest for freedom, in man himself, and in the world in which he lives, were quickly grasped by Buñuel and have become the source of the richness of his work.

Given Buñuel's uncompromising stance on so many

subjects, it is perhaps surprising that his cinematic style and technique should be relatively simple, straightforward and even conservative. Of all his films *Un Chien andalou* is still, technically, the most arresting, for its rapid succession of images, its violent juxtapositions and transitions and its liberal use of close-ups mark it out fifty years on as a highly experimental film. For the most part, though, Buñuel's cinematic style is devoid of eye-catching camera angles and of an over-indulgence in effects of slow motion and other tricks employed by more self-conscious exponents of the art of the cinema. Many of the explorations of the unconscious mind have, in fact, as in the case of Séverine's dreams and Tristana's vision of her uncle's severed head, the reality and solidity of the real world itself. The explanation lies quite simply in the fact that for Buñuel the irrational and instinctive are as real as any object we can feel or touch, and he does not distinguish between the two. In addition, his championing of a style that, more often than not, shows things as they are, without fantasy or sentiment, has much to do with Spanish temperament and thus with Buñuel's Spanishness, for a Spaniard will almost always call a spade a spade.

The influence of Spanish tradition on Buñuel should never be forgotten. He has himself drawn attention on many occasions to his love of the Spanish picareseque novel and Cervantes, and their impact can be seen very clearly in films like *Los olvidados* and *Nazarín*. Similarly, Buñuel's ruthless exposure of the evils of bourgeois society has its antecedent in the later paintings of Goya and in many of the novels of Galdós, where the theme of the stripping away of appearances acquires a particular ferocity. Buñuel's religious themes and images are also those of a man who, though he rejects the other worldliness and the futile idealism of religion, had been fully exposed to it in early life and who until the age of thirty, continued to return to Calanda to take part in the Easter Procession of the Drums. To be familiar with the Freudian and surrealist aspects of Buñuel's work and ignorant of his debt to his Spanish background is to do the man and his art less than justice. It is, in effect, Buñuel's Spanishness which colours his work so strongly and which so many critics, lacking a real knowledge of Spanish culture and attitudes, fail to grasp.

SELECT BIBLIOGRAPHY

Almendros, Nestor, 'Luis Buñuel: cineaste hispanique', *Objectif*, no. 21 (1963), pp. 15-20.

Aranda, J. Francisco, *Luis Buñuel: biografía crítica'*, Barcelona: Editorial Lumen, 1969.

Luis Buñuel: a Critical Biography, trans. David Robinson, London: Secker and Warburg, 1975.

'Buñuel español', *Cinema universitario*, no. 4 (1956), pp. 7-19.

'La passion selon Buñuel', *Cahiers du cinema*, no. 93 (1959), pp. 27-32.

'Surrealist and Spanish Giant', *Films and Filming*, vol. 8, no. 1 (1961), pp. 17-18.

'Back from the Wilderness', *Films and Filming*, vol. 8, no. 2 (1961), pp. 29-30.

Bazin, André, *'Los olvidados'*, in *Qu'est ce que le cinéma? III: Cinéma et Sociologie*, Paris: Editions du Cerf, 1961, pp. 22-28.

Brunius, Jacques, 'Quatrième période', in *En marge du cinéma français*, Paris: Arcanes, 1954, pp. 134-143.

Buache, Freddy, *Luis Buñuel*, Lausanne: La Cité, 1970.

The Cinema of Luis Buñuel, trans. Peter Graham, London and New York: Tantivy-Barnes, 1973.

Buñuel, Luis, 'The Cinema: an Instrument of Poetry', *New York Film Bulletin*, no. 28 (1961), pp. 4-6. Reprinted Joan Mellen (ed.), *The World of Luis Buñuel . . .*, New

York: Oxford University Press, 1978, pp. 105-110.
'Sur *Nazarín*', *Cinema 61*, no. 52 (1961).
'A Statement', *Film Culture,* no. 21 (1960).
'On *Viridiana*', *Film Culture,* no. 24 (1962). Reprinted Joan Mellen (ed.), *The World of Luis Buñuel* . . . New York: Oxford University Pres, 1978, pp. 216-218.
Carrière, Jean-Claude, 'The Buñuel Mystery', in Joan Mellen (ed.), *The World of Luis Buñuel* . . . , New York: Oxford University Press, 1978, pp. 90-102.
Cegretin, M., *'Los olvidados', Image et Son,* no. 153-154 (1962), pp. 50-53.
Chardère, Bernard, *'Los olvidados', Positif,* no. 1 (1952), pp. 11-22.
Delmas, Jean, 'Buñuel le mexicain', *Jeune Cinema,* no. 12 (1966), pp. 3-7.
Durgnat, Raymond, *Luis Buñuel,* London: Studio Vista, 1967.
'The Discreet Charm of the Bourgeoisie', in Joan Mellen (ed.), *The World of Luis Buñuel* . . . New York: Oxford University Press, 1978, pp. 373-396.
Esteve, Michel (ed.), *Luis Buñuel,* Paris: Lettres Modernes, 1962-63
'Nazarin et le journal d'un curé de campagne: la Passion refusée et acceptée', in *La Passion du Christ comme thème cinématographique,* Paris: Lettres Modernes, 1961, pp. 217-234.
'The Exterminating Angel: No Exit From the Human Condition', in Joan Mellen (ed.), *The World of Luis Buñuel* . . . , New York: Oxford University Press, 1978, pp. 244-254.
Fuentes, Carlos, 'The Discreet Charm of Luis Buñuel', in Joan Mellen (ed.), *The World of Luis Buñuel* . . . , New York: Oxford University Press, 1978, pp. 51-71.
Fieschi, Jean-André, 'L'ange et la bête: croquis mexicains de Luis Buñuel', *Cahiers du Cinema,* no. 176 (1966), pp. 33-40.
García Riera, Emilio, 'The Eternal Rebellion of Luis Buñuel',

Film Culture, no. 21 (1960).

'Viridiana', *Film Culture*, no. 24 (1962).

Gardier, René, 'L'ouvert et le clos', *Image et Son*, no. 250 (1971).

Gow, Gordon, *'Nazarin'*, *Films and Filming*, vol. 10, no. 1 (1963), p. 23.

Grange, Frèdèric (with Rebolledo, Carlos), *Luis Buñuel*, Paris: Editions Universitaires, 1964.

Hammond, Robert M., 'Luis Alcoriza and the Films of Luis Buñuel', *Film Heritage*. vol. 1, no. 1 (1965), pp. 25-34.

Haredurt, Peter, 'Luis Buñuel: Spaniard and Surrealist', in *Six European Directors*, London: Penguin, 1974, (pp. 102-134).

Hull, David Stewart, *'Viridiana'*, *Film Heritage*, vol. 15, no. 2 (1961-62), pp. 55-56.

Kanesaka, Kenji, 'A Visit to Luis Buñuel', *Film Culture*, no. 41 (1966), pp. 60-65.

Kast, Pierre, 'Un fonction de constat: notes sur l'oeuvre de Buñuel', *Cahiers du cinema*, no. 7 (1951), pp. 6-23.

Kyrou, Ado, *Luis Buñuel*, Paris: Edition Seghers, 1962.

Luis Buñuel: an Introduction, New York: Simon and Schuster, 1963.

'Luis Buñuel', *Le surréalisme au cinéma*, Paris: Le Terrain Vague, 2nd edn., 1963, pp. 207-268.

'La grande tendresse de Luis Buñuel', *Positif*, no. 10 (1954), pp. 39-56.

Lambert, Gavin, 'Buñuel and *Los olvidados*', *Sequence*, no. 14 (1952), pp. 30-32.

'Nazarín', *Film Quarterly*, vol. 13, no. 3 (1960), pp. 30-31.

Lefèvre, Raymond, '*Viridiana*, ou les infortunes de la charité', *Image et Son*, no. 152 (1962), pp. 34-35.

Lizalde, Eduardo, *Luis Buñuel: odisea del demoledor*, Mexico: Universidad autónoma de Mexico, 1962.

Lovell, Alan, 'Luis Buñuel', in *Anarchist Cinema*, London: Peace News, 1964, pp. 18-28.

Maddison, John, *'Los olvidados'*, *Sight and Sound*, vol. 21, no. 4 (1952), pp. 167-168.

Martin, Marcel, '*Viridiana*', *Cinema 62,* no. 65 (1962), pp. 98-100.
'The Priest and the Man', in Joan Mellen (ed.), *The World of Luis Buñuel . . .*, New York: Oxford University Press, 1978, pp. 209-213.
Matthews, J. H., *Surrealism and Film,* Michigan: University of Michigan Press, 1971.
Mauriac, Claude, 'Luis Buñuel', in *L'amour du cinéma,* Paris: Editions Albin Michel, 1954, pp. 58-65.
'Luis Buñuel', in *Petite littérature du cinéma,* Paris: Editions du Cerf, 1957, pp. 75-85.
Mellen, Joan (ed.), *The World of Luis Buñuel: Essays in Criticism,* New York: Oxford University Press, 1978.
Michel, Manuel, 'L'homme sans chaines', *Cinema 61,* no. 52 (1961), pp. 21-30.
Millar, Daniel, 'Luis Buñuel: Naturalist and Supernaturalist', *Screen Education,* no. 43 (1968), pp. 64-71.
Milne, Tom, 'The Mexican Buñuel', *Sight and Sound,* vol. 35, no. 1 (1965-66), pp. 37-39.
Moullet, Luc, *Luis Buñuel,* Brussels: Club Livre de Cinéma, 1957.
Nowell-Smith, Geoffrey, '*Nazarín*', *Sight and Sound,* vol. 32, no. 4 (1963), pp. 194-195.
Pena, José, (with Salachas, Gilbert). '*Viridiana*', *Telegine,* no. 106 (1962), pp. 15.
Philippe, Jean-Claude, (with Salachas, Gilbert). '*Nazarín*', *Telegine,* no. 96 (1961), pp. 16.
Prouse, Derek, 'Interviewing Buñuel', *Sight and Sound,* vol. 29, no. 3 (1960), pp. 118-119.
Richardson, Tony, 'The Films of Luis Buñuel', *Sight and Sound,* vol. 23, no. 3 (1954), pp. 125-130. Reprinted in Joan Mellen (ed.), *The World of Luis Buñuel . . .*, New York: Oxford University Press, 1978, pp. 125-138.
Richie, Donald, 'The Moral Code of Luis Buñuel', in Joan Mellen (ed.), *The World of Luis Buñuel . . .*, New York: Oxford University Press, 1978, pp. 111-115.
Robinson, David, 'The Old Surrealist', *London Magazine,*

1962, pp. 66-72.

'Thank God – I am still an Atheist', *Sight and Sound,* vol. 31, no. 3 (1962). Reprinted in Joan Mellen (ed.), *The World of Luis Buñuel . . .*, New York: Oxford University Press, 1978, pp. 235-243.

Rodríguez-Monegal, Emir, 'El mito Buñuel', *Tiempo de cine,* no. 14-15 (1963), pp. 54-66.

Rosenbaum, Jonathan, 'Interruption as Style', *Sight and Sound,* vol. 41, no. 1 (1972-73).

Rubia Barcia, J., 'Luis Buñuel's *Los olvidados*', *Quarterly of Film, Radio and Television,* vol. 7, no. 4 (1953), pp. 392-401.

Sarris, Andrew (ed.), 'Luis Buñuel', in *Interviews with Film Directors,* New York: Bobbs-Merrill, 1967, pp. 45-50.

'Luis Buñuel: the Devil and the Nun – *Viridiana*', *Movie,* no. 1 (1962), pp. 14-16.

'The Beauty of *Belle de Jour*', in Joan Mellen (ed.), *The World of Luis Buñuel . . .*, New York: Oxford University Press, 1978, pp. 289-296.

Seguin, Louis, '*Viridiana* et les critiques', *Positif,* no. 47 (1962), pp. 75-80. Reprinted in English translation in Joan Mellen, *The World of Luis Buñuel . . .*, New York: Oxford University Press, 1978, pp. 225-234.

Stein, Elliot, 'Buñuel's Golden Bowl', *Sight and Sound,* vol. 36, no. 4 (1967), pp. 173-175. Reprinted in Joan Mellen, *The World of Luis Buñuel . . .*, New York: Oxford University Press, 1978, pp. 278-288.

Thorok, Jean-Paul, 'La passion de *Nazarín*', *Positif,* no. 38 (1961), pp. 61-64.

Torres, Augusto, M., 'Luis Buñuel/Glauber Rocha: échos d'une conversation', *Cinema 68,* no. 123 (1968), pp. 48-53.

Trebouta, J., 'Une scandaleuse tendresse', *Cinema 56,* no. 13 (1956), pp. 8-12.

INDEX